Revisioning Writers' Talk

SUNY Series
Literature, Culture and Learning: *Theory and Practice*
Alan C. Purves, editor

Revisioning Writers' Talk:

Gender and Culture in Acts of Composing

MARY ANN CAIN

State University of New York Press

For my teachers,
Lil and Meta Susan

For George,
my partner in life, work, and love

Published by
State University of New York Press, Albany

© 1995 State University of New York

For information, address the State University of New York Press,
State University Plaza, Albany, NY 12246

Production by Bernadine Dawes · Marketing by Bernadette LaManna

Library of Congress Cataloging-in-Publication Data

Cain, Mary Ann.
Revisioning writers' talk: gender and culture in acts of composing
/ Mary Ann Cain.
p.   cm. — (SUNY series, literacy, culture, and learning)
Includes bibliographical references.
ISBN 0-7914-2075-2 (acid free). — ISBN 0-7914-2076-0 (pbk. : acid
free)
1. Women authors.   2. Public speaking.   [1. Authorship.]
I. Title.   II. Series.
PN151.C27   1995
808'.02—dc20   94-8007
                                                         CIP

1   2   3   4   5   6   7   8   9   10

Contents

Preface • ix

Writing the Subject: Representations of Experiential Knowledge • 1

What is "Social" about Social Constructivism? • 23

Composing Ourselves as Knowers: Women Writers in a Male Tradition • 41

The Academic Class • 69

The Self-Directed Group • 125

Representations of Power • 171

Epilogue: Writing, "That Old Classic" • 189

Works Consulted • 201

Index • 209

Preface

All writing is a social activity, but that's hard to remember when I close the office door, turn on the computer, and stare at the dark screen for hours at a time, decaf in hand. Fortunately, the conversations from which this book took shape and the relationships that enriched them were deeply sustaining—more than enough to remind me that I wasn't, after all, imprisoned in splendid isolation but responding, initiating, talking back, listening, pausing, and, at times, letting the silence speak.

I'd like to thank, as readers of an earlier version of this manuscript, Lil Brannon, Judy Johnson, and Cy Knoblauch for talking back to my text, helping me construct alternatives, resisting the formulaic, and relishing the unexpected. For their insights into stories in progress, in particular, and composing the story-world in general, I thank Gene Garber and Gene Mirabelli. I thank Judy Fetterley for showing me how much women's experience does matter. Without the following colleagues, there would have been no talk about writers' talk, and thus no dialogue from which to speak: Lâle Davidson, Sandy Deel, Penny Dugan, Patty Dunn, Julie Guttman, Jill Hanifan, Diane Lunde, Cindy Parrish, Jan Ramjerdi, Cecilia Rodríguez-Milanes, John Sandman, Beth Weatherby. I am also grateful to the Hudson Valley Writers' Guild poetry group, the graduate fiction class at SUNY Albany, and the members of the Writing Center fiction and poetry workshops at SUNY Albany for allowing me to participate not just as a workshop member but as a researcher, tape recorder in hand. I also owe much to Michelle Bobson, whose insight and enthusiasm helped me through the tangle of revision. Indiana University South Bend provided a Summer Faculty fellowship, which gave me the time and financial support to revise the manuscript. Priscilla Ross was instrumental in bringing this book into being at SUNY Press, a gift I will always cherish. I thank Bernadine Dawes and Wendy Nelson for their excellent production work.

Finally, I am grateful to my parents, Lester and Ruth Cain, for their patience, understanding, and support, and to my husband and partner, George Kalamaras, who encouraged me to keep going, provided dialogue to sustain the work, and offered silence when I needed it.

❧ Writing the Subject
Representations of Experiential Knowledge

This research began as my effort to bring into dialogue identities I negotiate as a writer, teacher, and scholar, whose relationships I felt intuitively but could not give voice to or simply did not recognize—even, at times, experienced as in conflict. But perhaps more importantly, what led me to such a dialogue was the need to understand how gender, as a culturally prescribed role, inscribed these other roles. I also sought to understand how, through an awareness of the complexities of these inscriptions, I might better construct alternatives for transforming and relating, to each other and to the personal identities I live, what seemed such disparate and sometimes conflicting professional identities, all of which are informed by my identity as woman.

The following pages set into motion the narratives through which I know the world in these various capacities, first from the felt, phenomenal sense of lived experience, to the metanarratives of interpreting those interpretations, through those layers of interpretation that constitute the larger context of culture, with its affirming rituals and informing myths that act as a background of beliefs woven invisibly into the fabric of daily life.

This chapter presents an overview of arguments within composition, feminism, literary theory, and myth studies that inform my methodology as well as my philosophical and ideological approaches to this work. I use these arguments to establish a framework for representing and interpreting the stories that follow in subsequent chapters.

A Phenomenological Approach to Research

My research methodology is phenomenological; its aim is to constitute the complexities and richness of lived experience, serving as a mode of inquiry into cultural representations of composing, of writers and teachers

1

of writing and their experience, and of women. I claim this work as research despite its nontraditional generic form, which blurs narration, self-
reflection, analysis, and fiction. These genres are no less modes of inquiry
than are those of conventional critical or analytic discourse, although the
label *research* might be more problematic than *inquiry*, since the discursive lines between "fact" and "fiction" are institutionally as well as culturally entrenched as self-evident truth. Fictions or myths are typically assigned derogatory connotations as something not only imagined but false.
Although researchers in many disciplines (for instance, Clifford Geertz in
anthropology, Hayden White in history, Lewis Thomas in biology, Loren
Eiseley in archaeology) have explored the "fictive" or literary dimensions
of their own knowledge making, "research" is still institutionally upheld
as what is real or truthful, as opposed to the imagined or false. Written
representations of research still fall within conventional exposition and
analysis; other genres are reserved for "literary" or "expressive" modes
that are perceived to fall outside of research. Thus, it is an ideological
move on my part to claim this work as research in order to create new
ways of relating narrative to other modes of inquiry and investigate how
they might better inform each other. Such a claim is not new, as I will
show in relation to M. M. Bakhtin's (1981) work on the novel as a genre,
but it does present ideological challenges to current arrangements of
power, prestige, and gender in English studies as well as between teacher-
writer practitioners and educational researchers, arrangements in which
women do most of the teaching and men most of the research about how
and what teachers should teach.

It is not my intention to suggest that traditional research is merely
"made up" or that it has nothing different to offer from blurred genres of
narration, reflection, and analysis. Nor would I suggest that the work represented in the following pages is unproblematically "research," because it
is also something Other, something that problematizes current research
practices, habits, and conventions by appropriating research discourse and
putting it into dialogue with these Other discourses. Blurred genres aren't
simply "new" or "special" discourses; instead, they are discourses that
"talk back" (Bakhtin 1981), transforming the cultural, institutional, and
historical processes that give dominant discourses their authority.

Some composition researchers, including those who promote teacher
research (for example, Goswami and Stillman 1987; Knoblauch and Brannon 1988; Heath 1987, 1988; Berthoff 1987; Ray 1993; Britton 1987;
Boomer 1987; Martin 1987), have already argued for the value of self-
reflective narrative as an appropriate genre for representing classroom

practice and the value of blurring research and narrative modes. Such views are based upon James Britton's (1982) theory of discourse in which transactional and poetic modes have their roots in expressive discourse; narrative as one facet of expressive discourse is thus fundamentally linked to the transactional modes of more traditional research as well as a bridge to poetic modes of literary discourse. Furthermore, the field of composition studies is beginning to recognize the value of narrative as a mode of knowing, by publishing expressive works such as autobiography and classroom narrative in research journals (see, for instance, Sommers 1992 and McQuade 1992), but has yet to give serious consideration to blurred genres incorporating poetic or literary modes other than autobiographical or ethnographic narratives as legitimate inquiry or to theorize their appropriate role in relation to theory and other forms of research. Furthermore, these narratives often are too readily interpreted in terms of positivistic assumptions, as if they reflected an empirical, unmediated reality (language as a "window" into reality), rather than as constructed identities and "thick descriptions" requiring interpretation rather than verification. In addition, when major journals and publishers do publish narratives, they are usually authored by established leaders in the field whose prestige consequently lends the appropriate "authority" to their (otherwise "personal") writing.

Mike Rose's *Lives on the Boundary* (1989) is one example of the professional license granted to established "authorities" to tell their life stories. Like many teacher-researchers, Rose blurs the boundaries between autobiography/memoir, anecdote, theory, and research. Yet his story reinscribes a masculinized identity of "master teacher" that overshadows the lives of those "on the boundaries" whose cause Rose advocates, including, as Penny Dugan (1991) has pointed out, the women in Rose's life. Rose has constructed himself as a tireless, hardworking, brilliant teacher standing up alone to a corrupt, mismanaged educational system. Thus, no one in this book (nor in the book's readership) "can be gifted or energetic or self-sacrificing enough," as Lil Brannon (1993, 461) has commented, to match Rose's success as a teacher/scholar. Because of this identity of "Romantic heroic teacher" (Brannon 1993, 461), *Lives on the Boundary* is valued and believed largely to the extent that the author is already a "success." Had Rose been a female adjunct faculty member at UCLA, the story might have been much different; an "unsuccessful" teacher's life would command less attention ("unsuccessful" teachers are common; "heroic" teachers are rare), and her insights and opinions less authority. Constructing himself as "master teacher" may have facilitated Rose's move to capture a broad public audience, but unfortunately that identity undermines the discussion of real problems of the marginalized student and the solutions Rose proposes so convincingly. Rose emerges as the "hero" who, by his transcendent example, will put the educational house in order.

Rose's construction of himself as romantic hero unfortunately obscures the more "common" heroism of other teachers who have struggled without the mentoring and privileges Rose was so fortunate to receive. Given the conditions that Rosalie Naumann faced in her school, for instance, it is perhaps more remarkable that she kept teaching, and teaching so well. It would be more remarkable, in fact, if Rose hadn't flourished, given the support he received. Unfortunately, the "smaller" efforts of others in his life appear "common" in comparison to his achievements, and thus easier to overlook. Teaching, except by a "master" teacher, becomes a "feminized" activity, lacking in authority; research and theory by the "master" subsequently save the day. In this way, he has earned the right to tell his story, and to tell it authoritatively.

The Feminization of Practice

One of the fundamental problems facing composition today is articulating relations between theory and practice. The field's ideal is praxis: theory-based, self-reflective practice in teaching, and research methodologies sensitive to the contexts of classroom life. However, the language practices of those who are trained in research and scholarship and those whose primary obligations are classroom instruction are often quite different. These differences reflect an institutionalized hierarchy of knowledge and professional status, with researcher-scholars dominating a field constituted largely by practitioners.

Not coincidentally, the fault lines between composition research and practice also fall along gender lines. Sue Ellen Holbrook (1991) has documented this phenomenon, noting that male compositionists are more likely than their female counterparts to write and publish, particularly on "harder" research topics such as theories of communication, research processes, and language/text/structure. Men are about even with women in areas such as composing processes and writing/literature across the curriculum. Women, on the other hand, dominate in "softer," more practice-oriented modes such as teacher development, processes of thought, student development, and nonacademic subjects. Holbrook (1991) points out that although women dominate composition as a whole, men dominate as knowledge makers. For instance, in Richard Larson's "Selected Bibliography of Scholarship on Composition and Rhetoric" 66 percent of the authors are male; in Barbara Weaver's "Bibliography of Writing Textbooks" 62 percent are male (Holbrook 1991). In addition, according to Holbrook, 65 percent of the articles accepted for *College English* were by men (61 percent of all articles were submitted by men) (Holbrook 1991, 228).

What accounts for the silence of practitioners in writing and writing instruction within composition research? Why the silence of so many women? Some practitioners respond to the dominant research discourse by expressing various degrees of alienation; the world of practice, when represented in the discourse of research, appears reduced and depleted of its richness. Some practitioners regard the language of research as oppressive and refuse to engage in it. Others perceive it as an acquisition necessary for gaining access to power. Yet others have embraced theory only to find their representations of practice appropriated or misread by the research community.

The problem of representing the world of practice is a problem shared by women in seeking to represent their subjectivities as women in a language that many perceive to be alienating, the product of domination. The dominant discourse renders their subjectivity as "feminized," a lesser "alternative" to a male-dominated culture. A feminized discourse is characterized by its partiality and particularity, in contrast to the assumed objectivity and universality of the dominant discourse. A system of binary oppositions maintains this hierarchy, making efforts to challenge or transform the status of practitioners and, in turn, most women, difficult.

Efforts at reforming the status of composition practice and, in turn, practitioners[1] have been aimed at the language by which practice is represented and through which it is interpreted institutionally, as well as within the research community, mirroring feminist arguments for rearticulating the experience of women through linguistic reform. Like some feminists, some compositionists, such as Maxine Hairston (1985) and Olivia Frey (1990), have sought to define their "difference" as practitioners and women from the dominant discourse ("critical theory," for Hairston; "argumentative discourse," for Frey) by claiming their language practices as unique (and even, at times, superior to those of the research/theory masculinist elite). Such arguments have called for valuing practitioner knowledge as a separate but equally valuable mode of knowing. Others, such as Susan Miller (1991) and Susan Jarratt (1991), have argued that, in defining "essential" differences, hegemonic institutional values are perpetuated, reinscribing the subordination of composition practice.

The arguments for better understanding and valuing a separate but equal practitioner discourse community are well represented by Stephen North (1987). North assigns practitioner discourse largely to the oral, as opposed to the written, realm—as "lore," an ambiguous term he applies in simultaneously admiring and (perhaps inadvertently) derogatory terms. "Composition's lore," according to North, is "a body of knowledge very much like those accumulated among practitioners of other arts. . . . not 'scientifically' rigorous. . . . driven . . . by a pragmatic logic. . . . [and] essentially experiential" (23).

North is well aware of the problems of representing experiential "lore" within written formats and criticizes other discourse communities within composition for misreading it as work by "bad Scholars or inadequate Researchers" (54–55). He clearly advocates valuing practitioner knowledge as something different from other knowledge-making within composition. North defines the limits of practitioner knowledge as being bound to a sense of "pragmatic" reality (what works and what doesn't), apparently outside larger social, cultural, and institutional practices and regulations. Practitioner knowledge is limited to what's local and practical; the problem, as North states it, is that we simply need to value the local and practical more than we already do.

Even as North seeks to revalue practitioner knowledge, he also chastises practitioners for misrepresenting their knowledge, trying to claim a more general and abstract authority for what North claims is essentially local and practical:

> Partly because of the medium, and partly because of pressure from institutions and other communities, when practitioners report on their inquiry in writing, they tend to misrepresent both its nature and authority, moving farther and farther from their pragmatic and experiential power base. (54)

North alternately admires practitioners for their "difference" yet wants to make sure that they know their place. He claims that lore is a powerful form of inquiry yet insists that practitioners should not try to make claims beyond lore's "essential" nature. Consequently, "lore," within North's definition, cannot challenge restrictive feminized inscriptions that North's essentialism reinscribes. North doesn't challenge how practitioners came to such a position in the first place; he only claims that the "difference" assigned by the research establishment and a public hostile to teacher-artists should be valued rather than scorned.

Practitioners, North acknowledges, are caught by the language of dominant research communities, which subverts their own purposes. This language overgeneralizes their experience, claims too much authority for their pragmatic testing of "what works," and misrepresents them to researchers. Like women, practitioners (most of whom are women, though North cites primarily men as writers of "lore") must confront a language of the dominant discourse community and use it in order to represent their ways of knowing in the research and academic community. Curiously, North suggests that practitioners seek to enter the dominant discourse out of insecurity over their status and a desire to improve it; by being more self-conscious about how they use language, North contends, they have a better chance of improving their marginal status.

North tends to dismiss the power relations that necessarily inform practitioners' use of scholarly discourse even as he acknowledges how readily practitioner knowledge can be appropriated and misread. He characterizes practitioners as victims of misrepresentation yet blames them for misusing a language that is not of their construction and that always leaves their meanings subject to appropriation and misinterpretation. Even if practitioners followed North's advice to be more self-conscious about using scholarly discourse to represent their knowledge, that would not, in the end, solve the problem of how scholarly research excludes practitioners, largely women.

North's argument falls into essentialist traps that feminist theorists such as Linda Alcoff (1988) have critiqued with regard to "cultural" feminism. North, like cultural feminists, believes that the status of marginalized groups can be improved simply by correction—of their own discourse as well as that of the dominant group. Practitioners and women can simply correct distortions in their images. Alcoff criticizes this approach, contending that a more "accurate" representation of women's experience is not possible within a hegemonically constructed discourse, and even if it were, the power that groups have to correct such distortions is limited by their *access* to the institutional regulations of the dominant discourses.

> Thus the cultural feminist reappraisal construes woman's passivity as her peacefulness, her sentimentality as her proclivity to nurture, her subjectiveness as her advanced self-awareness. . . . Cultural feminists have not challenged the defining of woman but only that definition given by men. (Alcoff 1988, 407)

North glosses issues of power (How did researchers get the power to define practitioner knowledge to begin with?) and access to institutions that regulate that discourse. Instead, he criticizes practitioners for their linguistic distortions, in contrast to Louise Phelps (1991), who claims that the silences and "distortions" may instead represent active resistance on the part of practitioners toward the discourse of the more powerful academic "elite." While Phelps might also be guilty of reproducing essentialist images of practitioners and "practical wisdom," she does suggest that practitioners are responding to their "feminized" status with appropriate resistance and not simply out of ignorance or insecurity.

In the end, North undermines his own project to "rescue" practitioner knowledge and place it firmly among the various "knowledge-making" communities within composition studies. By defining practitioner knowledge as essentially different from formal research rather than as a product of institutional inequities, especially of those toward women, he maintains binary oppositions between theory and practice, defining each as essentially separate but equal knowledge-making communities. He opposes the concrete, local, pragmatic inquiry of practitioners to the abstract, global, speculative knowledge of researchers—a formulation that maintains the subordination of the former to the latter. North assumes that language reflects, rather than constitutes, experience; like a mirror, it sustains distortions that are, however, correctable. If representations are "clear," then interpretations will, as a matter of course, fall into line as well.

Linguistic Determinism
in the Social Construction
of Meaning

North, of course, is not alone in his assumption that changes or corrections to language can empower marginalized groups. However, I would argue that language's role in the construction of meaning has been overemphasized. Although language plays an undeniably significant role in the shaping and reproduction of professional and gender hierarchies, it has been assigned too great a role in the *control* of such hierarchies. In fact, language itself, as a subject of study, has become "feminized," described as an instrument that either controls social processes or is controlled by them. In either case, language is perceived as an objective entity, a "thing" that either is dominated by or dominates social realities. Ann Berthoff (1991) observes this polarity with regard to theories of language: "Meaning [is perceived] as a two-valued relationship: it is 'thingy' and it comes from either within or without . . . [and] interpretation is either personal opinion or group thought" (280). Gender, too, has been culturally inscribed in similarly binary terms: either women as totally controlling, "bitchy," domineering; or women as completely controlled, victimized by a male-dominated system. Thus, these binary oppositions serve to maintain the values and beliefs of the dominant culture. "Language," as Berthoff observes, becomes "a substitute for reality" in either case (280).

Because language is perceived to be the primary means of social control over meaning, the project of reformers has been to capture control over language, to re-present their knowledge and experience "differently," as if meaning were a "thing" that could be wrestled and tamed. However, as feminist linguist Deborah Cameron (1985) points out, socially constructed meanings are a result of both linguistic and "metalinguistic" forces that Cameron claims are seldom adequately addressed in the study of language. The problem of representing women's experience, Cameron comments, is less a problem of language than of women's historical *relationship* to that language. According to Cameron, discourses are not inherently gendered but, historically speaking, shaped by men to the exclusion of women. The "essential" features of discourse are less relevant to women's exclusion than is women's access to that discourse, which historically has been limited by

> the institutions that regulate language use in our own society . . . [that] are deliberately oppressive to women. . . . Men control [these institutions as] . . . the prerogative of those with economic and political power to set up and regulate important social institutions. (145)

Cameron criticizes a "linguistic determinism" in the debate (characterized also by philosopher Linda Alcoff as a debate between cultural and poststructuralist feminists) over the representation of women's experience, a debate also echoed in composition studies between expressivist and social constructivist theories:

> Opponents of determinism appeal to notions of common sense and to free-will, which they accuse the radicals of denying: determinists, on the other hand, accuse non-believers of naviety [sic] and of clinging to an essentialist conception of human nature and experience which is inaccurate, outmoded, and irrevocably bourgeois. (169)

The binary terms of the debate over the language and representation of practice and gender differences converge in a shared assumption: language controls or is controlled by meaning. But, as Cameron points out, in the world of practice, meaning is also subject to metalinguistic forces such as institutional power structures that regulate a group's access to and control over discourses of power. Thus, language does not guarantee communication any more than silence automatically prevents it. And it is these dimensions of discourse, the metadiscursive activities of culture and social institutions—habits, myths, rituals, practices, historical and social processes—that are vital to the interpretation and representation of the meaning of experiential knowledge.

Unfortunately, the debate over the representation of practice is grounded in a linguistic determinism that, ironically, perpetuates the subordination of practice and practitioners; because language is described as the main means by which meaning is constructed, language rather than other cultural and institutional phenomena becomes the focus of study: "Because we use language to learn about and reflect on other social phenomena, the story goes, all those social phenomena must in the end reduce to language" (Cameron 1985, 164–65). To re-present "feminized" experience requires a redefinition of what constitutes "language." Cameron claims that linguistic research practices tend to treat all language as written rather than spoken and thus overlook the metalinguistic dimensions of language use and meaning making. Paradoxically, this calls for the representation of the nonrepresentational, or metadiscursive. This site is the intersection of discourse and image, as manifested in story and myth.

*The Role of Narrative
in Representations of
Experiential Knowledge*

I return now to my earlier argument that narrative is the appropriate mode for representing and interpreting experiential knowledge. However, the type of narrative that concerns me here is not simply the telling of events or actions. What interests me are the stories that pose questions related to hermeneutical inquiry: How do we know our knowledge? By what stories do we tell ourselves what we know? How is meaning constituted within a given discourse community? How is meaning possible? The stories I wish to tell ask questions that scientific or empirical inquiries cannot, by themselves, answer—namely, questions about the nature of experience and subjectivity or identity (i.e., "difference"). As Linda Alcoff (1988) observes,

There are questions of importance to human beings that science alone cannot answer (including what science is and how it functions), and yet these are questions that we can usefully address by combining scientific data with other logical, political, moral, pragmatic, and coherence considerations. (429)

This is not to advocate a return to an ontology that posits knowledge as independent from human agency, but to claim that questions such as these are part and parcel of the inquiry of practice and identity. The questions might not have answers based upon "fact"; rather, the activity of inquiring itself becomes a fact, an event as well as an object of study, leading to interpretation rather than verification: "knowing better" (Knoblauch and Brannon 1988) rather than "knowing more."

For a better understanding of the uses of story as a basis of inquiry, I turn to studies of mythography (see Doty 1986), which investigate not simply the content of myth (what they are or say) but how they function (what they do and how they mean). By understanding the "mythicity" of myths and mythmaking we might better comprehend the function of storytelling in relation to other modes of inquiry. As mythologist Wendy Doniger O'Flaherty (1988) states, stories are not designed as arguments; they do not assert propositional logic or offer solutions. They do, however, "provide us with metaphors that make the arguments real to us . . . [and] help us to approach certain problems of otherness" (2). Myths, as stories, are not simply *about* events; they are events in themselves. Consequently, the value of narrative in representing experiential knowledge is its self-reflexivity: stories become the events they narrate.

Stories of practice, then, provide a means by which to inquire into the nature of inquiry, specifically the myths by which research discourses narrate their own practices. Such stories don't merely tell about these myths; they enact them, they re-present them so as to make the familiar strange and the strange familiar. Through stories practitioners simultaneously engage in the discourse by which they are inscribed and "talk back" to it, reasserting an identity closer to the "truth" of their experience.

There are, however, some less "truthful" myths in the language of reform that require some closer examination to better understand how stories might transform the interpretation of experiential knowledge. As long as the meanings of story, and in turn myth, are regarded as constituted primarily through language, then story loses its power as an instrument of interpretation and returns to its ontological status as a window to the ineffable. Consequently, when compositionists and feminists discuss the appropriation and reinscription of alien or alienating discourses in the cause of social justice, they express a longing for a utopian control of meaning through language. Through language, cultural images and myths are regarded as revisable, vehicles for demythifying cultural values and beliefs and remythifying them toward a more egalitarian vision of experience.

But myths, as collectively authored and reproduced (or, perhaps more accurately, lacking authorship), are not subject to revision in the same ways as is an individually authored story. Myths, as Doniger O'Flaherty points out, achieve their meaning not only in the realm of discourse but in the nonverbal, visual realm. Myths acquire or lose power based upon their usefulness in interpreting experience; meaning comes from not simply what a myth says but how it functions, how it means. That is where the visual enters: a myth is as good as how well it helps one "see" or experience something, not just what it says about that something.

One can't, in fact, revise a myth, since a myth's powers come from both discursive and nondiscursive sources and its meaning is culturally and institutionally regulated rather than individually prescribed. As Doniger O'Flaherty (1988) humorously comments,

> One is . . . in danger of committing the basic sin of *hubris*—masquerading as a god—if one sets out to create a myth. Of course, this is a very common sin nowadays; many people seem to think that they can create new myths. But I don't think they can. (28)

Thus, one of the least true and least useful myths of the language reform movement to reappropriate the dominant discourse is that the myths (i.e., ideologies) that stories embody can be revised in an act of individual renaming. Ironically, by emphasizing language as the primary site of meaning making, the essential subject becomes reinscribed as the primary agent of this transformation. The political and economic systems by which meanings are institutionally regulated remain unchallenged, as do the limitations on access to these systems. This is because myths, as ways of seeing, are embodied even without language. According to Doniger O'Flaherty (1988),

> The myth, the core of meaning, may survive to some extent even without language; the myth can be recreated again and again, reinflated like a collapsible balloon. The story of the Trojan horse and the myth of Eden survive as myths, free-floating without words. (37–38)

This is not to deny that language has a significant role in mythic meaning making; stories, after all, are a principal vehicle by which myths are communicated. It is, however, to point out that the emphasis on language reform has diverted attention away from issues of power by which meanings are institutionally maintained and regulated. Consequently the essential subject, rather than the collective social struggle necessary to critique existing myths and posit alternatives for understanding and acting in the world, is reinscribed as the agent of transformation. I will say more in chapter 2 about specific myths that inform social constructivist theories in composition. For now, I want to note that the problem of representation, when considered in the context of how myths function, is not simply a problem of avoiding or correcting distortions of an otherwise free and accessible site of meaning, or a problem of individual acts of appropriating and reinscribing the dominant discourse. Instead, the problem of language is primarily a lack of access to discourses of power and the institutions that regulate them; as critical theorist Teresa Ebert (1992–93) states, socioeconomically marginalized groups

> have been denied access to those cultural and institutional subject positions and practices—such as education (including literacy), 'philosophy,' and 'theory' itself—through which individuals are enabled to produce new concepts and to legitimate those concepts they do generate (in short, to be 'heard'). (33)

Thus, the problem is not only to rework the language (or the story) but for groups to gain access to "subject positions" that allow the interpretive frameworks ("myths") by which they assign meaning to their experiences to be formulated and legitimated. Such a struggle, according to Ebert, requires collective action, which essentialist subjectivity and poststructuralist deconstruction of identities oppose.

By understanding the operations of myth/ideology in culture as a collective, yet institutionally regulated, activity of making sense of and enacting meanings of experience—an activity that is both discursive and nondiscursive, as a matter of both language and historically determined structures of power—then we can better understand the role of stories in enacting and reinscribing the myths that inform our inquiries about the nature of inquiry, or, in other words, the role of story to ask the unaskable, to talk back, to re-present "modes of intelligibility" (Ebert 1992–93, 14).

Dialogics and the Novel

What, then, is the power of narrative to challenge or transform its current gendered status as "other" or "different" as a mode of knowing without relying upon essentialist or deterministic definitions that maintain binary oppositions between experience and research, practice and theory, narration and proposition? As a gendered discursive practice, narrative is currently inscribed as an extension of, or complement to, existing discourses rather than as a unique mode of inquiry with its own structures, purposes, and interpretive codes. This is not to advance the "separate but equal" argument of cultural feminism, which affirms narrative "difference" without questioning the sociohistorical processes by which it has been constructed as such. However, it is to say that narratives can and do "talk back" rather than simply act as passive mirrors of the status quo, as illustrated by M. M. Bakhtin's theory of novelistic discourse.

Recognizing the marginalization of the novel as a literary form, Bakhtin, in *The Dialogic Imagination* (1981), argues that the novel as a genre is not simply an addition to or extension of the poetic genre that preceded it but an open-ended form that calls into question previous definitions of poetic form. Novels provide a reinterpretation of the reality represented in other genres and challenge the epic distance those genres place between authors and their subjects.

"Novelization," according to Bakhtin, occurs when one discourse represents and simultaneously speaks the discourse of another in order to bring those discourses into dialogue. Authors consequently "converse" with their subjects: "The hero [i.e., subject] is located in a zone of potential conversation with the author, in a zone of *dialogical contact*" (45, author's emphasis). Instead of simply *revealing* the subject's significance, as the hero is said to be revealed in epic poetry, novels reflect the world of contingency in which knowledge of the world is not limited by one, unified discourse but instead in its plasticity opens up to many genres, both poetic and rhetorical. Thus, the subject contributes to the construction of its (mediated, contingent) significance.

The novel represents a world of discourse that is open-ended and inexhaustible, always partial and ideologically motivated, yet full of possibilities: "Just as all there is to know about a man [*sic*] is not exhausted by his situation in life, so all there is to know about the world is not exhausted by a particular discourse about it" (45). The novel illustrates meaning as a product of unique and unrepeatable social, political, historical, meteorological, physiological (among other) forces—that is, "heteroglossia."

Bakhtin's view of the novel as a mode of inquiry into the languages of others is useful when considering the role of literary forms, specifically fiction, in relation to other modes of inquiry in composition research. Novels don't just passively reflect the pragmatic experience of their subjects, as North (1987) suggests of the narratives of practitioner lore, but actually reenvision that reality, probe it, "carnivalize" the received knowledge of authoritative discourse, laugh, mock, parody, and consume it in an effort to close the distance between subject and author, reader and subject, reader and author. Feminists such as Dale Bauer (1990) have found dialogical theories of discourse useful for the feminist project of using stories as powerful vehicles for reflection and action.

Novels bring widely varied discourses together within one genre. Their multivocality enacts the processes by which meanings are negotiated through interactions among various discourses, dependent upon context, and always shifting. Dialogical approaches to discourse also reclaim literary texts from their status as objects of inquiry (or, as Robert Scholes [1985] wryly notes, the modern substitute for sacred texts) and prompt rereadings of works of literature as responses to other discourses (which is what much feminist literary work continues to do; see, e.g., Patricia Yaeger's *Honey-Mad Women* [1988]) in which they are implicated. Finally, as Charles Schuster observes in "Mikhail Bakhtin as Rhetorical Theorist" (1985), a dialogical approach to rhetoric transforms the rhetorical triangle of speaker-listener-subject from the conventional rhetoric of analysis in which "subjects are actually conceived as objects" to a more dynamic view of discursive interplay:

> In Bakhtin's terms, the hero [subject] is as potent a determinant in the rhetorical paradigm as speaker or listener. The hero interacts with the speaker to shape the language and determine the form. At times, the hero becomes the dominant influence in verbal and written utterance. (595)

Such a dialogic approach to the subject has implications not only for strategies of interpretation but for research methodologies as well.

Objectivist Foundations
in Academic Research

Part of the project to legitimate the experiences and knowledge of practitioners within academe is to inquire into the institutional mechanisms by which practitioners have been excluded from discursive practices of the research community. Specifically, practitioners and researchers, practice and theory, teaching/writing and scholarship/analysis, as well as research methodologies (which assume a neutral, observable reality as the basis of all knowledge) and subjective, internal, nonempirical "creative" work have been institutionalized as binary oppositions. Furthermore, discourses of inquiry in the academy often rely upon false dichotomies between the object of inquiry and the observer as well as between the production and consumption of texts. A novel, for example, is still considered *only* a story, something imagined and constructed as opposed to something real and discovered; the mode of knowing of literary works is still, within the academy, less valued than those of more analytic, supposedly more disinterested, discourses whose emphasis is on the consumption (and objectification) of such texts.

Robert Scholes (1985) has commented upon this hierarchy of discourses as part of the larger "apparatus" of English departments in which the consumption of texts regarded as "literature" is valorized over the production of "pseudo-literary" or "pseudo-non-literary" works in creative writing and composition. In addition, interpretation and, in turn, critical discourse are privileged over the literary forms they study. English studies, according to Scholes, is structured upon binary oppositions of literature/nonliterature and consumption/production of texts that he believes must be deconstructed in order to reconceptualize the purposes, forms, and directions possible for the future of the discipline (7).

Phenomenological inquiry can assist in challenging this canonical hierarchy of discourses and the sociopolitical arrangements of academe (in this case, English departments and English studies) by delineating false dichotomies between subject and object, subjective and objective forms of inquiry, thereby making the dichtomies available for analysis and revision. According to Knoblauch and Brannon (1988),

> The concept of "objectivity" falsely reifies what is always profoundly human (and therefore interpretive) about our understanding [while] the concept of "subjectivity" falsely encloses consciousness, separating human understanding from the world that conditions its action even as, reciprocally, it is conditioned by that action. Human beings are not privileged observers outside of phenomenal reality but rather participants within it. (18)

Phenomenological inquiry assumes that the observer and the object of inquiry (i.e., the "subject") are joined by the instruments of inquiry—in this case, language. Language is the "speculative instrument," as Ann Berthoff describes it, that at once constructs knowledge and acts upon the knowledge that we construct. As Knoblauch and Brannon (1988) state, "The act of seeing . . . has a *material* effect on what is observed, altering it in the very process of focusing upon it" (17, authors' emphasis). We can know the world only through the mediation of symbolic forms, and therefore we are both observers *and* participants in the phenomena we study. In turn, what we write gives form to what we know.

Inquiring into the binary oppositions that maintain the subordinate status, and control the definitions of practice and the identities of (mostly female) practitioners is one step toward transforming institutional practice. Such inquiry cannot be limited to the linguistic practices of institutions but must include inquiry into the metalinguistic practices of power and authority in institutional structures and rituals. As Carl G. Herndl (1991) observes, "[D]isciplinary discourse appropriates the experience of the research subject and represents it in our institutions" (320). Consequently, inquiring into the mechanisms by which such appropriations are possible can subsequently make them available for critique and contestation.

Researching as a Woman

The problem of representing the research subject has been tied to problems of representing the researcher's subjectivity, which in positivist research has been posited as necessarily neutral and nonexistent. Representing the narrative, "subjective" knowledge of practice and practitioners, however, requires a reevaluation of the relation of subjects to researchers as well as of researchers' own subjectivities. Within composition, the question of subjective identities has also been raised in relation to feminist concerns, challenging the binary opposition between "objective" and "subjective" methods of research.

Since Elizabeth Flynn's "Composing as a Woman" appeared in 1988, more compositionists are beginning to question the specific ways in which composition studies is gendered and to identify how women, as primary agents of instruction, are marginalized. Flynn, like educational researcher Patti Lather, sees the problem as partly one of positivist assumptions underlying most research in the field. Flynn contends that to launch an inquiry that will be regarded as research, one must, paradoxically, exclude oneself as a woman. Otherwise, one's inquiry may meet the fate of being renamed as "merely" pedagogical, especially if one is a woman; as Flynn cites in her "Staffroom Interchange" (1990) response to "Composing as a Woman," reviewers of her original manuscript did not consider it legitimate research, requiring instead that she add a section entitled "Pedagogical Implications," as if to announce her work as valuable classroom practice but of little interest to the research community as research.

Flynn asks, just as Carol Gilligan (*In a Different Voice*) and Mary Belenky and colleagues (*Women's Ways of Knowing*) ask of their male predecessors, Are the models of ethical, intellectual, and writing development biased toward a male viewpoint? Lather (1991) would no doubt add, In what ways are the research methodologies themselves so biased, and how can we move into more "critical, praxis-oriented paradigm[s]"? (70).

What, in fact, is the relationship of models of composing to the "myths" of culture, of institutional arrangements of power and authority? What are the stories that inform our view of the "real world" outside of the classroom, where we know our students must go, both within and outside of academia? How do these stories affect our view of composing, the instruction we subsequently give, as well as the writing we do ourselves? And how can we, finally, act to change these stories and offer alternative views—for ourselves, our students, our field of study? Can we rewrite the history of composing to include "woman" as one who is not only composed but who composes?

To address these questions, one must adopt a research methodology that studies difference. This "difference," however, is not grounded in either the essentialism argued by North (a "difference between"—after Teresa Ebert—feminized practitioners and masculinized researchers) or the determinism of social constructivists (in which "difference" itself is a linguistic construct signifying a "difference within" the category of practice), but rather, as Teresa Ebert (1992–93) defines it, "*difference in relation . . . within a system of exploitation and the social struggle it engenders*" (16–17; author's emphasis). It must be a methodology that doesn't, at the start, require that one check one's own difference at the entryway, suppress the multiple identities one brings to bear upon any inquiry. As I have previously argued, I don't think most composition research seriously considers those who do this; and the published research that does do this doesn't offer a clear idea of how it might contribute to other research. I agree with Flynn's assessment about lingering positivist inclinations, even in ethnographic or "naturalistic" research, as discussed by Carl Herndl (1991).

But I also think, similar to Deborah Cameron (1985), that composition focuses too much on how meaning is constructed, maintained, and replicated through language, specifically the written word, to the exclusion of metalinguistic phenomena. The "linguistic determinism" cited by Cameron (1985) is perhaps another version of positivism. We confuse language with meaning instead of understanding meaning in broader contexts of symbolic form, including cultural and institutional forms of myth and ritual in the exercise and regulation of power and authority.

Flynn herself has since been criticized for essentialist definitions of "woman" in her research, reinscribing rather than challenging sexist concepts of gender in her observations that women write more about caring and connection in their narratives and men write more about adventure and separation (supporting Gilligan's research on differences in moral and ethical development between genders). Although Flynn's own research methodologies in this project may also be said to represent some lingering positivist assumptions in how she approaches the interpretation of student texts, her research is still, I believe, a landmark in its challenge to gendered research practices within composition and in creating links between practitioner knowledge and gendered identities. Similarly, Stephen North's (1987) attempt to resituate practitioner knowledge is highly significant in its attempt to change the status of a gendered practitioner knowledge. Although the critique of Flynn's and North's essentialization of practice and gender by social constructivists is instructive, social constructivists have not, I think, helped the cause of practitioners, or women, in particular, any more (and in some ways they have helped less) than Flynn or North, as I will discuss in chapter 2.

Writing the Subject

How might story, then, contribute to our understanding of how cultural and institutional myths derive their power and consequently give us some clues as to how to get out of our own heads and into the heads of Others, so to speak, without doing damage? How do we represent the Other—in our classrooms, ourselves as Other, those on the margins of society?

By reflecting on the ways in which the "myths" or "ideologies" of the academy shape the ways a writer comes to know her knowledge, we can begin to know better the assumptions that prevent writing from taking place by privileging some stories of composing over others. Although there exists an abundance of composing models from empirical, philosophical, cognitive, and other research perspectives, stories of composing are distinctly lacking from a writer's perspective. A writer's view of her own work is regarded as suspect, just as is a teacher's reflection on her own teaching, which is why neither are valued institutionally as real knowledge-making enterprises. As for the writer, and most particularly the woman writer, she is even more vulnerable to her text of composing being appropriated, because she has been socialized, as women in the culture generally have been, to mistrust what she knows—which models of conflict and separation reinforce.

I will tell, therefore, in the following chapters a writer's story, a woman's story, and in the telling resituate the prevailing story of master-apprentice, or, as Linda Brodkey (1987) has written, the "scene of writing" that, as Belenky and her colleagues (1986) have noted, highlights the "hero" story of education. Part of telling the woman writer's story, however, entails representing how the masculinist, "hero" story (as exemplified by Rose 1989) has inscribed her into its narrative structures, and how it is part of the web of stories that spin her and that she in turn spins.

Chapter 2 will focus on the prevailing stories of composition within social constructivism, examining the theories of Kenneth Bruffee, Patricia Bizzell, and David Bartholomae. Although their critique of the essential has been a useful perspective on much of the theory and pedagogy of expressivism, they rely upon images of romantic "hero" teachers and students recruited in the cause of social justice, reifying individual rationality and personal response as opposed to collective resistance and action.

Chapter 3 begins the woman writer's story, specifically my rereading of a draft of a short story I wrote several years ago. My rereading is through the interpretive framework of "romance" and "quest" plots noted by the feminist literary scholars Carolyn Heilbrun and Rachel Blau DuPlessis. Chapters 4 and 5 expand the writer's story to include stories of my experiences in two writing groups (a graduate fiction workshop and a self-directed student group) in which a draft of a second short story is discussed along with interpretations of the "mythic" or ideological frameworks informing the groups' talk. Chapter 6 returns to the question of representation, this time regarding representation of practitioners' power and authority. The book closes with an epilogue of reflections on the difference the experience of telling these stories has made to my own practice.

The value of a woman writer's stories is not in the "facts" that the narratives reveal but in the qualitative difference that the reading of such stories provides. Knoblauch and Brannon (1988) argue that we should value the ways of knowing that narratives provide for the same reasons we value literature; one does not know more as stories are added,

> but one does know 'better'; one's instincts and values, expectations and judgments mature. One's ability to read the world grows. Literature enhances the quality of understanding without presuming to add to its content. (28)

Narrative is a mode of knowing; the relational web of many texts complicates and enriches what we know of our experience. Instead of the reduction, isolation, and abstractions required in traditional scholarly discourse, narratives offer enlargement, inclusion, and enrichment, which are especially necessary to the development of women in the composition of themselves as knowers. Women writers are particularly vulnerable to the narratives that inscribe them; as Carolyn Heilbrun (1988) has noted in her work on women's biographies,

> We can only retell and live by the stories we have read or heard. We live our lives through texts. . . . Whatever their form or medium, these stories have formed us all; they are what we must use to make new fictions, new narratives. (37)

Patti Lather (1991) comments, "I conceptualize ideology as the stories a culture tells itself about itself" (2). In this sense, fictions shape our lives (and the stories we tell about our stories) in critical ways; therefore narratives of writers' talk, both within and outside the academy, deserve the serious attention we as readers of literature so willingly apply.

Note

1. By "practitioner" I refer to identities constructed through narratives of experience as opposed to abstract or propositional constructs. In this case, I refer specifically to teachers and students of writing as well as writers. But I also equate formal "practices" of teaching and writing with life "experiences" of women under the larger category of "experiential knowledge." Both require the construction of subjectivities that seek to re-create a verisimilitude of experience through narrative rather than to argue propositional "truths." In a sense, we are all "practitioners" in life, though our professional identities might sometimes amplify or obscure those practices.

❧ What is "Social" about Social Constructivism?

In chapter 1, I introduced theories of language that inform representations of experiential knowledge in composition and feminism, noting how essentialist and deterministic views of language and language practices share a common assumption: Changing language, whether by imbuing it with personal meaning or by correcting or appropriating it for the purposes of revising or subverting meaning, is the primary means by which to achieve personal and cultural empowerment. I have already discussed the limitations as well as the significances of essentialist views in composition, such as those of Stephen North and Elizabeth Flynn. I will now turn my attention to three social constructivists in composition to discuss the "linguistic determinism" of their approaches to composition theory and practice and explore the points at which they converge, diverge, and conflict with some feminist positions on language, representations of the self and individual and collective agency, and empowerment.

Social constructivism has provided a powerful critique of expressivist theory and practice in composition in its deconstruction of the essential definitions of self and subjectivity as textual constructions rather than "natural" attributes. However, social constructivists have in some ways diverted attention away from the historical inequities of composition teachers that theorists such as Flynn and North sought to address. By critiquing expressivists' desire to affirm and value the experiences of practitioners, social constructivists have left a vacuum as to how to intervene in transforming composition's feminized status in the academy and the oppressive material conditions within which practitioners (teachers and students alike) must work.

The contradictory and conflicting myths by which social constructivists interpret narratives of experience and subjectivity may themselves be implicated in the reproduction and maintenance of the binary oppositions that maintain current arrangements of institutional and cultural power.

Despite the fact that many teachers, students, and writers in general are restricted from access to and participation in the discourses by which cultural meanings are inscribed and regulated, social constructivists, taking their cue from postmodern theories of language, often treat change more as a matter of altering language practices than as a matter of social intervention and emancipation. As Teresa Ebert (1992–93) observes of what she terms "ludic postmodernism,"[1]

> [T]he dominant postmodern theories—what I have called "ludic" post-modernism—have problematized the notion of politics and rearticulated it as solely a cultural politic: that is, as a language-effect, a mode of rhetoric aimed at changing cultural representations, rather than as a collective practice through which existing social institutions are changed so that (economic) resources and cultural power can be distributed without regard to gender, race, class, sexuality. (6)

In ludic postmodernism, meaning is constructed in a "free" space where it is always subject to revision. Presumably, practitioners (whether teacher, student, writer, woman, or Others) move freely within the gaps in discourse in order to appropriate discourse for their own purposes. Changing language practices becomes, again, the primary mode of empowerment, even though, as Cameron (1985) has noted, meaning is not "freely" available to personal or social control, and myths, as Doniger O'Flaherty (1988) comments, are not simply things but practices—ways of seeing that are not authored but simply exist, to some extent, beyond language.

Thus, this chapter will primarily concern itself with the contradictory and conflicting myths by which social constructivists interpret and represent the realm of practice, particularly in relation to classroom practices of teachers and students of writing and modes of empowerment available to practitioners. I will inquire into representations of the "social" within these theories as both a textual construction and a deterministic set of relations. Finally, I will discuss the work of feminists seeking to define different views of the social and the systems and operations by which power is regulated.

A Response to Expressivism

Social constructivist classroom practices, as described by Kenneth Bruffee, at first greatly resembled the methods, if not the principles, of expressivists such as Peter Elbow (*Writing Without Teachers*, 1973) in their emphasis on collaborative learning. But in the 1980s, social constructivism became more a response and correction to expressivists whose theories and practices, constructivists argued, reinforce rather than challenge the institutional and cultural status quo by reinscribing the concept of a transcendent, autonomous self, thus maintaining inequities in the social order. Also, social constructivists argued against the cultural limitations of expressivist approaches and instead focused on the ways power and authority shape what teachers, students, and writers think and write as well as how to make cultural "codes of power" explicit to marginalized students of color (Delpit 1988).

Consequently, much social constructivist inquiry is focused on the social contexts of literacy and learning. Much of this concern for understanding the role of social contexts in literacy education came about from CUNY's open enrollments in the 1970s. Those who have looked to Mina Shaughnessy (1977) as a pioneer, such as Kenneth Bruffee, Patricia Bizzell, and David Bartholomae, continue her legacy, only now with more attention to students' participation in the shaping of meaning in discourses of power rather than to Shaughnessy's politics of accommodation (for more thorough critiques of Shaughnessy, see Bartholomae 1986b and Lu 1991).

Although social constructivists and feminists share the goal of transforming language practices by fostering active participation in the appropriation and transformation of discourses of power, the rhetoric of Bruffee, Bizzell, and Bartholomae represents the classroom within a masculine model of education that characterizes "reality" as primarily adversarial and requires, in turn, the production of "heroic" students who must overcome the "limitations" of their original communities. Alternative models of learning and reality, such as those suggested by Belenky and her colleagues (1986), Gilligan (1982), and others, are suppressed or denied in favor of a utopian vision of equal, autonomous, rational individuals who reason together freely to eliminate their differences and achieve consensus. The "differences" students bring to their educations are represented as limitations to overcome rather than as the starting point of their learning. Teachers, in contrast, are represented as shrinking away to invisibility or dwelling heroically above the partial, messy world of students, models of ideal, dispassionate, "free" inquiry. In this binary opposition, students are still limited by their home culture's biases, but teachers are supposedly "free" to "choose" positions (Ellsworth 1989). Teachers thus supply what students "lack"—another version of Freire's banking model. In this regard, social constructivists may undermine rather than assist feminist efforts at making educational institutions hospitable places for women to learn, by emphasizing a distancing from the knowledge of their lived experiences and a tacitly hierarchical rather than reciprocal relationship between teacher and student.

Bruffee and the Problem of Consensus

In Bruffee's collaborative model, two distinct populations exist: teacher and student. The teacher belongs to an apparently monolithic disciplinary discourse community that students are ultimately trying to approximate through their classroom talk. According to Bruffee (1984), this discourse is representative not only of the talk academics value, but also of that of "a community that approximates the one most students must eventually write for in everyday life, in business, government, and the professions" (642)—a discourse that takes place among peers. For Bruffee, it is such talk that makes up the "reality" into which students will be launched upon graduation, a reality with which, presumably, they are largely, if not entirely, unfamiliar.

In order for this conversation among peers to take place, it would seem that the role of the teacher in this context is to stay out of the discussion as much as possible. The role of teachers is to create contexts for talk, not to talk themselves, or to speak as little as possible so as to not jeopardize the interaction of equals speaking to equals. In fact, one might argue that the moment a teacher contributes anything to the peer discussion, the group's talk has been unduly influenced by a person of a higher status, namely, the teacher. Although I don't think Bruffee would ascribe to such rigid boundaries in practice, nonetheless it is teachers who initially have power in the classroom and, by "indirect" methods, "give" that power to their students in the form of collaborative learning contexts. What teachers contribute, the talk that they and, later, the outside world value, is presented by Bruffee as necessary and unproblematic. There is little consideration given to the "historical circumstances that greatly limited the group of people who had access to it in terms of race, sex, and social class" (Bizzell 1990a, 663).

The problem with this binary opposition between "students" or "peers" and "teacher" is that students are represented as a monolithic

"Other" in the text of Bruffee's classroom. This hierarchical model constructs the teacher as the master of a disciplinary discourse and students as apprentices who can hope only to approximate, with their "transitional" language, the master's voice. Teachers have access to a power that students need and see it as their task to "give" this power to students through collaborative methods of instruction. In contrast to their partial, emotional, subjective students, teachers are constructed as "free, rational, and objective . . . to choose positions on their own merits" (Ellsworth 1989, 306). Paradoxically, these "disinterested" teachers also see themselves, as Elizabeth Ellsworth (1989) comments with regard to critical pedagogy, as "mediator[s] on the side of an oppressed group" (309); one wonders how a "mediator" can also "take sides."

Bruffee's classroom is based upon a model of "energy drain," a concept discussed by Rosemary Deen (1986), in which power is perceived to flow in one direction, from teacher to student, without awareness of the source or of possibilities for renewal. In this model, the teacher is also jeopardized as a constant "power" giver who faces the likelihood of power drain or burnout because no new power is received—the ideal maternal image of the all-powerful, all-giving mother. Furthermore, differences in social status among "peers"—differences in gender, race, ethnicity, class— are not addressed in the supposedly egalitarian conversation among "equals."

Bruffee (1984) maintains that in the world of everyday life, this conversation among equals is also the normative discourse in the workplace and, presumably, the home. Certainly it can be argued that anyone seeking to participate in a discourse community will feel a pressure to conform to the conventions of that community. But it is misleading to suggest that "normal" discourse somehow transcends social hierarchies and is always purely informed by rational thought. In addition, if that "normal discourse" is, as Bruffee says, "pointed" and "explanatory and argumentative," then the discourse of many women and minorities, which follows different patterns of development, might not seem "normal" (and, as linguists Cameron [1985] and Labov [1970] have shown, transcripts of women's and African Americans' talk have frequently been misread by linguists as displaying a lack of "logic" and focus in speech and thought) and thus might seem superfluous in the collaborative classroom. What might seem to be a consensual discourse among equals is, in fact, the voice of a dominant group—white, middle-class, and male.

Thus Bruffee's model of a consensus resulting from an ideal conversation among autonomous individuals may, in fact, "accommodate its practices to the authority of knowledge it believes it is demystifying" (Trimbur

1989, 603). "Consensus," as Bruffee represents it, takes place outside of unequal power situations among "like-minded" people.

John Trimbur (1989) has critiqued Bruffee's concept of consensus as reinscribing power inequities among social groups in its depiction of consensus as something stable, the product of wholly rational, "normal" discourse. Trimbur notes that Bruffee's consensus does not adequately address the question of the relationship of "abnormal" discourse (borrowing from Richard Rorty's terms), which is outside the prevailing normative conversation, to its "normal" counterpoint, figuring such consensus as monolithic and thus unaware of "the set of power relations that organizes normal discourse: the acts of permission and prohibition, of incorporation and exclusion that institute the structure and practices of discourse communities" (608). Instead, abnormal discourse "offers a way to analyze the strategic moves by which discourse communities legitimize their own conversation by marginalizing others" (609). Thus Trimbur would invite those "others," including women, to exercise their "abnormal" discourses toward analyzing and discussing the ways their discourses are marginalized and thus impede the possibility of consensus.

Trimbur points to the problem of difference that already shapes classroom dynamics and offers a perspective on how to productively make use of differences instead of anticipating "an agreement that reconciles differences through an ideal conversation" (615). Rather, consensus should be regarded as "the desire of humans to live and work together with differences" (615). Students will struggle with the problems a teacher "orchestrates," and in the process they will learn how to appreciate and live with differences as they discuss shared concerns.

Trimbur's recasting of consensus in favor of "dissensus" is an important step toward opening the classroom up to all student voices. However, from a feminist perspective, I think he might not go far enough in addressing the role of the teacher's agency. With Trimbur, as with Bruffee, teachers are rhetorically inscribed as those who "orchestrate" classroom conversation, neutral, objective observers above their students' struggling subjectivities. Unlike Bruffee, Trimbur does construct the classroom conversation as a place where consensus occurs not as an "acculturative practice that reproduces business as usual" but rather as "a necessary fiction of reciprocity and mutual recognition, the dream of conversation as a perfect dialogue" (612). To this extent, Trimbur does hint at the possibility that such a reciprocity can occur between teachers and students, not only among students. Furthermore, Trimbur does say he believes the practice of "dissensus" "can release collective energies to turn the means of criticism into a means of transformation, to tap fundamental impulses towards emancipation and justice" (615). However, Trimbur's prose obscures teacher agency in favor of larger processes that apparently are supposed to just take over among students. The teacher is, once again, evacuated from Trimbur's prose when he contrasts Bruffee's "normal workings" of collaborative learning, in which teachers' analyses of writing represent a conversation that students aspire to join, to Trimbur's "utopian" view that "would abandon this expert-novice model of teaching and learning [and] [i]nstead . . . would provide students with a critical measure to identify the relations of power in the formation of expert judgment" (613). It is the "consensus" that provides the "critical measure"; this suggests the view that the teacher can somehow remain outside or above these processes and watch them unfold—a position similar to that of Bruffee. Teachers set up the conflicts but interestingly remain aloof from them. Students' struggles toward transformation don't include the teacher's subjectivity. Teachers "orchestrate" long enough for a "higher power" to take over in students' interactions and lead students toward liberatory ends.

Teachers take on a simultaneously powerful and voyeuristic role, for both Bruffee and Trimbur; because teachers are presumably freethinking, rational, and impartial, they can remain neutral and thus outside the struggle among students' differences, "orchestrating" conversation. But teachers, like students, are not totally free to engage in discourses of power, to choose positions "freely" and argue them objectively. To represent teachers as Bruffee and Trimbur do is to deny teachers their own history and subjectivities, a move that for women teachers can simply reinscribe their oppression by keeping them from critically examining their own status in the educational system.

Both Bruffee and Trimbur focus on the students' subjectivities in relation to each other. They do not, however, represent *intersubjectivity* between teachers and students, as if the teacher's power and authority over students were monolithic. In fact, for women and other Others, it is much more complex: Teachers can't orchestrate or distribute power when they don't have the stable, totalizing power ascribed to them by collaborative learning theorists.

Bizzell and the Problem of Agency

Patricia Bizzell has for many years inquired into the academic's roles and responsibilities in the classroom and in society as an agent of change and a model of civic responsibility. At the 1990 Conference on College Composition and Communication, Bizzell (1990b) critiqued (as Trimbur did later in *College English*) Bruffee's concept of peers as equals in response to his presentation on collaborative learning (Bruffee 1990; interestingly, little in Bruffee's theory or methodology seemed to have changed since his 1984 article in *College English*). In Bizzell's view, teachers, instead of striving to become invisible onlookers in the classroom conversations they set in motion, need to assert their authority as "strong" teachers to ensure that the social inequities that exist outside the classroom do not go unexamined in class. Bruffee's model of collaborative learning teachers, on the other hand, assumes that teachers' presences becomes more and more backgrounded as students learn to work together on the problems that teachers lay out. Like Ira Shor's ideally invisible teacher in *Critical Teaching and Everyday Life* (1987), the best teacher is one whose presence is no longer needed. Peter Elbow went so far as to describe a classroom without any teachers at all in *Writing without Teachers* (1973), a guidebook that, ironically, has been used as a basis for teacher-initiated instruction.

This model of the invisible teacher is in many ways counter to those feminist pedagogies that, on the one hand, seek to de-center authority and demystify the production of knowledge (similar to Bruffee 1984) but, on the other, represent the teacher as an active agent who models commitment and action (Bauer 1990 and Jarratt 1991). Thus, the problem with much collaborative or "process-oriented" learning models is that they, in portraying the teacher as an invisible agent, or worse, reinscribing her as a peacekeeper/nurturer, actually disempower both students and (mostly women) teachers. As Susan Jarratt (1991) observes of expressivist pedagogies such as Elbow's,

> [P]roblems occur when a female teacher takes a nurturing role in a class of men and women—replicating the traditional female role in our culture. A female teacher who takes a position of uncritical openness toward the male student, especially if social-class differences also apply, invites the exercise of patriarchal domination to which every man in our society is acculturated. (111)

Such approaches "feminize" the classroom negatively, so that, in Dale Bauer's words, students can avoid the ambivalence out of which true dialogue is possible and without which no "negotiation of meaning" or exploration of differences that are otherwise "buried deeply, already reconciled" (Bauer 1990, 387) will occur.

To this extent, I think Bizzell (1990b) is right to question the invisible teacher model as possibly contributing to, rather than alleviating, social hierarchies in peer group work. However, her solution of the "strong" teacher is only a modification of the model of education promoted by collaborative learning, which remains, even now, a model of assimilation into academic life (and the "real" world of work), in which thinking is represented by teacher talk and teacher values of intellectuality (though, as I will note momentarily, Bizzell [1990a; 1991] has since questioned her previous emphases on "antifoundationalism," which perpetuates the same binary oppositions as foundationalism). "Power" is still something teachers have and thus should "give" to students; power equals control, and control is always allied to force.

Nonetheless, I think Bizzell, unlike Bruffee, is very clear in her desire not to bamboozle students into believing that the kind of literacy that teachers promote is value-free. Teachers are not "value-neutral conveyers of truth," but "rhetors" who are "attempting to persuade [students] to accept our values, not simply inculcating our values" (Bizzell 1984, 454). As rhetors, teachers are obliged to teach not only ways of thinking, but thinking that conforms to values of the academic community. Bizzell (1984) uses William Perry's model of intellectual development in liberal education as a useful map of the kinds of changes teachers should strive for with their students. As she states, "The whole thrust of his developmental scheme is toward an increasing distance on [sic] the beliefs of one's childhood," beliefs that "can no longer be accepted uncritically as Absolutes" (453). Liberal education, then, seeks to distance the student from her or his home community by placing the values and beliefs of that community in relation to other values, particularly those of academia. It is a model that requires the renunciation of one way of thinking for another, presumably better, way. Bizzell believes in admitting up front that what we as academics value is better for students' intellectual development. We have ways of thinking (and thinking about thinking) that students do not have and that we know it is in their best interests for them to have.

Although Bizzell acknowledges that a student's intellectual development entails a process of socialization into the academic community, her model for that development is based upon one that Mary Belenky and her colleagues have argued in *Women's Ways of Knowing* (1986) is biased toward male-oriented representations of such development. Perry, they note, focused primarily upon male students in his study and consequently mirrors a process of what Belenky and her colleagues describe as separation and distance rather than the relational and "connected" values that form the basis of so many women's experience. If the values of liberal education that Bizzell says she wants for her students are based upon models of intellectual development that are male-biased, then students who do not fit the white, middle-class, male profile of that study are being asked to assimilate into a way of thinking that automatically excludes or erases their presence as disenfranchised groups. As John Trimbur (1989) implies, students assume a reality of "conflict and difference" without alternative spaces for identification and affirmation. For many women students, the research suggests, such a space can be critical in their continuing development.

Bizzell (1984) argues that what students need is "cultural literacy" (in a pre-Hirschian usage), which is "the objects of knowledge and the ways of thinking that one must master in order to participate in a particular community" (453). Students come to academia without these "objects of knowledge" or the "ways of thinking" required for intellectual development; it is the teacher's job to see that they get it. The goal of such literacy is displacement of a student from one community into another; as Bizzell notes, literacy in the form of reading and writing is peculiar to participation in the academic community, and that "literacy is not required for participation in every sort of community" (453). To become literate, then, means giving up one set of values for, presumably, a better, more significant set that will propel one forward through academia and subsequently through society.

While I agree that teaching should facilitate habits of mind that are particular to intellectual life, the models that Bizzell and Bruffee present tend to valorize the academic experience at the expense of a more critical awareness of the implications of an assimilationist view of entry into academic life. More recent work by Bizzell (1990a, 1990b, 1991), however, shows that she is constructing the role of the academic and of academic discourse in a more pluralistic context, seeking a third course of "positionality," using a feminist-oriented vantage point to critique the "Procrustean" foundationalist views of the conservative Right (as championed by E.D. Hirsch and Allan Bloom) as well as the "political quietism" of antifoundationalists of the Left. It is not enough to simply critique textual authority and power, as antifoundationalists do of foundationalists, nor is it adequate to call for a consensual discourse without considering the cultural and historical processes by which such a discourse is shaped and reshaped over time. Instead, Bizzell (1990a) calls for claiming a "rhetorical" authority that enables teachers to speak from a rhetorical (rather than "value-free") stance and persuade students to their viewpoints without imposing them:

> Thus the oratorical exercise of authority does recommend a positive position but does not impose it. The orator tries to achieve a consensus around the change in ideologies he or she advocates, but a consensus can only be achieved through collective participation in the rhetorical process. (673)

Consequently, teachers can exercise the authority of knowledge within the classroom but not from an authoritarian vantage point. Rather, teachers may explicitly identify themselves with certain "subject" positions, but as orators or rhetors they should engage students in the contradictions they express while at the same time modeling positive positions from which to construct personally meaningful and politically aware identifications.

Teacher as Hero:
David Bartholomae

Like Bruffee and Bizzell, David Bartholomae has extended Mina Shaughnessy's legacy, aiming to enfranchise "basic writers" who, as students from diverse cultural, class, and ethnic backgrounds, have been largely regarded as ineducable. Both Bizzell and Bartholomae have challenged Shaughnessy's assimilationist politics of literacy (i.e., that one must learn to "fit" unquestioningly into the dominant discourse), but they have also upheld her beliefs that students need to learn academic discourse, to "convert" to new values and habits of academe—in short, to become more like "us," the teachers. Language is the key to empowerment; by acquiring the language of those in power, one can "both imagine and write from a position of privilege" (Bartholomae 1985, 139). The paradox, as Bartholomae (1985) observes, is that students must speak in the academic voice "before . . . they have anything to say" (156).

Bartholomae redefines Shaughnessy's view of basic writers as "beginners" in a move that suggests a broader, more arbitrary, and less essential and pointed classification than Shaughnessy's. To Bartholomae (1985), basic writers are simply "university students traditionally placed in remedial composition courses" (136). Consequently, he blurs distinctions between "basic writers" and students in general by naming the difference in their ability to engage in academic discourse as one of degree, not kind, suggesting that that ability is a matter not simply of practice but of politics: "The writing, then, must somehow transform the political and social relationships between students and teachers" (140).

The assumption underlying the relationships between students and teachers is that students (i.e., basic writers) come from politically disenfranchised backgrounds. Teachers, in contrast, are privileged "insiders" who can give students access to discourses of privilege that they currently lack. Like Bruffee and Bizzell, the classroom is characterized in binary terms—the group "out of power" (students) is persuaded by the group "in power" (teachers) that academic ways of thinking, speaking, and writing will lead to a more equitable social order for those who acquire them.

In Bartholomae's rhetoric, teachers are "heroes" who can rescue students from the limits of their home discourses and bring them into a new, broader conversation of ideas. Teachers are advocates of the underclass, the disenfranchised, and as such encourage students to try on academic discourse "before they have anything to say," trusting that the teacher represents someone they can identify with and want to emulate. Clearly, such a relationship calls for no small measure of trust. The question is, What is the basis of that trust? Why should students want to become like "us"?

Bartholomae represents teachers' power and authority, as well as students' desire to appropriate it for themselves, as givens. Apparently the fact that students "don't have it" is enough to motivate them to "get it." This raises two problems: First, why should students trust another authority figure when presumably they've already encountered a long series of them who have kept them disenfranchised? Second, what are we really wanting students to become when we say we want them to become "like us"? What power and authority do most composition teachers have in the academy? Who, as Joseph Harris (1989) has asked, is the "us" that Bartholomae invokes?

With regard to the first problem, Bartholomae narrates a story of conversion in which "outsider" students must become "submerged" in the alien discourse of the academy, trusting that "we," their teachers, will help them work their way "within and against" their home and academic discourses. Like babes in the baptismal fount, students are supposed to relinquish prior language practices and allow themselves to be immersed in those of the more powerful "aliens." Students consequently are asked to open themselves to this "baptism" with the supposed guarantee that teachers will pull them out of the water before the alien discourse "drowns" them. The only risk that teachers apparently incur is that they might "drop the baby"—in other words, harm the student. Thus, teachers remain above the waters of the fount as objective spectators of their students' "progress."

Bartholomae insists that student writing will transform the student-teacher relationship by offering students the means to create an identity of privilege and power from which to speak and write. Yet in order to create such an identity, students must already trust the teacher to provide the appropriate models. Upon what is that trust based? Apparently, students are supposed to trust more-powerful teachers because they *are* powerful— a bit of circular logic that reinscribes teachers' authority as stable and continuous rather than partial and contingent. Furthermore, not all students will uniformly occupy positions out of power, since, as Bartholomae himself notes, basic writers are simply those placed in remedial classes and not monolithically of one particular class, race, gender, or ethnicity. In fact, one could argue that the profile of "basic" writers is relative to the overall student admissions of a given institution. In some cases, as Joseph Janangelo (1991) has pointed out, white, heterosexual, wealthy students might already have more social power and privilege than do their composition instructors. To construct students as a group monolithically out of power, and teachers as heroic power brokers, is to invite serious misreadings of either group's power and authority.

This brings us to the second problem: What are we really asking of students when we say we want them to become "like us"? On the one hand, students will often "read" the teacher through the binary opposition of their lack in relation to the teacher's possession of language. Consequently, teachers are constructed as stable entities to whom students, embroiled in the turmoil of their learning, can turn for wise, neutral, impartial counsel. But in fact teachers do not uniformly inhabit positions of privilege and power; they themselves are often excluded from dominant discourses of the academy because of gender, class, or status/rank. If teachers see themselves as heroic, above-the-fray, disinterested mediators, they risk denying their own problematic position in the academy as both powerful and powerless, tacitly passing on the same sense of powerlessness to their students. In the struggle for a sense of control, the old authoritarianism, or the old nurturing-peacekeeping, can find its way inside the classroom once again. As Kate Winter (1993) has written concerning the "trailing spouse" phenomenon in academe,

It appears that one's own writing history affects the way one teaches writing. A teacher who is so overburdened with composition classes that she cannot get on with her own work and who is in an adjunct position where her writing is devalued may skew the kind of instruction she gives in writing. A woman whose autonomy is restricted in life may try to reclaim it in the classroom. The erosion of her self-worth may create control issues for her and lead her away from her most effective student-centered teaching. (441)

Ultimately, I think it would be more useful to consider the student *in relation* to the teacher, who represents the authority of the institution yet also occupies a number of subject positions that might or might not be more powerful than those of the students. Furthermore, instead of casting student writers as lacking place, privilege, or authority, it might be more useful to invoke such qualities as something student writers already possess—and to see student writers' task as inquiring into the social and historical arrangements that have excluded and included students in both their "native" discourses and in academic discourses. Instead of perpetuating the master-apprentice metaphors—the powerful giving power to the powerless, the capitalistic exchange of one language for another as if language were a kind of intellectual currency (an image that is not far removed from the image of "codes" in functionalist rhetoric)—we could adopt a relational model of the educational enterprise, in which subjects (students, teachers, and so on) exist in a web of relations that can change but never entirely disappear.

Social constructivist theory has been useful, I think, in making a case for the view that literacy is very much a process of socialization and that teachers of writing need to consider the ways in which literacy is a cultural/textual construct rather than an "objective" accumulation of mechanized skills or a "subjective," personal meaningfulness. But the conversion myth underlying social constructivism, in which students are perceived as lacking or needy, and the teacher (the perpetual energy source) fills the lack, competes with the myths of empowerment and social justice. Consequently, students' ability to interpret and compose the significances of "the flow of social discourse," as Clifford Geertz (1983) calls it, in their own community is not valued. Students are taught that they must learn to think, not, as Ann Berthoff would say, *that* they think. And the teacher's energy source is represented as magically self-renewing, reifying an image of an all-giving and (in relation to students) all-powerful benevolence.

In contrast, Shirley Brice Heath's (1988) model of literacy instruction shows how students' ways with words and the contexts in which they learn in their local populations are studied in relation to school literacy. Their familiar ways of knowing are seen, through the "alien" eyes of the classroom, as strange and new, as inviting objects of study, and in turn the strange ways of the classroom become more familiar. It is a model of reciprocity, where both the teacher and the student learn from each other, rather than the energy source flowing unilaterally to the needy student. Perhaps more importantly, however, the reciprocity extends outside the classroom, between the institution and the community. No longer is it the students who must conform to the language practices of the school; in a radical ideological shift, the schools adapt to the language practices and cultures of its students and use them as a basis for shaping curricula and developing appropriate pedagogies. Students thus gain access to the dominant discourses *through* their cultures rather than by blindly immersing themselves in the alien tongue. "Difference" is defined in neither binary nor neutral frameworks; instead it is understood in the fluid, phenomenological contexts of daily life that are represented in the narratives of the local people Heath interviewed.

Feminist Critique
of "Empowerment"

Perhaps the most challenging issue social constructivists face is in representing how linguistic empowerment leads to social intervention to address inequities based upon differences in gender, race, class, ethnicity, and other "differences." In the rhetoric of social constructivism, the focus is primarily on changing the language practices of the student; changes on the part of the teacher, according to Elizabeth Ellsworth (1989) in her critique of liberatory pedagogy, are motivated largely "to enable the teacher to devise more effective strategies for bringing the student 'up' to the teacher's level of understanding" (306). The assumption underlying the "empowerment" of students is that once they can speak "within and against" the dominant discourse, they will automatically intervene in changing social inequities, either simply through their presence as a traditionally marginalized group or because they have been persuaded, through the teacher's "rhetorical authority," to think and act with more critical awareness. Thus it follows that a teacher's basis for intervention is activities in individual classrooms, rather than, as Heath advocates, also changing the institution to accommodate a more student-centered approach to literacy. Perhaps the reason Heath's work in the Piedmont was at once so successful and so threatening is that it effected more profound institutional change that any previous approaches (which perhaps is why her program was eventually abandoned). Social constructivists, however, construct intervention as reading the "texts" of classroom and culture; the rest, we assume, will simply happen—an assumption that further mystifies the social and historical forces by which power is gained and controlled.[2]

Feminists such as Elizabeth Ellsworth have questioned assumptions behind concepts of empowerment in liberatory pedagogies, which, on the one hand, encourage collective participation of students in critically examining the contradictions by which systems of power and privilege exclude them and, on the other, valorize rationality and "freethinking" individuals as the primary agents of social change and justice. Ultimately, as Ellsworth (1989) argues, the myth of rationality to liberate individuals obscures the larger processes by which various sociocultural groups are excluded from participation in the rational discourses that shape not only public policy but ways of seeing and interpreting reality. Paradoxically, emphasizing the teacher's role as a dispassionate arbitrator of student "differences" mystifies the contexts out of which rational discourse derives its power and subverts the very practices of social intervention and action that critical teachers wish to promote. It sets up a hierarchy of rational/irrational in which the voices of Others are subject to the dominant voice of the institution. Consequently, "strategies such as student empowerment and dialogue give the illusion of equality while in fact leaving the authoritarian nature of the teacher/student intact" (Ellsworth 1989, 306).

Perhaps most problematic for Ellsworth, as well as for feminist theorist Teresa Ebert, is the assumption that the classroom provides a "safe" haven for a dialogue about difference among students. The implication is that once teachers have set up the dialogue, students can speak freely, exercising the "tools" of critical discourse to develop positions. However, as Ellsworth points out, such a "free" or "safe" place cannot exist apart from an understanding of how all discourses not only are interested but have social consequences. Ellsworth (1989) urges a pedagogy that requires a critique of the implications of "difference" in student narratives "for other social movements and their struggles for self-definition" (305–6). If, in fact, all discourse is partial and self-interested in some way, then that partiality must be understood *in relation* to other discourses and the effects that each exerts upon the others. Consequently, it is not enough to simply change or develop access to discourses of power, as social constructivists assert; those discourses must be understood in relation to others and their social consequences. The practices of such theories must engage teachers and students in the struggle to define and negotiate their differences in relation to their effects on others and not simply against an ideal of rationality and "critical consciousness."

Narrating the Stories
We Live By

The narratives by which we know our knowledge are necessarily partial, interested, and bound by conscious and unconscious concealments of self-interest. However, to oppose them to a rationalist ideal in analyzing them only serves to maintain their subordination to the dominant ways of knowing. In chapter 3, I will narrate my story as a woman writer and a student through a rereading of a short story I composed several years earlier. When writers occupy a subject position, constructing meanings of their own stories, they begin to make practitioner knowledge understood *in relation to* (not simply in addition to) the scholarly discourses of power. That set of relations is necessarily complex; narratives serve to make those complexities more immediate and "real" as ways of seeing the world. By making such stories available, one can begin to "know better" the stories (myths) by which we, as a culture, live.

Notes

1. For a more detailed explanation of Ebert's concept of "ludic postmodernism," see Ebert 1991.

2. Patricia Bizzell (1990a, 1991) has recently sought to address the issue of the academy's participation in the development of a "national discourse" through which teachers, in their role as educators as well as citizens, would engage in dialogues with public groups ranging from government to labor unions to political caucuses. In this sense, she is interested in placing classroom dialogues in relation to other discourses teachers can intervene in, both within and outside the lacademy. Like Heath, Bizzell not only wants to bring students into discourses of power, but she attempts to work out strategies for how to intervene in changing those discourses by making them accessible and pluralistic—and subsequently changing the institutions that currently exclude them.

Composing Ourselves as Knowers
Women Writers in a Male Tradition

In this chapter I tell some stories about my experiences composing as a woman and the cultural myths that formed the contexts of my writing. My purpose in telling these stories is to offer insight into the ways a woman writer experiences the academic world as a student and a writer. These stories are "thick descriptions" of the narratives of the "native" subject that I use as the basis of an expanding interpretation of the cultural contexts of composing.

As the narrator of these stories, I do not claim objectivity over my own experiences in the sense of being "purely" an observer rather than a participant in constructing the significances of this story. Neither am I "purely" subjective; the point of rendering experience is neither objective nor subjective truth, not verification but interpretation. Thus, I make no special claims for the "truthfulness" of my account as "reality" in the sense of empirical or historical "fact," as opposed to something "made up." Instead, I present a story, a fiction, if you will, whose aim is to render experience convincingly, to create verisimilitude, to persuade of its life-likeness, rather than to prove a hypothesis or verify a fact. The "truthfulness" of this story lies not in its basis in "fact" but in its power to recreate these experiences as visible and immediate to the reader—providing readers with the means to construct an analogous experience. Consequently, the "factual" basis of the story is less important than its literary and rhetorical dimensions; its "truthfulness" lies in how well readers can construct these experiences for themselves and how persuasively they render that experience as "lifelike."

However, these are also stories about telling stories, about how a writer makes sense of her own experiences as a writer. In this respect, these are also metanarratives about the ways of seeing that stories provide, the shards of insight we gain into cultural stories of composing.

The first section of this chapter presents the interpretive frameworks

41

through which I tell my stories. The second section includes my stories about composing as well as a rereading of one of the short stories I wrote several years prior, which served as a metaphor for the ways I constructed myself as a writer. The last section is a draft of that short story, "Shelter." By juxtaposing the stories of my writing experiences with a draft of a short story I was composing during this time, readers may construct for themselves significances in the relationships between the two texts.

In subsequent chapters, I will expand the field of my attention to the talk of specific writing groups in which I was a participant; for now, I will begin with my experiences as writer and the institutional and cultural structures I negotiated in the process of coming to know my knowledge— as well as one of the stories I produced in that process.

In *Writing a Woman's Life*, Carolyn Heilbrun (1988) explores the problem of telling the stories of women's lives, given the cultural inscriptions that determine the shape and significance of women's experiences. Telling the lives of women who do not fit the traditional "marriage plot" is particularly difficult, because there is neither the language nor the form to represent their experiences; for instance, George Sand's contemporaries called her, for lack of a better description, a "man"—in honor of her intellect and independent thinking (Heilbrun 1988, 35–36). Because the language and, in turn, the narrative structures women use are driven by models from male experience, the stories that can be told of women's experiences are limited to stories about their relationship to male-dominant culture. Thus, much of women's lives remains unwritten.

Literary theorist Rachel Blau DuPlessis (1985) comments similarly on the ways existing narrative structures shape what can be told and thus known: "To compose a work is to negotiate with these questions: What stories can be told? How can plots be resolved? What is felt to be narratable by both literary and social conventions?" (3). For American women writers of the nineteenth and twentieth centuries, according to DuPlessis, the challenge has been in confronting oppositions between plots of romantic love and quest plots of inquiry and self-knowledge (*Bildung*), and to write "beyond" culturally sanctioned endings.

DuPlessis demonstrates in her explications of women's writing how potentialities for both romance and quest plots are generally present but, particularly in the case of nineteenth-century women, one plot is typically repressed in favor of another. A woman can marry and live happily ever after, or she can pursue the quest but die. The problem isn't merely textual (i.e., the failure of "old" plots) but ideological in the ways the dialogic between multiple discourses present in such texts is brought to a culturally sanctioned closure:

> Any artistic resolution . . . can, with greater or lesser success, attempt an ideological solution to the fundamental contradictions that animate the work. Any resolution can have traces of the conflicting materials that have been processed within it. It is where subtexts and repressed discourses can throw up one last flare of meaning; it is where the author may side-step and displace attention from the materials that a work has made available. (DuPlessis 1985, 3)

Consequently, when women writers set out to compose a story of women's experience, they face, as DuPlessis comments, "psychosocial" as well as narrative conventions in the plots through which they construct their identities as writers and women.

Similarly, the discourses writers use to represent acts of composition are themselves full of similar contradictions, but for ideological reasons they reflect resolutions preoccupied with masculine views of experience, in particular that of *Bildung* as part of the American literary heritage. Certainly other stories are present in this conflict, competing for attention. For instance, in her untitled poem in *The Writer on Her Work* (Sternburg 1991, 216–17), Ursula K. LeGuin refuses to valorize a singular identity over the many she experiences as a writer, deeply enmeshed in many other social and mythic identities:

> *The writer at her work*
> *is odd, is peculiar, is particular,*
> *certainly, but not, I think,*
> *singular.*
> *She tends to the plural.*

LeGuin's insistence upon plurality, however, competes with one of the prevailing myths of academic life: the scholarly *Bildung*; the academic as hero, as described in *Women of Academe* (Aisenberg and Harrington 1988):

> As with allegorical quests, professional service generally requires exacting training of the intellect, an apprenticeship, and then the performance of difficult tasks calling for the intelligent use of initiative, stamina, de-

termination, resourcefulness, integrity, and often, creativity. The performers of these tasks—Albert Einstein, Jonas Salk, John Dewey, Alfred North Whitehead, Franklin Roosevelt, Andrew Carnegie, Albert Camus, Thomas Edison—are our modern heroes. And like the heroes of an earlier age, they are, for the most part, men. (14)

It is my contention that the story of a writer's *Bildung* is one of the most valorized myths within American culture and that, because of that fact, the ways writers construct their identities as writers continue to be influenced by that myth, both within and outside the academy. As literary critic Nina Baym (1985) notes, our American literary tradition has been preoccupied with developing a canon of works that defines not simply what is best aesthetically but what is best *culturally*—that is, most "American." Thus, the history of American literature, if we take Baym's observations a step further, is a history of *Bildung*—a search for identity separate from European origins, for what is "essentially" American. And as Baym demonstrates, that essence has been construed as essentially male, a "beset manhood" in which the prevailing myth represents society in an adversarial relationship to the individual. This opposition is decidedly gendered:

> [T]he entrammeling society and the promising landscape [are] . . . both . . . depicted in unmistakably feminine terms, and this gives a sexual character to the protagonist's story which does, indeed, limit its applicability to women. (Baym 1985, 72)

In turn, composing is also valorized as a heroic act of *Bildung* from which women as subjects are culturally excluded, inscribed as they are in plots of romantic love. This heroic myth is so powerful, according to Baym, that even when "the woman writer creates a story that conforms to the expected myth, it is not recognized for what it is because of a superfluous sexual specialization in the myth in the critics' minds" (76). And when a woman writer doesn't conform, "she is understood to be writing minor or trivial literature" (76). That is the double bind that Baym says women writers must confront in the context of this myth.

Scenes of Writing

The "heroic," valorized, masculine self signifies a construction of self and identity apart or in isolation from culture, autonomous, self-contained, ahistorical. As such, this myth is set in opposition to, rather than in dialogue with, other identities, other plots through which experience is ordered and interpreted. Linda Brodkey observes a primary heroic myth of composing, "the scene of writing," in which "a solitary writer alone in a cold garret [is] working into the small hours of the morning by the thin light of a candle . . . the writer is an Author and the writing is Literature" (quoted in Haake 1989, 2).

Bakhtin (1981) is also concerned with the demystification of such "scenes of writing." His example is instructive for reimagining the myths of composing. As noted in chapter 1, Bakhtin critiques the heroic discourse of epic poetry as part of a centripetal impulse in discourse that focuses on unity of character, plot, focus, and, ultimately, ideology, distancing itself from history and repressing alternative plots and points of view. This impulse, as he notes, is part of the construction of national identity and ideology that represses local and regional identities and languages as debased, all in the cause of national unity.

The implications of Bakhtin's theories of discourse for women writers, then, is that centripetal impulses in discourse create pressures for women to define themselves in relation to a cultural ideology that privileges male experience as the norm. Centrifugal impulses, however, are simultaneously present and represent potential discourses of resistance. Baym describes centripetal impulses in American literature and culture, showing how the formation of American cultural identity has exerted a similarly hegemonic force on women writers, who, although dominating the commercial publishing scene of the nineteenth century, were largely excluded from the male literary canon, regarded as "trivial," at best, and, at worst, as dangerous, diluting true American "art."

Stories of other such "scenes of writing" are common today in popular culture; read, for instance, the ways in which this American male poet, quoted in an article by a male reporter in the "Living Today" section of an Albany, New York, newspaper, composes himself as a writer:

"People like to classify, catalogue and index everybody," [Bern] Porter says. "I reject being classified, but I guess avant-guarde is the best term. It's breaking from the norm. It's a lonely, desolate business. You have to like being the lone wolf." (Grondahl 1989)

Several writerly myths intersect in this statement: the lone wolf; the writer in the lonely garret; the clever hero unbowed in the face of an indifferent or hostile society; the genius laboring in obscurity. Of course, in the context of the article, the writer is also cast as privileged and elite, having touched greatness in his associations with Einstein, Henry Miller, and

Robert Oppenheimer, admirable for his disciplined solitude and private struggles toward new knowledge.

What's hard, isolating, and lonely in the creative life is also what the reporter finds admirable about Porter: He's tough; he's survived; he no longer cares what people think of him. "The local people [in his home state of Maine] don't know and don't care what we do there and that's all right with me," Porter says (Grondahl 1989). Although he admits to being considered a "crackpot" in Maine, the apparent implication is that the "locals" are fools. His associations with nationally known "heroes" enshrine in him the cultural mythos of "creative" and unconventional types too big to be understood by the smaller, local minds. He doesn't care if anyone cares about what he does—he is a rock against rejection, the consummate artist in his "art for art's sake" attitude, the most rugged of New England individualists. His work might not mean a thing to anyone, but that doesn't matter. Consequently the reporter omits information about the poet's family, his immediate friends, and other forms of support or community, or even about the relevance of the writer's work to others, because the artist "alone" makes a "better" story.

Writers are thus culturally inscribed as heroes on a quest for meaning, fighting the dragons of doubt, criticism, and rejection. The hero typically affirms the triumph of the individual over society, the power of the singular voice rising above the ordinary, the man who, like Odysseus, is elevated to a godlike stature. (In the case of living figures like Porter, the stature might be less than godlike, but it is similarly singular.) Ironically, women writers may be writing themselves out of their own stories by valorizing the heroic quest as a metaphor for composing their experiences, because women's experience is traditionally marginalized in those stories.

"To change a story," as DuPlessis (1985) points out, "signals a dissent from social norms as well as narrative forms" (20). Thus "writing beyond the [prescribed] ending" means examining where "ideology meets narrative" (19). The following narrative is my attempt to write beyond the ending of a quest story I first drafted many years ago.

Romancing the Mountain

What happens when a woman composes herself and her experience as a writer through the quest narrative? In 1984, I began writing a short story that became a metaphor for my struggles as a writer and as a woman to give form to my experiences. The story, entitled "Shelter," was inspired by my experience climbing Long's Peak, a 14,251-foot mountain in Colorado's Rocky Mountain National Park.

Martha, the protagonist, was in her mid twenties, obsessed with climbing Long's Peak. She believed that in doing so she would somehow transform the drudgery and confusion of her current life into something meaningful. That seemed to me what the heroic quest was all about—to see beyond one's "personal" point of view, toward something transpersonal. It was also the romantic plot revisited—the desire for a merging with the Other (in this case the mountain-as-father) who will complete the Self.

This obsession to climb/write the mountain was so intense in Martha (and in myself) that the writing became a form of survival: "What I write and how I write is done in order to save my own life . . . a way of knowing that I am not hallucinating, that whatever I feel/know is" (Barbara Christian, quoted in Ellsworth 1989, 302). Writing the mountain became "a reality check for survival" (Barbara Christian, quoted in Ellsworth 1989, 302). Unlike the hero's call to a "higher" calling and a wider meaningfulness, composing this story provided me with a means to affirm whatever meaning was already in place rather than, like the hero, transcend it. In this struggle for affirmation, I discovered a listening Other, a doubling of my voice and self.

Because I wrote for survival and not simply for "play" (*jouissance*), my "obsession" might have been fueled by my perception that I lacked options: there was only this story, and I had to "get it right." As Ellsworth (1989) writes, "Words spoken for survival come already validated in a radically different arena of proof and carry no option or luxury of choice" (302). The choices were there, but they were not available to me, because I could not construct myself as one having such choices, of knowing other stories.

bell hooks (1989) comments on how oppressive structures of race and class affect the ways poor, rural blacks valued their own, potentially counterhegemonic worldviews "more as a survival strategy determined less by conscious efforts to oppose oppressive race and class biases than by circumstance" (76). Of course as a white person from a middle-class background, I speak from privileges that neither hooks nor Ellworth's minority students could claim. Still, I did not see my "quest" story as oppositional to oppressive "biases" as much as I saw myself living out cultural expectations as a writer, reinscribing the culturally accepted story despite its persistent "failure." The story, I felt, was not the problem; but, as the writer, I hadn't yet "mastered" it.

In reality, my first attempt to climb Long's Peak had failed because of adverse weather. A year later, on my second attempt, my friends and I made it to the summit. However, I continued to write the story of a failed, solo venture, more interested in why I had "failed" than in the fact that later I had "succeeded" with friends. Here is how the story begins:

> At 12,000 feet, wind carves my face in sharp edges, fills my ears with its ragged voice. It's said young Indian boys once climbed this mountain to seek their spirit guides for life. As for Kath and me, the spirits have resisted us all the way up. The harder I push forward, the stronger the wind pushes back, as if we're not allowed to enter this realm of clouds.

It was not a particularly auspicious moment of the hike, nor was it a particularly fortunate omen for the composing of this story. For just as Martha, the narrator, and her companion, Kath, push on into an ever more resistant wind, I, the writer, kept running into resistance in the composing of the story. My story seemed to be writing itself, and with every sentence it narrowed into a seemingly inevitable conclusion: Martha trapped on the mountain, alone, having abandoned Kath.

Yet if the "spirits" resisted the two women hikers at the beginning of the story, prohibiting them from entering "this realm of clouds," that resistance, it seemed to me, provided all the more reason to forge ahead, to resist resistance. If young Indian boys could find their spirit guides at the top of the mountain, why should two women be denied the same?

The only way Martha knew how to reach the top of the mountain was through an act of will or force; getting to the end of the story seemed to require the same. In the heroic quest, obstacles are meant to strengthen the hero's determination. Thus, it seemed that Martha and I simply had to be more determined. I was deep in the throes of oppositional discourse. Martha was going to *argue* herself to the top of that mountain; I, in turn, would *reason* myself to a finished draft. If I can write one draft, I told myself, then I can write past all the blocks that are appearing. If only I try harder. If only I become more disciplined at my writing. If only I had more time/money to write. If only I were more perceptive, smarter, luckier.

Martha and I had internalized an ideal for the "right" course of our self-development. Unfortunately that development depended upon us being something other than what we already were—namely, women. The heroic quest is so often regarded as a *universal* rather than a gendered pattern of human development, whether in Kohlberg's (1984) models of ethical and moral development or in Perry's (1970) views on intellectual progress. In popular culture, it's not surprising that the work of myth scholar Joseph Campbell has captured the public imagination because of its emphasis on the underlying universality of myths as indicative of pyschic processes of integration or "wholeness," thus "transcending" gender.

In *The Hero with a Thousand Faces*, Campbell (1968) writes that stories of heroic adventure represent a "universal" pattern of individuation that cuts across all cultures at all periods of history. The heroic quest represents a search for meaningfulness and purpose that leads to the psychic integration of the hero. All quest stories represent some portion of the larger monomyth that Campbell describes as a predetermined cycle of departure and return.

Martha, it seemed to me at the time, was preoccupied with a similar purpose as the classic hero; climbing the mountain and, in turn, writing the story represented her search for a psychic integration that seemed available to her only upon gaining the view at the summit. Martha and I drew upon a mystical memory of an Edenic moment that we sensed we could regain through the view at the top of Long's Peak. This is how Martha remembers that view:

> I hear my father's voice in this wind, from the mountains he first brought me to as a child on one of our family's endless cross-country car trips. While he focused his camera for yet another family portrait, I saw from the summits red canyons undulate in their soft sleep of sand, the lithe body of a river embrace a valley of farms checkerboarded green and gold. Clouds tangled in our hair; birds perched fearlessly on the car. I repeated their names, dark and rich on my tongue: Sangre de Cristos, Sierra Nevada, San Juan, Never Summer, and savored the memories of the world spread open at my feet.

Going up the mountain, composing the story, would, then, return Martha to something that had been lost from childhood—the memory of a more fluid world, a world without boundaries. What Martha needed seemed to be outside of herself, and I also sensed I was lacking something attainable only outside of myself, but in the trying I believed we would somehow get it. We both wanted access to a vision of a larger, more inclusive world. "Vision" emerged as a controlling metaphor to the story of Martha's ascent and to my composing: What we lacked was vision.

What we sought was vision. But to get that vision, we needed a vision of how to proceed.

I wrote a version of the story and submitted it to a graduate fiction workshop as a postgraduate student. If I'd already found treacherous my identity as an "apprentice" to the "master" writers, now, as someone "outside" the program and the graduate community, it was even more problematic; I wasn't an "apprentice" anymore, but at the same time I wasn't a "master," either—or else why would I be back? Mainly, I hoped that the meaning of Martha's ascension and, in turn, my meaning making as a writer (not to mention my identity as a sort of writer-in-progress) would be clarified with the assistance of other readers.

As a group, the workshop acknowledged some sort of vision in the draft I'd turned in. Readers tried hard to tell me what to do to make the draft express better whatever I was after. But the general response was that the vision wasn't "focused." The story had to get focused before they could make sense of it.

I knew they were right. I knew the story lacked focus. That seemed to be the point of the whole enterprise—Martha was seeking vision through her climb, and I was seeking vision through the writing of the story. But for some reason, the vision was faulty—out of focus. I wondered, "How do I correct a faulty focus? If I am the lens through which my story is projected, does that mean I am faulty?" That seemed to confirm a fear I'd had about Martha all along—that she was "warped" by her obsession with climbing this mountain and therefore had to meet with death. So would my life as a writer meet with a similar fate, because like Martha, I was obsessed with getting this story "right"?

It seems that Martha and I were caught in the double bind created by contradictions in the romance and quest plots: We needed to be single-minded to gain what we apparently lacked, yet because we were single-minded, we met ambiguous fates as a woman and as a writer. Or, as Baym (1985) might say, I tried to conform to the expected heroic myth, but "because of a superfluous sexual specialization . . . as entertained in the critic's mind," my story wasn't understood. Perhaps it was also a clash between a personal identity that still observed the old romance plot and the professional identity that required a "process of transformation . . . an intellectual and emotional process whereby women acquire a new identity . . . [that] can make different and conflicting demands" (Aisenberg and Harrington 1988, 20).

Martha and I both got stuck in this "process." We could neither forge ahead nor retreat. As Martha observes:

Somehow I got off the trail. My knees shake. I don't know if I can get back on from here. I lower one foot to start back down, but my leg is weak, as if the bone has melted. . . . The only way out is to feel my way down and I'm already so numb I can barely feel the crevice where I've jammed my boot.

I think the main story that I was inscribed by, the story that I, in turn, inscribed Martha into, was a story I'd encountered frequently in my education as a writer: a story of control. That, it seemed to me, was the hero story—gaining control over oneself, over one's inner life. Joseph Campbell reinforced this view: The heroic journey was the way to gain control over one's desires instead of being ruled by them. One was supposed to shed material concerns in favor of a higher, more expansive consciousness. One should not be controlled by one's desires; one should learn how to control them.

This is a story that I now recognize as institutionalized in the academy, in writing workshops as well as other classrooms of my academic career: point out what a student lacks and proceed from there. One thing a student is almost always lacking is control. A school's function is to socialize students so that they will acquire the control and discipline appropriate to their future roles in society.

The lesson of Long's Peak for Martha, like the lesson of school for students, is to not trust what you know; as Martha observes, "Long's Peak is not kind, but kindness is not what I seek." School might not be kind, but it is necessary, a time of separation, a time to doubt what you know through lived experience in order to enter the larger world of intellectual life. It is what Peter Elbow (1986) has named "the doubting game." School will give you what you lack.

However, as Belenky and her colleagues (1986) point out in *Women's Ways of Knowing*, it is difficult for many women (and men) students to begin their educations constructed as persons lacking knowledge. What women know from their lived experiences is not valued; thus they are made to feel as if they are working from a deficit that will never be reconciled, a deficit that male students might also experience, but differently. The story that inscribes women learners who want a larger, more expansive life is a story of the peril and penalty of that desire: with every gain in control comes a lack of power.

The mythos that drives the story of control is that of the autonomous self, the hero who rises above history and culture to become more than human, even godlike. The "real" world is not a safe place. To prepare for the adversarial climate of the world out there, schools provide temporary domiciles where students practice becoming self-sufficient, independent, and self-supporting. *Practice* is the key word—students are not doing "real" work, but only warming up for what's to come. They read about the triumphs of real writers, thinkers, scientists, artists, though to claim to be one themselves is an act of daring that only the boldest might attempt. And the shelter that schools provide is necessarily temporary, because sooner or later everyone must face the challenge of the "real" world, sink or swim. The system can't support those who want to hang on and "practice."

As a writer schooled in this model of the "real" world, I imagined that to survive as a writer I would need to be able to write alone, in isolation, because the academic workshops I was accustomed to were simply fleeting communities that apparently had little to do with how "real" writers operated. The point of going to a workshop was to learn how to operate without it: a literary apprenticeship. Real writers knew how to identify and correct problems by themselves. Real writers (like Bern Porter) didn't listen to critics, certain of their own meanings and purposes. Real writers came up with original ideas and inspiration on their own. They didn't need a workshop for stimulation or input.

Martha was simply an extension of the mythos I lived out as a writer—she believed that to be a knower in this world, in control of one's destiny, she had to be able to find her way up the mountain alone. She had to leave behind her guide, Kath, and the shelter that Kath seeks out, to face the real world of the mountain. She tells herself that unlike Kath, who needed a boyfriend to "coax" her along the trail, she is "glad to be alone." To seek or desire the assistance of others, as Kath does, is to give up one's autonomy.

The workshops I enrolled in operated within this model of the real world. Ironically, instead of offering a safe place for writers to try out their emerging meanings, it became a microcosm of the "real" world it was meant to prepare students for. The writer had to learn to listen to all kinds of criticism, in silence, then afterward sift through the dross of all the commentary to garner the gold that was useful. To make this transformation, the writer, it was presumed, already knew her own meanings and purposes. Consequently, this sifting always took place outside the workshop—an act of autonomy that the writer would also have to perform in the "real" world, instead of in conversation with others. It was also presumed that the readers likewise had fully realized meanings of their readings and it was simply a matter of exchanging and debating those meanings in the workshop.

This model, then, assumes that the construction of meaning necessarily takes place in the private world of the individual writer and reader. It assumes that students will know how to make these transformations, to construct and construe the contexts that make meaning possible, before they even enter the classroom. The act of making meaning is assumed to be "obvious" and "natural" and not in any way specific to a particular way of knowing the world. Only an individual can make meaning, and meaning is always individual and private—the sole property of that individual.

The heroic quest follows a similar model that focuses on the individual's ability to comprehend the meanings of events, people, and things. Sometimes the hero has a helper or sidekick to provide clues, but ultimately the hero is the final "reader" of a situation. We don't know how the hero learned to become such a powerful meaning maker; it seems he was born to the task. It isn't something that can be learned. And perhaps that's also the message of the hero model of education: Schools (including writing workshops) can't teach you how to learn—you either know or you don't. The teacher's task isn't to teach students how to learn—it's to teach the ones who already know. Frequently such teachers see their role not as being someone who teaches (thus generating esoteric debates around such questions as "Can creative writing really be taught?" [Bishop 1990, 11]) but instead, as Bishop notes, as being a presence to be absorbed, a model for living. Those students who "don't make it," who don't live up to the master model, "are dismissed too easily as 'not real writers'" (Bishop 1989, 6).

Unfortunately for Martha, she was one of those who were not born knowing how to learn to make meaning out of a mountain. She tried hard to live up to the hero model, but in the trying got stuck and endangered her life. She perceived that she was not a knower, but thought that if she tried hard enough she would become one.

I think Martha *does* learn something, however, in the midst of all the conflicts and contradictions, in the process of getting stuck, something I did not claim when I abandoned the story several years ago. In a sense I am glad that she left the trail, though of course that was part of the quest plot—the woman gets lost and dies. Yet Martha doesn't, finally, die; she hangs on; she learns that to save herself, she must recast her relationship with the mountain. The mountain is not wholly Other than herself—it is also herself. Thus, when Martha says, "My leg is weak, as if the bone has melted," it is the beginning of her transformation. She is and is not the mountain. In the midst of a snow squall, she realizes that her face and hands are "burning": the boundaries between self and other are dissolving in the heat of her awakening memory of a safe place—the shelter she passed on the way up, where she told Kath to wait for her. A bull's-eye that marks the trail she has strayed from glows far off. Martha says,

> I open my eyes and stare at the bull's-eye. I stare until it grows larger. Kath's face glows from its red center. I blink, and she retreats, so I stare again until I can feel the heat from her face warming my face, my hands. She is tucked safely inside the stone hut, sheltered from the blizzard outside, a bright circle of fire warming her, her boots kicked off. She is curled up, asleep. I peer into the tiny, eye-like window, the wind numbing my back.

Martha can finally remember a place of safety by staring the bull in the eye, so to speak. Waiting for her is Kath, who, like Martha's mother, has been present but inaccessible in her silence. It is as if Martha has always known there was this shelter but, in her heroic quest, has been obstructed from access to that knowledge. She didn't "know her knowledge."

In a model of education in which the real world is constructed as an unsafe place, and school is a microcosm of a world of separation and conflict, there is no shelter, no place students can go if they don't already know how to learn within prescribed institutional boundaries. If they don't already know, they will always be climbing to gain a control they can't, finally, achieve. As Martha says, "I'm wondering what's at the top of this rock, if, in fact, there really is an end. As if I've been climbing all my life and now can't stop even if I want to."

Fortunately for Martha, she does stop climbing and finally stares at the bull's-eye for a clue. Staring at the bull's-eye, the eye of patriarchy, naming the stories that oppress us and keep us from knowing our knowledge while at the same time recognizing that we are and are not part of that patriarchy, just as Martha realizes that she is and is not the mountain—that seems to be the first step toward re-membering that safe place that mothers made for us as we learned to live in the world. When Martha stares at the bull's-eye, the wind literally and figuratively changes directions, is at her back instead of ahead of her. The wind is the voice of the father, the patriarchy, and has been reversed.

Martha has yet to tell her story to Kath, who waits for her inside the shelter, beside the fire. But by recognizing the patriarchal wind she was resisting and, in turn, the patriarchal script she was enacting, Martha has begun to reconnect with that part of herself that knows. The oppressor is now visible, and it is and is not herself. There remains for her and Kath the task of negotiating these limitations to tell the stories of their experiences as women and establish safe places for all learners.

When women tell the stories of their experiences, we know the world differently; we "demystify the original scene that has worked so well to silence us" (Haake 1989, 2). We can then construct a place in which we can "[hold] a wide diversity of scenes to be compatible, to coexist, to enhance and redefine each other" (Haake 1989, 2). We can reconstruct the world as a place that both women and men safely inhabit.

The Story

Shelter

At 12,000 feet, wind carves my face in sharp edges, fills my ears with its ragged voice. It's said young Indian boys once climbed this mountain to seek their spirit guides for life. As for Kath and me, the spirits have resisted us all the way up. The harder I push forward, the stronger the wind pushes back, as if we're not allowed to enter this realm of clouds.

I hear my father's voice in this wind, from the mountains he first brought me to as a child on one of our family's endless cross-country car trips. While he focused his camera for yet another family portrait, I saw from the summits red canyons undulate in their soft sleep of sand, the lithe body of a river embrace a valley of farms checkerboarded green and gold. Clouds tangled in our hair; birds perched fearlessly on the car. I repeated the names, dark and rich on my tongue: Sangre de Cristo, Sierra Nevada, Rocky Mountains, Never Summer, and savored the memories of the world spread open at my feet.

Below, on the last stretch of the steep boulder field, Kath is shouting something. She stops to adjust a thin yellow bandanna over her ears, cups her hands around her mouth, and leans once more into the wind. I shake my head, wave her up.

As I straighten from a crouch, the wind nearly casts me down. It's like standing before an open mouth, the keyhole, as it's called, a jagged gap in the mountain where south and west winds conspire to flush all life not firmly anchored on the granite skin. Nothing like the benevolent mountains of our summer trips when all we had to do was pile out of the car,

road-weary and limp, and lean over "scenic overlooks" handily
carved out of the road. Then my father snapped a few pictures
before we had to climb back in for more hours of driving. I'm
always looking past the white borders of his pictures, as if I can
see something beyond the boundaries of the horizon.

Long's Peak is not kind, but kindness is not what I seek. I
crouch back down, watching Kath struggle up each massive
boulder.

Finally she pulls herself up to the ledge, out of breath, her
face wind-scorched. We huddle together at one edge of the
keyhole's jaw. Head bowed, she rubs her reddened ears then
slowly eases off her pack. I offer her my water bottle and press a
bag of peanuts and raisins into one hand while she drinks.

She lowers the bottle stiffly, picks out a few nuts, staring
wearily down the boulder field. It's taken two hours to hike the
same distance she and her boyfriend had hiked in 45 minutes in
July. I twist the belly strap of my pack tightly around one finger
then another. She is dressed for mid-July, not early September.
Her legs burn bright red below her cotton shorts. I massage my
thighs quickly, barely warm in my jeans.

Miles below at the trailhead, aspen shiver gold medallions
against a gentle autumn. On the plains, the grass is burned from
late summer drought, untouched yet by frost. But on this
mountain, spring and fall are too gentle a transition; overnight,
the wind breathes arctic and frost forms crystals in small tundra
puddles that the day before the sun had embraced. Winter is
patient—it retreats to the summit for a few weeks in July and
August, creeping down the mountain until it ices the plains
once more.

Kath sighs, leaning back against a boulder, and mumbles
something.

"What?" I shout.

She points to the right and down. I scan cliff shadows, the
litter of rock and scree, until a smooth shape emerges: first two
square eyes, then a conical head from flat, even stones among
the chaotic spill—a stone hut wedged below the keyhole.

"Saw it last time. Someone struck by lightning. There's a
plaque," she yells. She cups her ears, shivers. "Sure you want to
go on?"

"You?"

She peers from under straight black bangs, silent. She has a round face like a Navajo and an impressive silence to match, a silence I want to split open like a boulder cracked by lightning. I might just as well ask the mountain what to do as ask her.

"You need a hat," I holler over the wind. If only I could turn the wind around, grab hold and let it pull me to the top.

She nods, shoulders hunching like a scolded child.

"And long pants. What now?" I ask.

Her elbows dig into her thighs, chin resting on clenched hands.

"Be rough," she says. "This wind's tricky."

"Want to quit or what?"

For a moment the wind eases, as if catching its breath, then bears down all the harder. She clutches her bandanna just before it can whisk off her sunburned scalp. She gazes mournfully down the boulder field, its uneven layers of broken rock, then up at the keyhole, then at me for a moment before inspecting the dust on her boots.

"Long way to go yet."

"Nothing like last time, I bet."

She shakes her head, laughs in her slow way as if unsure she should laugh. "In July it was thunderstorms. Hot. Cold when clouds took over. But no wind." She shades her eyes, looks up. "Might even snow today."

"At least you know the way."

She tucks her chin into one shoulder then peeks up from under her bangs, a tentative smile spreading. I laugh, then she laughs, and we both shake our heads, smiling.

"Some guide," she says. "You lit out before I even got my pack strapped."

"But really," I say, and suddenly the whole mood has switched. "I want to go to the top." She sinks into her Navajo silence. "Will you keep going?" My voice cracks, impatient, almost pleading.

Every morning for three years I've looked out the window from my house on the plains and seen Long's Peak, the only snowcap visible above the dry foothills. It pierces the clear sky, a blue wedge sometimes sharp as an arrowhead, other times blurred as an ancient memory, the tallest mountain in northern Colorado. I've climbed other mountains, only to reach the summit and see Long's Peak, snow spotting its arched back, staring back at me.

She takes another long sip from my water bottle, staring down the trail to scrub trees far below.

"The wind does slow you down, but I sort of like it, too," I say. She looks over at me. "It pounds against your skin, into your muscle and bone. All that matters is the next step, keeping one foot ahead of the other."

She considers this for a moment, stroking her chin lightly.

"Do you know what I mean?" I press my hands tight against my stomach, clench my knees together.

Her head sinks to her chest, eyes widened as if in a trance. Under her swirling bangs, in her broad forehead, furrows of something like pity carve her skin.

"Just wait for me in the shelter," I blurt out.

Her head bobs up, bangs twirling. The silence between us tightens.

"It's at least a couple hours more up, Martha."

"Will you wait?"

She stares at me a long time then crawls across the ledge, dark but for the yellow bandanna that soon disappears into the smooth stones of the shelter.

I think of that yellow bandanna, a small aspen leaf skipping over the naked slope, as I cross the keyhole onto the other side of the mountain.

Clouds race overhead like a movie on fast forward, circling the distant peak, fierce wind about to rip me off the rocks as I creep alone onto the narrow ledge. Hundreds of feet below, the dark eye of a lake dilates. I inch forward, giddy with altitude, wanting to laugh at my slowness, instead keeping my eyes on each rough hold, so the wind won't pluck me from the mountain's spine and toss me into the dark canyons below.

Every few minutes I stop to hunt for the bright orange and red bull's-eyes Kath said mark the trail from here on. Shortcuts can be deadly. She and her boyfriend found a man struggling to get back down to the ledge after ignoring the bull's-eyes. The climb back to where he'd come from was too steep; to get down, it seemed he'd have to slide down a smooth rock face, and possibly slide right over the ledge and fall hundreds of feet.

But the danger up here isn't just the mountain itself—it's your perception of danger that causes most problems. From the man's point of view, he was stuck, so he panicked. But Kath saw a way down, if only he could calm himself enough to try. A narrow crevice lined the smooth rock, just wide enough for the toe of his boot. She told him to feel his way down, that she'd guide him.

At first he didn't want to try it. His hands quivered, raw from clutching rock all day, and his knees bobbed. He was afraid because he couldn't see the crevice—only Kath could see it. She coached him on where to put his foot, one step at a time. She praised him every time he got a little closer. Once he made it to the ledge, he said a quick thanks and rushed off, perhaps embarrassed by his predicament.

I pause, grab onto a boulder. I can't tell where my fingers end and rock begins. An ocean of mountains breaks to the south, heaving west, some crested white with the first snow. Wind strips earth to ancient forms with its chiseled breath: rock, water, sky, trees no longer trees but some dark mosaic that ripples and arches into the horizon. Breath within me struggles to meet the larger breath around me.

This wind is the rough timbre of my father's voice, not smooth like Sam's voice, dragging across my cheeks, numbing me, a chill I struggle against, a sleep that draws me down.

"Martha! Come down off that rock!"
"But Dad, you should see the view."
"Stand next to your brother and sister."
"Why do we have to take so many pictures?"
"Stand still."
"It'll only take a minute," my mother adds.
"But then we'll have to leave right away."
"Yeah, that's all we ever do on vacation—drive and take pictures. We never get to see anything," says Carol.
"Quit your bellyaching. Bobby, look over here."

"Can't we ever just be somewhere?" I ask. The sun over my father's head makes my eyes water. I squint and wipe my nose with the back of my hand.

"Look at me. Smile. Stop blinking. Get ready. Here we go."

I always do smile: it's the one thing I know for certain he wants. He invites the neighbors over for slide shows of our trips and wants them to see what a good time we had.

"There we are in the Sangre de Cristo," he narrates.

"Good slides, top-notch," they tell him.

"And there's Old Tucson, where they used to make cowboy movies."

The light from the projector flashes onto his face, and that same look hovers in his eyes as when he was taking the picture, his vision fixed on some point in the horizon over our heads.

I get more daring as I get older, wandering farther and farther away as he focuses the camera, walking the narrow ledge of a stone retaining wall. Climbing a pile of precarious rock, dangling from a tree limb, hoping he'll take a quick picture of me, smile at my courage. But he never takes candids. And the farther away I wander, the louder he hollers for me to come back and pose with the family.

"No one in their right mind would tackle that mountain with you," Sam grins, lower lip spreading full. "They'd drop dead from exhaustion before you were even warmed up."

"Come with me."

"You know I don't like to work that hard."

Clay on the potter's wheel spins neatly between his hands. He presses a finger in deeply to open the clay, wide and smooth. A spike of blonde hair slides into one eye; I resist the urge to brush it aside.

"Work? It's not work. It's fun."

"To you, maybe."

He cups the sides gently until they rise, tall and slender. His hands glide up and down until the vase emerges, a smooth, narrow-necked oval.

"This is work. It'll do you good to get out in the fresh air. You look like a ghost from staying in all day."

One finger dives at my nose, leaving a wet print. I wipe it off with the back of my hand.

"Please, Sam, just try it."

"What, and spoil your fun? You know you aren't satisfied unless you've covered the trail from end to end. Then you want to do it all over again."

"A slight exaggeration?"

"I don't like to race around like you."

"That's for sure. The one hike you came along, all you wanted to do was look at the colors of columbines in different lights. It took us an hour just to go one mile!"

"I don't care about finishing the trail. I liked being where I was."

"But's that no challenge!"

He arches one eyebrow and looks at me out the corner of his eyes. "I think we'd both be happier if each of us did what *she* likes and didn't worry about the other person."

With a quick twist, he arches the oval into a thin spiral.

"The trouble with you is that you only do what comes easily. You were born a good potter, and what you weren't born with, your father taught you. You don't know what it's like to struggle for something you want."

He turns off the wheel and, covering my hands, looks straight at me. "Always looking for a good fight, aren't you, Martha?" His lips pucker in a half-smile; he shakes his head. "Something *you* picked up from *your* father, no doubt." He inspects the clay spiral before scooping it up and tossing it into a bucket of slip at his feet. "Well, I don't want to fight. I've got work to do."

"Don't work too hard or it won't be fun anymore."

He rests his hands on either side of the wheel and leans over.

"Go climb a mountain," he sighs, kissing me, tasting of clay.

He's right, sometimes I long for a good fight. But he is so clever at making peace.

The wind cuts into the mountain from the west, propelling me along the ledge as I creep eastward. Its heavy breath numbs my back. I am careful not to move one hand, one foot, before the other is firmly planted.

I used to think of mountains as friendly beings, offering cool stands of yellow pine just when the sun becomes unbearable, revealing a secret valley just when I think I can't hike another foot.

But on Long's, there is no shelter from the rocky skin, the naked slopes battered ceaselessly by wind, by storms of rain, hail, and snow, baked by day in a sun nearly close enough to hold its spears of light in my hand, frozen by darkness each night. The sky is open in three directions, but those are three directions in which I may fall. Stripped of trees, meadows, water, the mountain reveals its massive indifference.

No matter how cautiously I proceed, I seem to be going too fast. At one moment I cling to the image of a rock just out of reach, at another I am in the Sierra Nevada, and at another I disappear altogether, bound only by a thin cord of instinct to the ledge. As if my father has set up his slide projector inside me—I don't know what will flash upon the screen next.

"Here are the Rockies. Lot of snow up there in July."

"Dad. I'm moving to Colorado."

"No."

"No? Just like that?"

"That's right."

"But why?"

"Here's the Arches National Monument. Utah has a lot of desert. Here're the salt flats outside Salt Lake City."

"Stop. You're going too fast."

He advances the next slide, a family portrait from when I was 11 years old. We're all squint-frowning into the sun at a riding stable in Cheyenne. My mother has her arm around my shoulders; I am hunched up.

"You were such a good girl."

He stares past me to this still life, and his voice catches just the tiniest bit. He presses his hands on top of the warm projector.

Another picture from the same trip flashes onto the screen. I am standing next to him, on a hill outside Denver, the Rockies rising like blue ghosts behind us—one of the few shots he allowed my mother to take. Bobby is next to me, then Carol. My father stands with his arms at his side, head thrust forward, a thin smile, or perhaps just a shadow, across his lips. My arms are crossed, as if hugging myself, my head tipped slightly toward him, my eyes focused somewhere beyond the borders of the slide, in the same direction as my father's eyes.

My boot slips a little and I grab for a boulder, digging my fingers into its rough surface. I half expect to see Kath's yellow kerchief fluttering just ahead toward the next bull's-eye, even though I know she is back at the shelter, waiting for me.

We are driving to Cheyenne on a narrow road that splits hills of summer grass, sun balanced on the rim of earth. Cigar smoke hangs in the car. My father has the air conditioning turned up, won't let us open the windows, the air burning, thick-sweet.

I am sitting behind him, my doll on my lap. He can't reach me as easily when I sit right behind him. So now his attention is fixed upon my brother and sister, who are fighting again, this time over the radio. My sister orders my mother to leave on the Who; my brother wants it off. I hug my doll, whisper in her ear, comb her hair carefully.

I look out the window. Shadows lengthen; pastures are spotted with sheep like small gray shrubs. Cattle stand with heads low, grazing.

My father yells over his shoulder at my brother and sister to shut up or he'll pull the car over and give us something to yell about. He grabs my mother's hand from the dial and races across static until a "beautiful music" station rasps through the speakers.

"There," he says, "now your mother can have some peace."

"Daddy," I say, "can we stop for ice cream tonight?"

Silence. A plume of smoke curls over his shoulder. I wait a minute, wondering if he heard me. I rock on the seat's edge, clutching my doll.

"Daddy . . ."

"I've had enough of you kids!" He doesn't turn around.

"I just asked."

"Never mind," my mother says, stretching out a hand to me. I pull away, press my face against the window.

The sun has dipped below the rim. No cars pass. I stare at the back of my father's head, the thinning hair, rough skin at the neck leathery like an elephant's hide. But the place where the hair looks so soft, skin a shade paler. I think of times when I was very small that he'd take me with him to the barbershop. I'd wait for what seemed a long, long time with my doll, whispering to her, hoping he'd ask the barber for a lollipop for me.

Now, sitting behind him, I trace the pale rim of skin below his sunburned neck with my eyes and reach out to touch its softness, but at the last second pull back.

"When are you going to give up that doll?" my sister says. She's a high school freshman and wears circles of red blush on her cheeks. "For God's sake, you're 11 years old."

"Shut up!"

My father twists around. "I'm going to slap the next person who says one word."

My sister leans across my brother who fidgets and makes a face but is otherwise quiet. "Wait'll you're my age. It gets worse," she whispers to me.

We pull into a Holiday Inn so my father can call in reservations at Cheyenne, still hours away. I grab my doll and rush to the bathroom before anyone sees me. My mother soon follows, and I hear her in the next stall. The bathroom vibrates with her movements.

"You all right, honey?" I see her sandaled feet, long toes beneath the stall's yellow walls.

Tears run down my face. I clutch my doll against my chest, her hard plastic fingers digging into my neck. I don't want to go on.

"Uh-huh," I answer.

She flushes the toilet. I hear water running, paper towel crumpling, see her feet glide past.

"Your dad's calling," she says quietly, the door swinging open.

I stare at the yellow walls, unblinking, until they begin to quiver, until they are right next to me, until I am intimate with every scratch, every dent, every message scrawled in faint ink on their surface. Until the yellow has embraced me like a shaft of light, flowing, restless, yet so very quiet.

"You don't even notice when I'm gone, do you?" I persist.

He's spinning a jar nearly as wide as his arms with a tiny blow hole at the top, as if a big belly laugh got trapped inside and can only squeak out a little at a time. It's already mid-morning, and I'm anxious to get going, yet I'm tantalized at the prospect of an argument.

"I do, too, notice," he says mildly.

"You only like me when I'm around, when I fit into your routine. When I shut up and behave myself."

"You want to jump up and down? Let out a few primal screams? Go ahead. I won't stop you."

"It doesn't mean you'll pay a bit of attention. You're always so preoccupied. Even now. Pots on the brain."

He switches off the wheel, leans forward, his nose headed for mine. But the pot is too fat, and he stops short.

"See? Always your damn pots between us."

He grins, taking in the situation, then laughs and laughs. I smile unwillingly, edge backward.

"But really, Martha." He straightens up. "You know what you say when I do pay attention? 'Let's go ride bikes along the river.' Or, 'Let's go visit somebody.' As soon as you get my attention you don't want it anymore."

"That's not true."

"What about when we went out for dinner last week? We go to a candlelit restaurant, quiet music, and all you can do is talk about Long's Peak. 'Did you know 25 people died there this century?' 'After the keyhole is the hardest part.' Real romantic."

"Well what about when I get up early and shop because you never have any food, and I come back and make a nice breakfast, and you say, 'No thanks, I'm not hungry.' Because you're too busy with your pots."

"Ok, so we're both obsessed. But my point is that when I do make time to be with you, you're not there. You're restless,

Martha. Like you're always racing ahead to catch up with something. It's easier to let you go your own way while I go mine. Besides, God knows what you'd do if I tried to hold you back."

"Easier. That figures. You always take the easy way out."

"Face it, Martha. The only times you even try to connect with me are when you've just come in and when you're about to go. Safer that way. Doesn't tie you down."

For a moment, I don't know what to say. Then I say lamely, "I'm sick of your friends telling me what a great guy you are."

"I *am* a great guy." He switches on the wheel, leans over to peer into the jar's tiny mouth. "I care for you as much as you'll let me, but part of you may never be satisfied."

All I can think of is ramming my fist through that fat pot between us, punching the wind out of its ugly laugh. But something stops me, maybe the sadness in his eyes, the color of the gunpowder tea he drinks in the afternoons. He reaches around and strokes my clenched hand with cold clay slip.

Clouds boil, thick and gray, blocking the sun. I am near the end of the ledge. The trail cuts up from here into a tall crevasse. This must be the chute Kath described, a thousand-foot climb straight up to another ledge, then over a smooth face to the top. I don't have much time, snow threatening.

A glacier spreads at the foot of the chute like a rumpled robe. The wind has swept it clear of other hikers' footprints, its surface gray, crusty from a summer of melting rain. I step across to begin the ascent.

My back aches from creeping hunched over for so long. A few hard pellets of snow bounce against the rocks onto my bare hands. I have mittens but I couldn't grab hold as well wearing them. I search for the bull's-eyes up ahead but can't see my father than the next step.

Each step now is a trial. I have to pull myself up instead of just scrambling along the ledge: first one foot secured, one hand firm, boost up, then the other foot, the other hand, grasping forward. My eyes water, snow stinging.

Kath said she hadn't expected to reach the summit in July

even when the weather was good. She had to rest a lot, and her boyfriend coaxed her over the hardest spots. She said she couldn't have done it alone. Me, I'm glad to be alone.

I keep to the left where holds come easiest, the rocks more stable. I can't see the bull's-eyes, but at this point, any way I can keep going is the right way. Then I reach a rock face about ten feet high, straight up, cracked through the middle like a big egg, speckled pink and green with lichens.

In the past, I've hiked up steep grades and sometimes scrambled over a few rocks. But this sudden vertical climb is something I've never attempted before. I test one foot and find a solid grip, grab on with fingers rough from so much scraping on rock, and pull up. I close my eyes, and the dark world spins around me, or perhaps I am spinning, like one of Sam's pots, in the wind's shadow, its echo wedged in my throat.

Kath's yellow scarf skips across the boulder field again before disappearing into the stone shelter, like a small flame extinguished on the rock. Something in me wants to cry out; then I do: "Kath!" I yell. The sound of my own voice, of her name, calms me a little.

I jam in my other foot, grip one edge of the crack and pull up again. My fingers are frozen into claws. The next steps are shakier. I'm wondering what's at the top of this rock, if, in fact, there really is an end. As if I've been climbing all my life and now can't stop even if I want to.

Another step up and I see a bull's-eye glowing far off to the right. Somehow I got off the trail. My knees shake. I don't know if I get back on from here. I lower one foot to start back down, but my leg is weak, as if the bone has melted.

Snow pellets fall faster, burning my face and hands. I let my body curve into the rocks, let my head fall forward. I close my eyes and I can see myself as if in one of my father's slides, clinging to rock, the wind about to either fling me down or numb me until I can't even feel whether or not I'm holding on. The only way out is to feel my way down and I'm already so numb I can barely feel the crevice where I've jammed my boot.

I open my eyes and stare at the bull's-eye. I stare until it grows larger. Kath's face glows from its red center. I blink, and she retreats, so I stare again until I can feel the heat from her face warming my face, my hands. She is tucked safely inside the stone hut, sheltered from the blizzard outside, a bright circle of fire warming her, her boots kicked off. She is curled up, asleep. I peer into the tiny, eye-like window, the wind numbing my back, and she wakes as I stare, her round face contracting in silence, the heat dissipating into the cold gray rock. I ask her again if she wants to keep going.

🎼 The Academic Class

*Myths do not tell us how, they simply
give us the invisible background which
starts us imagining, questioning, going
deeper.*

—JAMES HILLMAN

In the previous chapter, I narrated my experiences of what Carolyn Heilbrun (1988) calls "cultural inscriptions" in the composition of a short story. The ways I constructed my identities as a writer, student, and woman were affected by cultural myths informing education and the conflicts they generated. In this chapter, I will examine more specifically how these cultural myths were enacted in a graduate fiction workshop through the talk of students and the instructor.

The particular discussion I will focus upon concerns a draft of a short story, "Bridge of Flowers, Bridge of Iron," that I submitted as a member of the class. Students included both master's and doctoral candidates as well as selected nonmatriculated students from the community. I taped this discussion then listened to the recording on a number of occasions. I also talked to students and the instructor before and after the discussion in an effort to understand their various responses to my story, to the discussion, and to my (other) role as researcher.

At first, I had expected to use the recordings as empirical evidence in a more traditional case study or ethnography. However, it became apparent to me, as I began to transcribe portions of the tapes, that my interpretation, rather than remaining implicit in my representation of the transcript, needed to be rendered visible as part of what shaped that reality. I was not, after all, researching "from the outside in," as a traditional eth-

69

nographer, but rather "from the inside out," as a member of the class. Like teacher-researchers, I sought to recompose the familiarities of this classroom as "strange" and its "strangeness" as more familiar. Consequently, to truthfully recreate what I experienced as multilayered contexts within contexts, I needed to explore my interpretation on many levels. The forms for doing so, however, were more readily available within the blurred genres of postmodern fiction, which makes its constructedness a subject of inquiry. In contrast, traditional empirical research genres emphasize the discovery of knowledge and the limitation of ambiguity rather than the role of the subject in the construction of knowledge and the uncertainties of discourse.

To represent the phenomenal world truthfully, it is thus important to draw the reader's attention to the constructedness of representation. That is why, for instance, in this narrative, the student writer is given a different name than mine—my characterization of her is no less a construction than that of the instructor. Consequently, readers must construct for themselves the murkiness, contradictions, sudden illuminations, and continual change of this talk. They will experience the reciprocal, nonlinear path that changes in consciousness and identity follow, so as to better understand those processes.

I have borrowed a blurred generic form that draws from fiction as well as analytic writing, namely Ann Berthoff's dialectical notes, to represent a dialogue between two discourses, the instructor's and the student writer's. In this two-column format, these discourses "speak" simultaneously and recursively, as well as linearly. Readers can construct for themselves many approaches to the text; they might read one column at a time, switch columns as the text shifts, read from left column to right column or vice versa, and so on. In this more self-conscious approach to reading, gaps between the two discourses, as well as overlaps, disruptions, and continuities, are rendered visible in ways that traditional ethnographic narratives (written through a central narrative voice) tend to efface. Thus, readers must become active participants in the construction of meaning during this discussion, because, like the class, they must create patterns of meaningfulness in a situation where any number of patterns are possible. Like the class, readers will read the student text prior to the discussion, developing interpretations before and during the discussion.

In an earlier draft, I had written this dialogue from a single, omniscient point of view. However, my voice as author/interpreter of events was much too central; I found myself "filling in" or explaining differences in interpretations between individuals rather than problematizing them.

Even in this revised version, there are moments in which it may seem that narrative commentary is more an authorial intrusion than part of the dialogue between each character's discourse. Of course, within each column are multiple languages that modulate closer to and farther from the character's "own" language; therefore, sometimes the more "distant" languages might seem more intrusive. I've tried to lessen those moments by including phrases like *she thinks* and *he believes* when appropriate to indicate they are the character's perceptions, not simply the narrator's "filling in" of meaning. Finally, I've tried to juxtapose sections where each character has separate, sometimes similar, sometimes different, perceptions of the same moment to further de-center authorial intrusion or commentary and subsequently heighten the "de-centeredness" of the text and my role as author.

By representing this event as dialogical, I wish to call into question conventional assumptions about the representation of classroom discourse as a unified, continuous, coherent, and linear text rather than an event with gaps, reversals, serendipity, simultaneity, chaos—something that can't, finally, be controlled or even entirely understood, contrary to the educational myths that say it can and should. Certainly control is part of the story, but in this dialogue it has been de-centered and devalorized. Certainly teachers want their students to change for the better, sometimes to even convert to beliefs we hold dear—but again, that is only part of the story, a part that must be understood in relation to other, less visible parts. Will, effort, even force may be part of the story—but not in the absence of reciprocity and receptivity. Thus the task of representation is not simply a matter of adding missing elements to an otherwise coherent story. As Foucault says, such discursive transformations leave gaps or chasms that remain unbridgeable. We need to imagine a new story altogether in which the parts have a much different relationship to the whole of our knowledge.

Following the narrative is an analysis that expands the representation of the class to my interpretation of it, interpreting that interpretation through cultural myths about writers and women and, in turn, interpreting those cultural myths through an informing mythos of Western culture, the heroic quest. By representing the multilayered contexts of culture that inform this classroom story, I wish to deepen readers' understandings of the complexities they may face in "revisioning" these myths and at the same time demonstrate why such a "revisioning" is important, to start us all "imagining, questioning, going deeper" into our classroom experiences.

To begin this dialogue, readers must first construct themselves as participants in, as well as observers of, this classroom. Therefore, what follows next is the short-story draft, "Bridge of Flowers, Bridge of Iron," which class members also read prior to the discussion. Following the short-story draft is the narrative "dialogue" of the class's talk. A cultural interpretation of the forms of that talk ends the chapter.

The Story

Bridge of Flowers, Bridge of Iron

She was willing to do about anything to make him smile. Even now, as he sat on the rocks away from the falls, absorbing sunlight. Especially now, because he never seemed so locked into himself, so heavy, as he did at that moment. His smile was rare and therefore precious, more so now that they lived apart.

The times he did, finally, smile, she wasn't sure how she did it, or if it was even her doing at all—if, instead, he was really watching something across the room or out the window. Or now, catching a reflection of something on a pool out of reach of the waterfall. In fact, he seemed determined to frustrate her as soon as he saw what she was up to. She considered diving in to break up the mirrored surface below, thinking that might please him. But as she looked at him again she saw a slight smile lurking about his lips, the way a salamander smiles, not really a smile unless you see it a certain way. She had to catch him off guard, vigilant salamander that he was.

When Tom and Susan called to say they wanted to visit over the weekend, she thought it would be good for him to get out of town for the afternoon. At first, he didn't want to come. He said he was in the middle of some poems and wanted to keep at them. But as they spoke, him with his arms stretched across the doorway to his small studio apartment, it turned out he could use a break from the poems, after all. The pressure in his head was getting to him from spending so much time in that cramped, rather barren, as she saw it, space. He also wanted to be with Tom and Susan, whom he hadn't seen since the winter.

Tom was talking to him now, sitting beside him on the rocks. Susan was below, next to the water, taking off her shoes.

Carrie decided to rejoin them, leaping lightly over smooth granite the river waters had carved into deep pools the locals called potholes. It was her favorite place all summer. The granite erupted from the soft green landscape like bone, bone that over time had been swirled in deep currents of the river so that its surface reflected the circuitous flow of water. On steamy July days, she liked to lie out on the rocks in her swimsuit and, when she was so hot she couldn't stand it any more, leap into the potholes with a huge splash. Sometimes she brought a sketch pad.

She had thought it would be good for him to come out here and let the sun pour into his light-starved body. It seemed to be working. She sat next to Susan, looking up at him, noticing an animation in his face she hadn't seen during her weekly breakfasts with him in town. They were talking about his new poems.

She listened in for a moment, staring across the rocks at a younger couple in bathing suits jumping in the water together, meeting in the deepest part of the pothole then turning on their backs to float. She said to Susan, still dangling her feet in the water, "Let's go swimming." She said it loud enough for the men to hear.

"I didn't bring a suit."

"We can swim in our underwear. I've done it before."

Susan looked around. The potholes were far enough below the falls that the streets and bridges of the small village were out of sight. Still, people had been coming and going on the small path that led down the rocks behind the antiques store.

"Go ahead, Carrie. I don't want to swim in my clothes. If we're going out to eat, I'd better stay dry."

Carrie looked uncertainly at the young couple, comfortable as seals as they stretched out on the rock in their wet, shining suits.

"What about you guys?" she asked the men.

They shook their heads and continued their poetry talk.

She stood up next to Susan. "Well, I'm going to go in," she said, unbuttoning her shirt to the tank top underneath. "I really want to go in there. I'm at least going to try it."

"Water's cold." Susan pointed to her feet, which she lifted out of the water, white and slightly shriveled.

"I'll get used to it. Do you think I'll look funny in my underwear?"

Susan shrugged.

"Nobody'll notice. I'm just a little stick. I've got nothing to hide."

Laughing, Susan got up. "I don't think anyone would ever accuse you of hiding anything." She stepped out with her long, muscular legs and gingerly made her way on the slippery rocks to the waterfall.

Watching Susan go, she sank down onto her rock seat again, rubbing her hands along her thighs. Compared to Susan's solid contours, her own body seemed weightless, the flesh transparent, the veins in her hands and arms intertwined like rivers with the muscles she'd gained from her swimming and gardening and hiking, and from handling the bedridden clients whose homes she visited each week. Whenever she came to the potholes, as she did often the last few weeks, since the separation had been, after many months, made official, she could easily imagine herself, as she lay on the rocks, filling with warm light, and rising, rising until she dissolved into the green Berkshires, until her bone merged with the bony rock that erupted unexpectedly at this bend in the river.

She wanted to go into the water, but in the end she didn't want to swim alone. She listened again to the two men's poetry talk, or tried to, because the longer she listened, the more distracted she became. He had that smile in his eyes that she didn't know how to summon herself; he was writing the best poetry of his life, he was telling Tom, and she knew it was because he wasn't living with her in their house. He was living in town in a little sweatbox apartment, which was what he seemed to need in order to write these days. And the poems were coming not from her, but from Emma.

When she looked at him lately, as she did now, all the lightness inside her that she tried so hard to capture compressed under the weight of his dark eyes looking past her into some primordial grief that both nourished and devastated him. That Emma appeared should not have surprised her, since she was only the embodiment of that grief that Carrie tried so hard to disperse, but the harder she tried, the more stubbornly he resisted.

Susan had reached the waterfall and was searching for a place to sit. Carrie wondered if she hadn't gotten bored with the poetry conversation. Susan was a writer, too, and a teacher, as was Tom, but she rarely talked about her own work. She seemed more interested in the potholes and the land around her than in the conversation at hand. In fact, Susan's first words on seeing the potholes were, "They're like O'Keeffe's bones." Which was what she had thought, too. When she had brought them across the Bridge of Flowers, a pedestrian bridge on the other side of the river that ran parallel to the rusted iron roadway bridge, Susan stopped to look at the names of flowers that the Shelbourne Falls people had labeled with small tags. Susan kept pulling Tom away from Michael to show him different blossoms, which he duly admired. Michael, on the other hand, said little about the outrageous colors and shapes of those flowers in the peak of their season. She had thought if she got Michael interested in something outside of himself, she could distract him at least for a while from his brooding.

Susan eased down by the falling water, legs crossed in a lotus, head tilted forward as though eavesdropping on a conversation between the granite and the falling river. Carrie wished she had brought her sketch pad.

Her attention drifted back to the two men. Now Tom was talking about teaching. Phrases like "empowering the student," "student-centered classroom," "non-judgmental response" snagged her attention. And then the two of them argued about it.

She stood up and stretched her arms taut overhead and yawned. "You guys want to eat here or go home and make something?" she asked. She met Michael's eyes when she said "home."

"I don't care," Tom smiled. "Whatever's easiest for you." He glanced at Michael. "I don't want to make a big production out of it."

"Let's eat here," Michael said, and looked across the water.

"OK," she sighed.

"Whatever you guys want to do," Tom said.

She wanted to contradict Michael but caught herself. She hated to argue. She usually found it easier to agree with him, especially over trivial things like where they should eat dinner.

Yet in spite of herself, she'd say things she knew would irritate him when they met for breakfast each week. Deliberately provoke a fight then instantly regret it. Once she started, she didn't back down as much or as easily as she used to.

Susan was coming back across the rocks, her footing more assured this time. "Hey, Susan," Carrie called, "where d'you want to eat tonight?"

Susan stepped up next to Tom and Michael, looked at Tom as if soliciting his response, glanced at Michael, who was staring past her to the falls, then moved over to hug Tom around the shoulders. Tom hugged her back. "It's up to you," he said. "I'm open to suggestion."

She rubbed up and down his back a couple times before she turned to Carrie. "I thought you said you wanted to eat at the River House? We could get a table that looks out on the water."

"We can fix something at home, too, if you're short on cash." She couldn't help it, but she found herself searching Michael's face. She never asked, but she knew money had to be tight for him now that he was on his own, without work for the summer. She thought he didn't want her to know, because he knew she would give him anything he needed.

"Let's eat here," Michael said again, clasping his hands behind his head and twisting with his elbows from side to side in a quick, jabbing stretch.

"Good," Susan said. "That's what I want to do." She smiled at Michael. "Did you want to eat now?" she asked Carrie.

"Uh-uh." She sat down again, testing the water with her toe.

"Great. I wanted to spend some more time with these rocks."

Susan took off for a small cove just behind them where a trickle of water slid down into a glassy pool, one of the deepest of the potholes, Carrie knew. Tom and Michael stretched out their legs as they repositioned themselves overhead. Tom pointed to the small whirlpools the rocks created against the flow of the river. She closed her eyes, letting the sun probe her lids, tilting her head far back against her neck. In the winter she felt starved for this bone-melting heat, this brilliant light, and she thought if she could remember this moment clearly enough, drink it in with her entire body till she overflowed with it, she could conjure it to counter the spell of December.

That had been the worst time, last winter. When the cold had seeped into every crevice of the house, snow piling up on the driveway. She began closing off rooms one by one: his study, its ransacked look, a few papers scattered on the makeshift desk; the basement with all his books; her small room with the easel and dried paint on the pallet, paintings so old she barely remembered doing them. That had been the worst time. Not the fall, when her friends in town told her about Emma, when the leaves had turned. Then, her friends were supportive, curious, ready to hurt Emma to show their fierce loyalty to her, the disgust they had for her best friend who had chosen her husband over her.

She had asked them to leave Emma alone. When they realized she meant it, they stopped calling as often. Then snow came, and it was difficult for them to simply drop by any more. As the cold deepened and the days shortened, she felt Emma's wounded blue eyes on her. She dreamed about her often, at first merely observing her, then arguing with her, and then striking her with her fist. The last terrified her; she was afraid she might actually do that. So she avoided her whenever she went to town, and stayed home more and more. Sometimes she lay on the sofa at night, closer to the wood stove, instead of in bed, and listened to the roof creak in the wind, feeling a strange comfort in Emma's cold presence.

Tom and Susan had come in January, when her grief was heaviest and yet almost pleasant in its familiarity. Tom had been Michael's friend out West before he and Susan moved to the Northeast. Since then, everything they did together had been as couples. They stayed in the house with her, since Michael had no room for them, and tried their best not to be angry at Michael or blame her for telling him to leave. Susan, who usually had little to say to Michael, said even less when he came to the house during that visit. Tom, on the other hand, went out of his way to seek Michael out and talk privately. She was glad Tom did, because Michael wasn't talking to any of their friends in town, and she worried about him. She, on the other hand, talked to Susan alone, and Tom alone, and then to the both of them, sifting through her feelings, the events of the separation, her fears and hopes of what lay ahead. Tom helped her hang a small show of her work in the hallway gallery of an office;

Susan had brought her skis and they tromped around the fresh snow in the woods behind the house. After they left, the solitude seemed refreshing. She didn't need Emma's company as much. She started some new pictures, this time with pastels.

When she opened her eyes into the afternoon again, she noticed the light had changed from its white brilliance to a mellower, golden color reminiscent of fall skies not far away. Susan was on her knees, bending over the water. Carrie leaped over to the smooth place where Susan balanced herself with her left arm reaching into the air while her right hand dove for the glistening rocks at the bottom of the pool.

"They never look as good after you bring them up and they dry," she told Carrie, "but I like them just the same."

"This place is incredible." Carrie waved her arms. "Uh-huh. I want to take a little bit of it back with me. To get me through the school year." She laughed. "I think I got one. Here we go." Susan held up the rock on her open palm. "It looks like a potato. Look at this, Tom. A potato rock."

"Let me see."

She hopped up, cradling the rock in her right hand while using her left to balance against the granite. As Tom stroked the rock, Michael smiled at Susan, shaking his head slightly. "Potato rock, huh?"

Susan smiled back. "Yeah. It even smells like one." Tom handed her the rock back, and she gave it to Michael.

"Looks good enough to eat," Tom joked.

"Potato rock," Michael repeated, returning it to Susan's upraised palm.

"Yes." Her fingers curled around the brown rock. "Only it's a little too smooth for a real potato. But it's a potato in every other way."

Carrie knew that look in his eyes, the writing-a-poem stare he gave Susan before she came back to the cove where Carrie was waiting. Susan was dark-haired and fair-skinned like Emma but without the look of tragedy in her eyes, the color of water. She realized she might have been jealous of that moment between Susan and Michael had it happened last winter. Then it occurred to her that Susan needed Michael's smile, too. Because when Susan settled back beside her and yawned and stretched out her arms, it was clear she was feeling some relief from

Michael's stoic silence. And even Tom, she understood now, played for that smile, whether it was to praise Michael's poetry or to make silly jokes about rocks. And sometimes it was the two of them teamed up, a comedy routine for Michael's benefit.

Susan had put her potato rock aside and was now caressing the large mound of granite they shared, her fingers following the intricate swirls in its surface, smoky gray currents penetrating the lighter gray, like an overcast sky. Then she rubbed the surface in broad, sweeping strokes with the flat of her palm, rubbed and rubbed as if to polish it.

"I feel like I could stay here forever," she sighed.

"This place saved me this summer."

Susan nodded, her head in rhythm with the slow circles she worked upon the granite.

"I'm hardly ever at the house any more. I'm either here or at Ben's." She looked over at Michael and Tom. They were just far enough away that, with the sound of the falls in the background, they wouldn't hear her.

Carrie's fingers discovered a bump in the otherwise smooth rock face and moved across it, testing its shape. There was so much more to tell than she had told Susan over the phone, and yet something in her resisted the telling. That it was not the truth, somehow, even though it had all happened.

Overhead, the sky was so clear and sharp it hurt to look at it. So she turned her attention to the rock she sat on, its solidity reassuring in the midst of the falling water.

"Do you come here alone?"

"Sometimes. Sometimes with Ben. Mostly alone. It's a good place to let my body take over, y'know? Lie in the sun and stop thinking."

Susan nodded.

"He's been good for me." She considered the taste of those words then repeated them for another taste. "He's been very good for me."

"You make him sound like medicine. 'I don't like him, but I know he's good for me.'"

Carrie laughed. "That's good, that's good. You know, he was my doctor. That's how I met him." She heard her laugh ringing across the water and, liking the sound, laughed some more.

"Really? You met him through your job?"

"No, actually I went to him on my own. For that numbness on my left side I've had for a few years. He does acupuncture."

"Good deal. A built-in acupuncturist. He gives you freebies now that you stay with him?"

"I'm going to have to find another one soon."

"Why?"

"I think I'm going to cool things off."

"Does Michael know?"

She nodded.

"Is he still seeing Emma?"

She sighed.

"Then why—"

"I don't know." Her fingers collected strands of her short, light hair. Usually it was quite straight and lay smoothly against her head, like it did today, but during July, the humidity curled the ends so it stood out a little from her scalp. Ben had liked it that way. She liked the wildness about it, tendrils curling out all over instead of lying sedately like feathers.

"I told him we had to stop," Carrie continued. "I need some time to be alone. He said let's wait until your birthday. End of September. Go out with a bang, is what he said."

Susan was quiet for a moment, rolling her river rock between her palms. "But you told me on the phone how good he made you feel. Michael's upset, isn't he? When did you finally tell him about Ben?"

"Yeah, that's another story. Me with my great timing. Michael comes over right around our anniversary, the beginning of July. He comes to the house. I have these new pastels of landscapes which I show him. They're from the woods around Ben's place. He thinks they're great, my best work ever. Amazed, really. Even before I tell him he knows something's up. But I let him talk first, being his idea and all." Her fingers worry pieces of amber around her neck as she continues. "He tells me he wants to come home. This out of the blue, really, after a couple weeks before we had agreed to making the separation official. Live like single people, we'd decided. So I went out and threw myself at my doctor. Aargh!" She pulls her hair in mock despair. "I didn't mean to make them both want me."

"But it's great that they do," Susan insisted. "Don't you feel wanted?"

"Hah. 'Wanted for theft' more like it. Stealing love." Still, she smiled. In the winter, when Emma's presence loomed large in the house, she felt herself shrinking. Michael was always staring over her shoulder at Emma, who was always with them even though he never spoke a word about her. It was precisely because he didn't that her presence was so immense. She, on the other hand, was like a tiny bird pecking and swooping to get his attention away from this woman who was everywhere: in his poems, his bed, everywhere he looked, even with his wife. She pecked: Are you still seeing her? Even though she knew the answer already. And pecked: When are you coming home? And when he kissed her good-by, she'd peck him coldly and turn away.

But with summer came Ben and the sharp edge winter had honed in her softened. She opened up the house again, cleaned out the wood stoves. As soon as it was warm enough to leave the doors open, she left and rarely came back, spending her days at the potholes or at Ben's place drawing, and nights at his side. As long as she stayed in the house, Emma would stay. So she left the doors open, hoping Emma would take the hint and leave. She planted a garden, half-heartedly, because they had always planted a garden. But she forgot to water it, and then there was drought. The failed garden became another reason to stay away. Ben told her, "Move in with me."

"I have a marriage to figure out."

"Move in anyway."

He had two dogs, a mother and a daughter, the mother overbearing, barking whenever Ben did not give her attention, the daughter sweet and mischievous. She and Michael had brought a three-legged cat from the West who was getting old and couldn't stand the aggressive curiosity of two large dogs. His place was torn up with the remodeling he'd been doing on his 1870 mill house for seven years now.

She told him she'd think about it.

"He wants me to move in with him," she told Susan.

"Whew! That was fast. You've known him all of six weeks?"

"He's ready to settle down. He's going on 40. Michael's in midlife crisis and this guy's just getting started. Funny."

"He sounds a little—desperate."

"Thing is, I could do it. I could raise his Jewish children.

Help him finish his house. Sell my—our—house. I could stay
with anyone who loved me. Like a dog—just pet me and talk
sweet and I'll follow you anywhere."

"You and Michael didn't want children?"

"We could never decide." She sighed. "I don't know what I
want, and I'm afraid I'll just take whatever comes along."

"Then spending some time alone will be good for you."

Susan was trying so hard to help her she felt bad that she
was holding back. She thought of Susan bending over an
especially beautiful flower on the Bridge of Flowers, an electric
orange and yellow one, its center thick with pollen, Susan
holding its face gently in her hands, bending low to smell it, the
tip of her nose dusted bright yellow. And then Tom tapping her
nose, grinning, then wiping the smudge off with his fingertip.
Susan's quick glance at Michael, then at her, as Tom touched
the pollen. Michael looking away, as usual. But Carrie saw it,
though until now she didn't understand it. Susan's look was
fear.

What was it that Susan had told them last fall? She and
Tom had been to a poetry reading of a husband and wife. The
husband had had lung surgery and his voice was raspy and his
breath short. They read poems about their marriage, poems of
great tenderness, Susan said, because the man was obviously
dying and their days left together were few. No one knew how
bad off he was until he read poems instead of a story because
his breath was so short.

Until now, she thought Susan was simply being a good
friend, listening, encouraging. But it was really that she needed
to know. Knowing made it less scary for her, the failure of a
marriage. Knowing helped her make sense of it, made it
manageable.

What she was going to say would probably blow that apart.

"Susan, I might be pregnant."

"Really?"

Susan wasn't shocked, after all. In fact, she had that writing-
a-poem look like Michael's on her face. The look her friends in
town had when they told her about Emma.

"I'm not sure. I'm only two weeks late."

"I bet it's nerves."

"Maybe I'll have to move in with Ben after all."

"You're thinking of having it?"

She shrugged. "Sometimes I think it'd be easier that way. Just let things happen."

They talked about it for a while until Susan declared she was hungry, and they all got up and stretched. Michael led them up the rocks to Main Street. Most of the shops were closed and dark; few people passed on the village street. Michael was taking them back on a different route. Susan hung back, peering into storefronts, her hands cupped to the glass. Michael had stopped Tom to get his bearings when Carrie spotted, right there in the middle of the walkway, a small brown bird.

"Oh, look, I think it's hurt!" she cried.

Michael and Tom turned around as Susan and Carrie bent over the bird, which sat motionless.

"It must be scared to death of us," Susan said, leaning over to touch its smooth head.

Michael had already started walking away when Carrie stood up. Susan was wondering aloud what to do with it, but Carrie didn't want to do anything. It wanted to be left alone. Birds like that, she knew, seldom recovered, no matter how you nursed them. Besides, she had a cat. Her and Michael's cat, the three-legged one they brought from the West.

She started walking ahead, leaving Susan to say her last few words to the frightened bird. She had wanted to cross the Bridge of Flowers again, but that wasn't the way Michael was headed. The iron bridge was old and rusty, a remnant of the industrial past of a village that now lived for tourists. But it would get them across just the same.

The Class

Beth:

Sunlight has nearly run its course as Beth watches the other students filter into the classroom, one by one, in pairs, or small clusters. It is mid October, when evenings fade quickly into night, midpoint in the season, midterms on campus, a time when activity is high, even frantic, as faculty and student energies are cresting.

Beth had arrived early to choose a good seat for the evening's discussion. A few people had arrived before her, observing the weekly ritual of breaking desks out of rows and into a three-quarter circle that begins and ends on either side of a large gunmetal-green desk.

Someone turned on the overhead lights, which bleach the last traces of sunset while exposing every gouge and nick in the frayed classroom carpet, cinderblock walls, and chalk-covered blackboard. The shortening days remind her of the paper due next week, the books left to read, the student essays to respond to before the end of the week. Her fingernail works a groove in the desk; her foot nervously taps the desk's metal leg.

Beth sits at the end of the circle nearest the window, at the front of the room. Gerald would usually sit on the other side of the circle's head, somewhat apart from yet still within the circle's boundaries. Sometimes he would put copies of stories on the teacher's desk next to him but otherwise would not use it.

Gerald:

By the time Gerald arrives, the lights are on, the desks have been plucked from their rigid rows, and most of the students are present, chatting congenially. He slips into a seat nearest the door then quickly takes note of who is missing. He likes to begin promptly, since with such a large class—twelve in all—time is at a premium. The commentary of this group, a mix of experienced "workshoppers" and novice writers from the community, tends to become long and involved. He has to make sure everyone has a chance to speak, and everyone gets equal time for the critique of their writing. Not a simple task with such a diversity of students.

Of the two stories scheduled for this evening, Gerald chooses Beth's to begin. This is the second story he has seen of hers; so far she is one of the strongest writers in class. He remembers her graduate school application, having selected her for a teaching assistantship over a year ago.

Opening with Beth's story, he thinks, might spark a lively enough discussion to carry the class through the second story, which isn't nearly as interesting—the less said, the better. Besides, he has already taught another class this afternoon, conferenced with several students in his office—all following a morning committee meeting and two hours of class prep time at home. Ten P.M., no matter how absorbing the discussion, never seems to come soon enough.

So far Gerald likes this group, despite its obvious challenges. The mix of backgrounds, talents, and levels of experience has generated some exciting talk. He sees wheels turning, especially in the eyes of the novice writers, some of whom have never before participated in a workshop. At first, some of them seemed put off by the informality

Beth was too nervous to wait at the campus center between classes, as she usually does, to join classmates in a preclass discussion of the night's stories. Her second story of the semester will be discussed tonight; she decided to forego the early reviews in favor of a little preclass solitude.

In most workshops Beth has attended, the writers do not usually know each other or each other's work before the semester begins, so the small rituals of rearranging desks, choosing seats, and handing out manuscripts help smooth some of the initial awkwardness. Breaks during the three hours of class give students further opportunity to talk and share their experiences.

In chatting with other students, Beth discovered some have workshop experience, while others have never shared their work publicly. Karen, a newswriter for the local paper, is familiar with having her reporting "sliced up," as she says, under the editor's pen. Yet she has never shown her short stories to anyone but her boyfriend. As Karen describes it, these stories are spun from a different thread than her reporting, about which she says she can be more "objective." Karen told Beth she enrolled in this class because without deadlines, without someone to write for, her own stories just didn't get written.

During the first night's introductions, Jane told the class she'd given up a tenure-track appointment in business to return to school full-time and become a writer. For years, she had longed to write, but between raising a daughter on her own and surviving, which she is proud to have done quite well, there was no time to dig in and learn her craft.

Barry arrives late, as usual. Beth has noticed that he almost always leaves as soon as class is over. During breaks, he talks about his life as a salesman, riding the train several hours each day to and from the city. He looks for-

of the workshop—no instructor at the head of the class, no lectures or note taking, just another writer among many, offering comments.

ward to class time as a respite from the "real world," his writing an escape valve relieving the pressures of everyday life. In contrast, Kathy, who is usually at the campus center previewing the night's stories with others before class, has come directly from an undergraduate career and is seeking guidance on her first novel. Beth herself, after several years of workshops in bachelor's and master's degree programs, is in her second year of full-time studies. After holding various civil service jobs, she moved across the country to return to academia to begin doctoral work.

In all, there are a dozen students plus the instructor, brought together by the promise of having a place to meet and talk about their writing. Except for Kathy, whom Beth knows from another class, they are strangers to her. The small rituals—meeting in the same place each week at the same time, the constancy of membership—create a stability and continuity that enables talk in an otherwise awkward enterprise: to comment on real, live writers' writing in their presence. Despite her years of workshop experience, Beth has never been entirely comfortable with the immediacy of it, which she is reminded of every time she leaves her literary theory class and returns to the workshop.

Gerald is generally satisfied with this class's responsiveness to his workshop style. He likes to encourage not only literary analysis but the expression of feelings—the "gut" reactions uncensored by the brain. These students have been refreshingly honest—disagreements have been heated at times, but good-natured.

They seem to be pulling together as a class. Beth, one of the more experienced workshoppers, helps with thoughtful, incisive comments. Gerald expects students will critique her work with the same feeling and care she demonstrates toward theirs. That is part of what Gerald sees as the politics of workshops—students often get the same kind of comments they give.

Beth assumes all her classmates have felt this shift between their literature classes and the workshop, since all writers sooner or later study literature. Everyone freely uses and understands standard lit-crit terms such as *plot, character, theme,* and various *points-of-view,* so Beth concludes that they share, on some levels, a background in reading literature. But with living authors in the midst of their critics, something more feels at stake than reading Joyce or Woolf, or even contemporary authors like Morrison and Silko.

One of the established rituals is that Gerald is usually the last to arrive. When he does, the chatter dies down in anticipation of the evening's work. Tonight, though, Gerald doesn't seem to be in as much of a hurry to get started. A few students haven't yet arrived, and he waits, inquiring about their absence. He sits in the desk at the front of the circle, across the gap from Beth. Some take the opportunity to ask him questions about class business.

On any other night, Beth would welcome the chance to ease the transition from the world outside to this ritualized space they construct every week. However, tonight she would rather just get on with it.

Finally, Gerald introduces the two stories to be discussed, which

That causes a problem when everyone gives nothing but praise, afraid to say what they really think.

Twenty-five years ago, when Gerald was a graduate student in the Yale M.F.A. program, writing workshops were a relatively new phenomenon. Mostly New Critics ran them, conducting class as if the stories were literary artifacts subject to analysis rather than artistic creations that required the responses of both head and heart. They acted as if the writer weren't even in the room, slicing the stories apart with a detached, surgical precision. They seemed afraid to respond openly and honestly, trapped in "the text itself," not in how it affected them as living, breathing human beings. That wasn't the way real editors and readers read in the real world.

everyone has read and prepared notes for in advance. Beth rocks back and forth in her seat, anxious to hear the verdict on her work. When the last student arrives, Gerald suggests starting with Beth's story.

"OK with you, Beth?"
She nods.

"Sure." She wonders why he picked hers first. Sometimes he used the weaker stories as warm-ups for the better ones.

"Good. Who'd like to start? What were your initial reactions to this story?"

The silence that follows doesn't bother Beth, at first, marking the passage between social talk and workshop business. Sometimes someone would crack a joke to ease the tension.

Tonight, however, the silence drags on. The right words, those that will maintain the tenuous ties between strangers, struggle to materialize. Not a good omen, Beth thinks. In this group, someone always starts off with a bit of praise to grease the wheels of talk.

Gerald is about to ask another question when Kathy jumps in. "The focus on the man in the story is so intense." She reads the first line of the story out loud:

She was willing to do about anything to make him smile.

Kathy glances at Beth, as if to

Gerald is glad someone has fi-

gauge her reaction. Kathy doesn't seem sure what she wants to say about this intensity, only that it's there. The comment is so open-ended that Beth can't tell if the statement is a criticism—in other words, is there *too* much emphasis on the man?—or a description that might lead to an interpretation of the character—is Carrie too intensely preoccupied with Michael? Whose focus does she mean, Beth wonders, the writer's or Carrie's? She sits quietly, listening for an answer.

It doesn't occur to Beth to ask Kathy what she means, since the workshop rules were established long ago: the writer doesn't speak until the end. Also, Kathy is still exploring her reaction, early as it is in the discussion.

The word, *obsessed* surprises Beth; Barry and Kathy think this is a story about a woman obsessed with pleasing a man. But it isn't supposed to be a story about their marriage; instead, it is about Carrie, the messy process of coming to know herself as a result of this critical moment in her life.

nally broken the ice. He prefers not to be the lead voice, because students sometimes measure their reactions against his instead of coming up with their own.

And fortunately, it's a good reaction. Kathy is critiquing the writer's emphasis on Michael, a rather uninteresting, one-dimensional character. He could count on Kathy to point out important ambiguities: Michael is a flat, even offensive character to readers, but to Carrie he's the center of the universe.

Barry responds to Kathy's comment: "I didn't see any reason for this woman to be obsessed with this guy. He's so thoroughly unlikable—"

"—So I asked myself why," Kathy cuts in. "Why would she be so obsessed with pleasing this guy?"

Gerald thinks the class is off to a particularly strong start tonight. Usually, they have to warm up to the major issues of a story, offering polite or tepid praise to open the discussion. But clearly this story has hit readers' nerves, as he predicted. Kathy and Barry have raised the same issue: What makes Michael so important to Carrie when he's so dull and unlikable to readers? Teasing out these ambiguities is something Gerald seeks to train students to do as both writers and editors.

Beth is disappointed that both Kathy and Barry label Carrie "obsessed." Yet their underlying responses still seem quite different; Kathy poses an exploratory question to herself by way of further developing her interpretation. She implies that there must be some reason for Carrie's "obsession." Barry, on the other hand, states an assertion as a judgment about the reasonableness of Carrie's motives and, in turn, the clarity of the writer's intentions—in other words, there *shouldn't* be any ambiguity about why Michael is so important to either Carrie or the reader.

Barry's comment seems more of a judgment about the believability of the story, while Kathy's question suggests she is willing to believe a woman could behave this way, with further clarification. But Beth is not certain whether Kathy thinks clarification should come from the writer or from further consideration of her own interpretation.

Gerald fills the silence following Kathy's comment. Kathy has turned the discussion away from the text and into speculation about what it could mean rather than what it actually says. Gerald wants to stick to what's on the page, in search of further clues to the mystery of this relationship. Gerald rephrases Kathy's question to lead the class back to a close reading of the story.

"Why *does* Carrie care, and

That's not what Kathy was asking, Beth thinks. Kathy had turned the question onto herself rather than the text, probing her interpretation. Gerald's question, on the other hand, seems to assume that a problem exists within the story. Thus, ambiguity is more a problem of the text than a challenge to a reader to go deeper into her interpretation. Kathy's uncertainty, Gerald implies, is caused by an unnecessary gap in the text.

why does she want to make Michael smile? Why does she want to do all these things for him?"

Gerald thinks the key might lie in understanding Carrie's behavior. Right now, she caters to a total jerk for no apparent reason. Gerald's hunch is that the real story might be in their relationship, which is currently portrayed in one-dimensional images. This is the mystery for the class to unravel, the static in the signal that the writer must clear up.

Silence settles over the group, tightening the air. Fingers grip whatever is handy—pen caps, manuscript corners, the edges of desks whose seats are hard and confining, especially to Gerald who has already put in a full day and would have liked a hot shower and a glass of wine, or at least a cigarette (which will have to wait until break). Instead, he and his students, other adults, are trapped in a setting better suited for the youthful, impervious bodies of 18- to 21-year-olds.

The silence winds Gerald into a daydream of comfort, even as he tightens against the miserable seat, his elbows sliding painfully against the formica desktop. For some, he knows, there is at least the bar to look forward to after class. For others, there are spouses and children waiting, morning trains to catch, and, for him, classes to prepare.

Gerald doesn't think Kathy is asking the right question, since workshop questions are supposed to discover and clarify problems, not explore interpretations. Yet even Kathy's question, open-ended as it seems, assumes a deficiency. In Beth's experience, workshops are supposed to help writers frame problems so they can go home and solve them. The trick is to do that without destroying everyone's goodwill, being honest without alienating anyone. Consensus is the ideal, as distant a horizon as it sometimes may be, as it is now.

Gerald prefers talk to silence, yet he knows silence also has a way of heightening the urgency for someone to speak. So he allows his question to remain suspended a moment. Silence rarely lasts long in this group. But this is a tough problem, first just to frame it, then to try to resolve it.

Even though the class started with a problem rather than the obligatory praise, Beth knows they don't want her to think her story is hopelessly bad. If it *were* that bad, little or no response would be given. That is, unless the writer is so purely negative in his own comments as a reader that no one holds back when his story comes up. Such was the case with Charles, the assumption being that Charles dished out the kind of critique he

Why would Carrie care at all for Michael after he slept with her best friend? The question frustrates yet tantalizes the sleuth in Gerald. Some of the students' frustration seems located in the plot as unbelievable; Barry, for instance, wonders why a woman would be so stupid as to stay with a cretin like Michael. Also, there's a question of characterization—Michael is too flat to be believable. One solution is obvious, Gerald thinks: make Mi-

wanted and expected for himself.

Kathy believes that women like Carrie, who attach themselves to oppressive men, exist. The mystery is why. Kathy suggests some abuse is at work, but isn't sure exactly what.

But Carrie *isn't* abused, Beth thinks. She's not a victim. She's not crazy. She is *normal*. A lot of women are like Carrie. Thus, when Linda changes the subject, Beth is relieved.

That's exactly right. This is a story about Carrie, not Carrie and somebody, but Carrie and her own nature, herself as reflected in her perceptions of the landscape. Michael is just a prop to get to this place.

As Linda reads, Beth wonders why readers care so much about Michael's characterization. Plenty of stories have flat or stock characters. She has heard many stories about husbands and boyfriends who fit the same pattern.

chael more believable. Make him as complex as the rest of the story.

Gerald is about to offer his solution when Linda switches the topic to setting.

"I'm interested in what's happening at the water's edge, with the rubbing of rocks, crossing bridges, getting on," she says. "I don't mind not knowing why Carrie acts the way she does. I'm more attracted to the landscape of the story, like Carrie, than the human interactions. Look at the energy she puts into observing the rocks and the water."

Linda reads:

Carrie leapt lightly over the smooth granite the river waters had carved into deep pools the locals had called potholes. It was her favorite place all summer. The granite erupted from the soft green landscape like bone, bone that over time had been swirled in deep currents of the river so that its surface reflected the circuitous flow of water. On steamy July days, she liked to lie out on the rocks in her swimsuit and, when she was so hot she couldn't stand it anymore, leap into the potholes with a huge splash.

"That's an interesting point," Gerald says. Linda is a lyrical, descriptive writer, so her attentiveness to this passage is not surprising. "Carrie's attraction to this landscape, like her attraction to Michael, *is* puzzling. Why *does* she pay so much attention to the detail of the rocks? What is the significance of these rocks?"

Gerald's questions seem to come from frustration, as if he believes the writer is deliberately holding back the evidence needed to solve the mystery. Not playing fair. Not enough clues. He confronts a lot of false leads and dead ends, and the landscape just seems to be another avenue leading nowhere.

Linda's comment is just another example of an emerging pattern: Carrie's intense projections onto certain subjects, out of proportion to what these subjects merit in readers' eyes.

Gerald wants the class to see the contradiction between Carrie's obsession with Michael and the writer's flat characterization of him. It might help readers understand the story better if Michael were a more complex character, since he has such importance, at least to Carrie. Certain questions of interpretation, such as Kathy's, can't be answered until this contradiction is resolved.

Jane responds wryly to Gerald's question, "The rocks made me think of the way all the characters are trying to make this rock-faced guy smile."

The class laughs. Gerald shifts in his seat. Beth is glad for the diversion.

That's right, Gerald thinks, Tom and Susan are also "playing for Michael's smile."

Jane's comment only reinforces

Gerald's point—another mystery. Why does everyone want to make Michael smile? Or at least why does Carrie think they do?

"Why?" Gerald asks Jane.

"I don't know why."

And she doesn't care, Beth thinks. Jane and Linda don't need to know why to believe it. And neither do I.

But she *does* know why. If Jane would only say so it might help the writer clarify her character's motivations. This is potentially such a compelling story. Michael has a lot of undeveloped charisma; so many people want to please him, after all. He must be very enigmatic. But it just doesn't come out on the page. There's more to this relationship than the writer lets on.

And then there's Carrie. She's hardly a doormat. She's trying to manipulate Michael; she wants to *make* him smile. She decides what's "good" for him. There's a very strong, determined woman here, but again, she doesn't come across on the page.

Jane smiles enigmatically. Beth wonders if Gerald will be able to keep control over the discussion, which seems especially volatile tonight. Will he keep the talk moving toward the horizon of consensus? Can he ensure that no one is ruthlessly raked over the collective coals of critique, as Charles was last week?

Because of more tension than usual, the goodwill and camaraderie developed over several weeks suddenly feel tenuous. As Jane tells Beth the next day, "I'm surprised at how few positive

Gerald glances at Beth. He doesn't want to lose her goodwill—or anyone else's—despite the productive tension. The class is resisting what's on the page, persuaded by Kathy's speculation about what the story *could* mean. No one wants to find clues in the text and work from that. But if they want to solve the puzzle, they have to look for the missing pieces.

surprised at how few positive comments people made. Usually someone always says something encouraging, at least at the beginning, and then again at the end. I don't know why it was so different this time." Later Beth learns that some of the other students feel uncomfortable about this lack of praise, too. It's as if once the "negative" critique has been set in motion, it's a long, hard slide to the end of discussion, where no cushion of "redeeming qualities" is waiting for the writer.

So Carrie is not perceived as a trustworthy narrator. And Carrie's motives for making such a revelation are questionable, as if she just wants attention.

Beth realizes that to some readers, Carrie is not a reliable character and therefore her "revelation" must be read with some doubt about whether or not she's telling the truth, whether the baby is her lover's, as she claims, or Michael's, whether she's even pregnant or just vying for attention. In fact, Carrie seems so incredibly childlike and insecure

Fortunately, Carl returns to the text in search of more of the contradictions Gerald has been trying to point out.

Carl cites the page, then comments, "Here Carrie is, telling Susan she might be pregnant, when she's only two weeks late with her period."

Yet another example of how Carrie attaches a mysterious significance to otherwise mundane events.

Aside from a few groans, no one responds to Carl. Though the groans are justified, Gerald doesn't want to entirely discourage Carl, one of the younger students, from developing an alternative reading of Carrie. An aficionado of postmodernist fiction, especially John Barth, Carl is proposing a postmodernist reading of Carrie as an unreliable narrator. Perhaps the so-that she is unbelievable, defying conventional reading or understanding.

Kathy now seems determined to make a case for how Carrie *might* be understood, for which Beth is grateful.

But her interpretation is double-edged, nonetheless; even as Kathy tries to raise sympathy for Carrie as victim, others are convinced that no normal person could feel anything but revulsion or hatred for Michael, the cold, stoic, dark man. If there is any consensus so far, it is that Michael is portrayed as a wretched human being, a "rock" or dead weight on Carrie's existence. Consequently, Carrie's character is the one in question. She must be unbelievably flawed as a human being—so unbelievably flawed that the class casts around for more reasonable alternatives—perhaps it's her *view* of Michael, and not Michael himself, that is flawed. There had to be a reason why she stayed with

lution is to make Carrie the narrator of the story?

At any rate, Carl's line of thinking has some merit, despite its naivete about menstrual cycles. When is Carrie telling the truth, and when is she exaggerating? Without clear knowledge of her motives, it's hard to judge.

Happily for the discussion, which Gerald feared had stalled again, Kathy offers a counterinterpretation to Carl's.

"Carrie doesn't have control, so she looks to other people for it."

So Kathy sees Carrie as a passive woman ruled by her desire for the "dark" man, Michael, the brooding poet. Gerald notes that from this view, Carrie's story would focus on the ways in which she lacks control. Carrie would be the victim of her sexuality, which leads to her suffering and the end of her selfhood. Had she not succumbed to Michael's dark eroticism, had she not sought to satisfy her desire, she would never have become a prisoner of Michael's brooding universe. Carrie is thus captive to Michael's "salamander smile."

Interesting theory, Gerald thinks, but it doesn't account for the strong, aggressive side of Carrie, the side that wants to *make* Michael smile and bend to her will. Carl might be off-base about the pregnancy announcement as a ploy for attention, but Carrie *is*, nonetheless, manipulative. So she isn't a

him. He could not possibly be as oppressive as Carrie (and the writer) makes him out to be. Carrie distorts reality in her passivity and dependency. She is completely overwhelmed by him.

Carrie is the problem, not Michael. Carrie is the one who cannot be trusted. Her attachment to Michael is unthinkable and must be rejected, at least by some of the group, in face of more human evidence.

Carrie's behavior is under scrutiny, Beth believes, only with the deepening doubt that she can be trusted as a reliable reader of her own circumstances.

completely reliable point-of-view character.

Karen brings the discussion back full circle to the question of motivation: "Why is Carrie so involved in making this jerk smile?" Gerald is pleased. This is a bright group, he thinks; even newcomers like Karen are alert to the central issues.

In the meantime, Carl doggedly pursues his postmodernist interpretation. "Carrie is thinking nasty things about Michael even as she tries to make him smile," he says, implying that Carrie might not be the victim-as-doormat that Kathy's reading suggests. Finally, someone sees Carrie as a strong person in her own right.

Carl supports his statement by reading a passage from the story:

The times he did, finally, smile, she wasn't sure how she

did it, or if it was even her doing
at all—if, instead, he was really
watching something across the
room or out the window. Or
now, catching a reflection of
something on a pool out of
reachof the waterfall. In fact, he
seemed determined to frustrate
her as soon as he saw what she
was up to. She considered diving
in to break up the mirrored surface below, thinking that might
please him. But as she looked at
him again she saw a slight smile
lurking about his lips, the way a
salamander smiles, not really a
smile unless you see it a certain
way. She had to catch him off
guard, vigilant salamander that
he was.

"She's making a qualitative
judgment about Michael," Carl observes.

Carl's reading of Carrie poses a
direct challenge to Kathy's. On the
one hand, Carl sees her as someone
capable of making a "qualitative
judgment"—as opposed to Kathy's
passive victim. Carl points to a control in Carrie that no one, not even
the most sympathetic reader, is
willing to grant Carrie. Carrie's
"qualitative judgment" might seem
to some readers as significant as a
flea barking at a lion, and yet nonetheless it is an act of judgment, indicative of an autonomous mind,
however untrustworthy, capable of
forming its own views.

Gerald scans the room. Beth is writing furiously. Everyone else seems to be on the edges of their seats. He has no idea what will happen next. Charles, for instance, could open his mouth and say something so trivial and blunt that the energy could come crashing down. But Charles, too, seems captured by these contradictions. Gerald waits for the next comment.

"Carrie's anger is so squashed and yet it comes out in these diffused ways," Kathy says.

Kathy's leap from passive resistance to anger is not large, and to Beth quite obvious.

Kathy's move to resolve the contradictions may be premature. The idea that Carrie is capable of a clear, direct emotion such as anger flies in the face of either reading presented so far: Carrie as either passive victim or active, though mightily frustrated, woman. Anger, after all, is power, and that is clearly something everyone agrees Carrie lacks. If she were truly angry, she would have left Michael long ago. The class consensus seems to be that Carrie's problem is that she *isn't* angry. If she were a "normal" person, she would have left Michael and never looked back.

A long, charged pause follows.

The silence implicates Kathy's comment as subversive, threatening the fragile bonds of goodwill and camaraderie the class has worked so hard to maintain, despite moments such as this when the careful consensus they have developed is suddenly and unexpectedly jeopardized.

Anger? Gerald thinks. Passive women are victims because they *aren't* angry. Carrie's "nasty thoughts" about Michael were more a sign of frustration or unhappiness. But surely not anger.

Kathy's view is not the only one implicated. Beth, who has thus far sat silently, intent upon listening, now finds herself also doubted. Perhaps Carrie seems unreliable, Beth speculates, because the writer has an unreliable interpretation of Carrie's situation. It goes back to the missing clues in the mystery, the mystery of Carrie's behavior.

For Kathy to claim "anger" is like a detective to point to a nonexistent clue. Gerald sees no visible evidence of anger in Carrie. That would make it another story altogether. That is not the story on the page, but simply a speculation on Kathy's part. It is not the story of the class's consensus. If, in fact, Carrie really is angry, then she has betrayed Michael by concealing it. But the anger, to Gerald's mind, simply can't be substantiated within the text as it currently exists.

An opportunity to explain her intentions and resolve the class's dilemma has presented itself to Beth, but she declines to speak. Readers are supposed to draw their own conclusions, untainted by the "intentional fallacy" of the writer. For her to speak now would constitute a criticism of the class's sincere effort to understand her story.

The class's goodwill has already been stretched a bit thin by Kathy's challenge to the class's consensus; Beth doesn't want to risk it any further. Charles did last week, and, deservedly or not, received a verbal pummeling in return.

Karen, perhaps in a gesture of appeasement, suggests a change in the subject. Beth is both relieved and disappointed.

Everyone hurriedly shuffles their copies to find the beginning of the end. Beth pictures some squinting at marginal notes scribbled over coffee at home, little hieroglyphic fragments that make little sense in the fluorescent overhead light, or longer comments squeezed between the double-spaced text. Hunting for clues. Everyone, including Beth, trying to recollect their original thoughts. But things have been stirred around so much in the discussion no one can tell her own thoughts from anyone else's. Going back to the text, something solid and real in the face of so many contradictions, provides everyone a moment of grounding.

Beth flips quickly to the passage in question.

Laughing, Karen says, "Let's look at something else. What did you think of the end of the story?"

Anxious to get the discussion back on track and into the text once more, Gerald adds, "Where does the ending start, where is the ending? Page 17?"

"It's the page with the bird,"
Linda says. Trust Linda to remem-
ber the imagery, Gerald thinks.
Linda reads,

Michael led them up to the rocks
to Main Street. Most of the shops
were closed and dark; few people
passed on the village street. Michael was taking them back on a
different route. Susan hung back,
peering into storefronts, her
hands cupped to the glass. Michael stopped Tom to get his
bearings when Carrie spotted,
right there in the middle of the
walkway, a small brown bird.

"Strange, all of a sudden Carrie
has this confidence," Linda observes with a certain surprise. "She
sees—well, it's confusing—she decides to compromise. But," she
squints at her notations, "I wondered why."
As if to answer her own question, Linda reads on:

"Oh, look, I think it's hurt!"
Carrie cried.
Michael and Tom turned
around as Susan and Carrie bent
over the bird, which sat motionless.
"It must be scared to death
of us," Susan said, leaning over
to touch its smooth head.
Michael had already started
walking away when Carrie stood
up. Susan was wondering aloud
what to do with it, but Carrie

didn't want to do anything. It wanted to be left alone. Birds like that, she knew, seldom recovered, no matter how you nursed them. Besides, she had a cat. Her and Michael's cat, the three-legged one they'd brought from the West.

She started walking ahead, leaving Susan to say her last few words to the frightened bird. She had wanted to cross the Bridge of Flowers again, but that wasn't the way Michael was headed. The iron bridge was old and rusty, a remnant of the industrial past of a village that now lived for tourists. But it would get them across just the same.

"What do you think of the bird? Do you think it's significant?" Gerald asks, hoping Linda will elaborate.

This question has the same double-edged quality as Gerald's opening question, asking for an interpretation, but at the same time questioning whether the bird *is* significant or just another dead end in the search for clues.

Kathy answers first. "Here on page 14, it says,"

Carrie was like a tiny bird pecking and swooping to get Michael's attention away from this woman, his lover (and her best friend), who was everywhere: in his poems, his bed, everywhere he looked, even with his wife.

Carrie pecked: Are you still seeing her? Even though she knew
the answer already. And pecked:
When are you coming home to
stay? And when he kissed her
goodby, she'd peck him coldly
and turn away.

"There's a lot of bird imagery
scattered throughout the story.
Carrie also refers to herself as
'weightless,' somewhere, as I recall.
Like *she's* a bird."

"I think you're onto something
here," Gerald says, eager for clues.
"I hadn't noticed this pattern before."

Still, he questions why he
hadn't noticed. The symbolism is
there, but he's not sure it adds up
to anything. There are hints, but
perhaps that's all they are. Vapor
trails, tracings of something still in
the writer's mind that hasn't yet
materialized on the page.

The mystery remains a mystery, only heightened by the possibility of meaning. He returns to
Carl's inference that Carrie is an
unreliable point-of-view character.
Maybe the announcement of pregnancy really *is* meant as a ploy for
attention?

Barry apparently has been
thinking along similar lines as Gerald. "I thought she had already
ruled out having kids, and here she
is deciding all over again."

"But Carrie and Michael never
could decide if they wanted children," says Gerald.

"No, *he* never could decide," Kathy says excitedly. "If *he* had decided, she would have had one. That's the whole point. Carrie doesn't decide *anything*. She needs a man to make decisions for her. If not Michael, then her lover. That's her identity. *She* is the bird. She's giving up on herself."

Kathy slumps hard against the back of her seat, as if she's found the breakthrough in her reading. Gerald senses she is alone in her satisfaction, as Linda, rereading her notes once again, says, almost apologetically, "Actually I'd connected the bird more to Michael."

"The pregnancy was something she was just making up," says Barry. "She was only two weeks late."

"She wants to be a mother so bad she's making it up," adds Carl.

"I want Carrie to go over the flower bridge, not the iron bridge at the end," Kathy sighs.

Kathy is not the only one who wishes Carrie would go her own way instead of compromising, following Michael, as she always has, over the ugly, rusted iron bridge. Jane and Linda, too, say they want Carrie not to "give up on herself."

Gerald, too, would like a different resolution of the dynamic between Carrie and Michael. He refers the class to another passage, which they read silently:

"Susan, I might be pregnant."

So they think Carrie is giving in to Michael's desires and giving up on her own. Kathy seems to see the flower bridge as a symbol of Carrie's sexuality, its "outrageous shapes and colors" represented by the flowers that remind them of "erotic Georgia O'Keeffe flower paintings," as Jane says, echoing Kathy's frustration. And thus, to them, Carrie is giving up on her own vision and crossing the river into the unknown, at the dark man's heels.

"Really?"

Susan wasn't shocked, after all. In fact, she had that writing-a-poem look like Michael's on her face. The look her friends in town had when they told her about Emma.

"I'm not sure. I'm only two weeks late."

"I bet it's nerves."

"Maybe I'll have to move in with Ben after all."

"You're thinking of having it?"

She shrugged. "Sometimes I think it'd be easier that way. Just let things happen."

"I can't tell if Carrie is telling the truth or deliberately lying about her pregnancy. And then Susan's 'writing-a-poem' look when Carrie tells her—that seems like distortion on Carrie's part," Gerald says.

"It's fear. Susan's afraid to hear the truth about Carrie," Kathy counters. "She may look distracted, but really, she's afraid."

"You know, I've known women like Carrie," says Jane. "Who knows why, but they keep hanging on. I took the story as it is now, accepted it totally, like Linda." Linda glances up from her notes briefly. "She's hanging on because she doesn't know anything else. So to let things just happen is a survival tactic."

"I still want to know what made Carrie and Michael come to-

Karen can't believe that any woman would hang on to someone as thoroughly unacceptable as Michael. To cling to someone characterized as an absence, impervious to light, a weight and an oppression, doesn't make sense, as unimaginable as a woman loving her rapist. Michael, therefore, must be lovable in some way. Why else would Carrie stay with him?

The light from the brief October evening has long since disappeared, and the tall, narrow windows that Beth now stares out are dark except for occasional headlights streaming past. Everyone, including Beth, seems tired, and there is still another story to discuss.

It is clear that no consensus will be reached about this story. That is not unusual nor even necessarily unexpected, though tonight the lack of agreement weighs a little heavier than usual, the cushion of praise having long since been withdrawn.

Beth thinks that they are not sure how she is taking this. She gave up on writing notes long before. Notes are usually a sign to readers that the feedback is worth

gether," says Karen. "There must be something redeeming about their past, some love exchanged that would make Carrie work so hard to make him smile."

"It's more devastating if there is nothing," Jane replies.

"Carrie is tired of making decisions," Linda says. "Look at page 16. She says, 'Sometimes I think it'd be easier that way. Just let things happen.' I thought of Carrie as depressed. Seeing her as a bird, though, changes things."

"There's a lot of anger not stated. You can see that in her intense need to watch how Susan reacts to her," says Kathy, glancing at Beth.

Gerald has to make a decision. The discussion has taken a turn into murkier waters than the group has time or energy for, so he steps in to wrap things up.

recording. The writer merely listening is more ambiguous.

The word *anger* again seems to send everyone scrambling, as if someone might become confrontational, as Charles did. To acknowledge Carrie's anger is to invite the possibility that Carrie's author or some of her readers might share that anger.

In Beth's experiences over the years, it has always been part of the workshop ritual to invite the writer to speak at the end of the discussion. The writer can ask questions, even comment on the comments, though that is a maneuver that requires the utmost tact in order to maintain everyone's goodwill. She's not sure what her questions are at this point, and her comments about the comments don't come easily to mind, either. And another story is yet to be discussed, another 90 minutes to go.

"You may be right," he says to Kathy. "But the story you describe isn't actually on the page. This is your interpretation of it."

"Yeah, you've pointed out a lot of neat things, but I don't feel that interpretation," says Karen.

"There's just not enough information in the story to support that reading," says Barry. "Kathy has a nice story, but I need more information—why she's attracted to Michael, then Ben, whether or not she's really pregnant, and so on."

"At least Kathy is trying to find a road out for Carrie by reading the absences in the story," says Linda.

"Would you like to say anything?" Gerald asks Beth.

"No, but thanks for the comments," Beth smiles. "I have a lot of ideas to sort through."

"Let's take a break," says Gerald.

Beth stretches slowly as the others break up once again into pairs or groups, or stray alone into the hall, outside, crossing the courtyard to the campus center without her. She stretches away the tightness of the small, hard desk, the discipline of holding herself at attention, like a yoga posture or a warm-up stretch before a race, when her body ached for the comfort of an old, familiar chair.

She watches them scatter but expects they will return, because the ritual has taken hold; it is harder to break form and call it a night than to stay and complete what has already begun.

One by one, they rise from the desks designed for shorter class periods and younger bodies, stretching out stiffness and cramps. Gerald checks his shirt pocket for cigarettes and a lighter. He follows some of the other students headed outdoors, to the campus center for coffee, or a smoke, or a snack. Some people duck into the bathroom, to reappear in ten minutes, back in their seats.

Hard work tonight. Although he had anticipated some tension, the discussion wasn't, finally, what he'd expected. He'll talk to Beth about it later, in private.

The Woman in the Text

In the following sections of this chapter, I will interpret the classroom dialogue through narratives of gender and culture. Of course, many interpretations are possible; I present mine from the position of one who is both participant in the construction of this story and observer of that construction. This is not to say my interpretation is not privileged; in fact, I think my bias toward the writer's experience is inescapable and thus should be carefully considered. It is to say, however, that the writer's story should not be excluded in constructing the meanings of the contexts in which writers talk about their work.

One of the most notable features of this discussion was the emphasis, almost to the exclusion of any other issue, on the character of Carrie. (As you will see in chapter 5, the self-directed group had a similar emphasis.) Of particular interest to the class was Carrie's relationship to her husband, Michael, whom everyone agreed was a thoroughly unlikable character. From the beginning, the primary problem readers identified was confusion over why Carrie behaved the way she did—why, in other words, she chose to stay with a man who clearly did not return her love, who went out of his way to deny her the approval (in the form of a smile) she needed so badly, and who deeply violated her trust by having an affair with her best friend. To some members of the class, it was inconceivable that Carrie would, in fact, stay with Michael.

The axis around which the class's debate circled was the question of whether Carrie was a believable character, or whether, instead, the story was being narrated by a distorted or otherwise "unreliable" narrator. Several women in the class, including Kathy, Jane, and Linda, supported the view not only that Carrie was believable, but that the question itself was a moot point, based on their personal experiences. As Jane said, she'd known many women like Carrie, victims of the gravitational pull of bad relationships.

But others, including Barry, Gerald, Carl, and Karen, insisted on the need for a further explanation of Carrie's behavior. To Karen, the relationship had to have originated as love; thus Karen believed that the author's representation of Michael as entirely oppressive and unlikable needed to be balanced with information about why Carrie had married him in the first place. In contrast, Jane raised the possibility that there might never have been any love between Carrie and Michael at all. The argument's axis, then, was weighted on one end with doubt about Carrie's believability as a character and on the other end with belief, based largely on personal experience. Both ends, however, reflected some difficulty in understanding Carrie's motivation to appease Michael and win his approval and love.

As a whole, the class reacted to Carrie in ways analogous to societal responses to abused women; though physical abuse was never suggested, those who found Carrie credible did imply she was emotionally abused by Michael. On the other hand, those who doubted her believability were skeptical about her purported victimization. Instead they regarded Carrie as a psychologically damaged person who distorted, exaggerated, and even lied (as Carl said, she might have been lying about her pregnancy) for attention and approval.

This raises a familiar social dilemma, for if a woman, as a result of her abuse, is psychologically impaired, then how can one prove such impairment was not there to begin with? How can one trust the judgment of one who is "sick" enough to "let" herself be abused in the first place? To the doubters, there was no visible evidence that Carrie was a victim of anything but her own troubled psyche; she was not a normal person, because normal people, like those in the class, would never have remained with someone as awful as Michael.

The problem, as Gerald and others framed it, is one of evidence that could prove Carrie was, in fact, a victim of Michael's domination. The believers didn't require such evidence, drawing from their own experiences as women and with women of their acquaintance. The mechanisms for why Carrie would choose to stay with Michael might not have been clear in the story, but the fact that she was a victim, depressed, passive, unable to make decisions, was clear to believers, who could easily imagine the possible reasons Carrie was bound to this relationship. Doubters, on the other hand, questioned the soundness of Carrie's perception. Because no physical evidence of abuse existed, only evidence of a relationship that, for some reason, had fallen apart, they questioned Carrie's sanity and maturity. The problem, contrary to believers' suggestions, might not be Michael; the problem could very well be Carrie, who seemed unable to distinguish reality from fantasy.

These two poles of the argument share a common question about the story's interpretation—is this a story of love gone sour or is it about power and domination? Even though each side, doubters and believers, took apparently opposing positions (Carrie as demented; Carrie as victim), they actually constitute two sides of the same representation, joined by a common assumption: Carrie is a woman out of control. The former position, Carrie as a "woman scorned," whose love has been rejected and whose mind has been distorted, nonetheless maintains the possibility of a story of power—a woman seeking power over the man whose love she is "obsessed" with regaining. This possibility was hinted at by Carl when he noted that Carrie was "thinking nasty things" about Michael even as she tried to win his smile (and thus his love and approval). So in the background of Carrie's play for affection is the possibility that she was also playing for power in the form of control over Michael.

Yet the other position also invites a similar reading of control, posing the possibility of Carrie's "obsession" for love and approval. Both positions, though different in what they chose to foreground—Carrie as deranged, Carrie as helpless victim—are actually quite similar to the extent that Carrie is represented as someone obsessed with gaining something she once had. Whether that "something" is love or power is the ambiguous center around which the argument revolves.

The class regarded Carrie's announcement of pregnancy as a highly significant moment, a critical key to the story's interpretation. Just as it was significant that the class discussed Carrie almost exclusively in relation to a man (either Michael or Ben, her lover), perhaps even more significant is the importance of the ambiguity that surrounded the truth or falsity of Carrie's announcement.

Carl was skeptical, as were Gerald and Barry, to some extent, of Carrie's "premature" revelation to Susan about her pregnancy; Carl's hunch was that Carrie lied from a pathological need for attention. Those who believed that Carrie might have been pregnant (or at least believed that Carrie thought so) also regarded the pregnancy as representative of her lack of control over her life—falling into situations, letting them take over her life rather than making her own decisions.

The ambiguity of whether or not Carrie was pregnant was overshadowed by the frustration experienced by both doubters and believers over Carrie's lack of control, as represented by her bizarre obsession with getting attention, or her unmitigated passivity in face of personal crises. Both sides wanted her to be different, less obsessed, more in control of her emotions and her life. For the class as a whole, whether or not individuals sympathized, no one finally empathized with Carrie, because of the ambiguity surrounding her characterization. She was too much Other, too much unlike how the class saw itself. They could neither gain a clear understanding of her motives and desires nor verify the clarity or distortion of her perceptions.

The Writer in the Class

Just as the class projected an object rather than a subject status onto Carrie because of her obsession with gaining love and approval, her lack of control, and her possible pregnancy, they also projected an object status onto the writer of the story, whose motives, like Carrie's, were ambiguous and thus in need of clarification. For, as the class understood its task, these ambiguities had to be framed as problems to assist the writer in resolving the tensions the ambiguities generated.

A secondary task was to make concrete recommendations as to what might assist clarification, as some of the class did toward the end (during other discussions, such recommendations took up substantially more of the conversation). While most class members agreed that such "suggestions" were welcome, they were also quite aware that such commentary blurred the already murky boundaries between the production and the consumption of texts.

The boundaries between production and consumption of texts were carefully maintained through the class's talk. No one believed she or he was capable of rewriting another writer's story; for example, the ritual of asking the writer to speak at the end of each discussion was, in part, a symbolic gesture of returning the text to the writer, reinforcing the belief that only the writer, finally, could understand her motives in writing a given work. Thus, the mystery, the Otherness, of the story's production remained just that—Other. To discuss the genesis of a composition would have been outside the realm of what the class as readers could know and was therefore not considered relevant.

Consequently, in such a workshop there is considerable pressure against the writer's speaking during discussion of the story, whether this is formally announced as a rule of class operations, as it was in this class at the beginning of the term, or simply discouraged through a variety of social mechanisms designed to maintain peace and goodwill, at least on the surface of the class's interactions. A writer's talk would only jeopardize an already cloudy boundary between what readers know as consumers and what the writer knows as the producer of the story.

The principle evoked in keeping production/consumption boundaries clear is the "intentional fallacy," which stipulates that an author's statement of intention should not influence a reader's interpretation of a text. In this context, a text is represented as an autonomous object of scrutiny whose origins and history must be suppressed in order to render the most accurate assessment of its quality and value. Thus, to confuse the mode of production with the mode of consumption is to risk domination by the writer's or reader's control of the textual territories. To suggest that not only the writer but her readers may enter into the composition of a text, that composing might in fact be a collaborative rather than solely individual enterprise, is to violate the territorial arrangement that keeps the two factions, writers and critics, at peace.

The cultural myth of the writer or critic as autonomous is strong, and the fear of losing autonomy is pervasive, as the workshop dialogue demonstrates. In turn, writing workshops serve to control that fear through a ritual enactment of the very loss of control and individual autonomy that both critics and writers dread. As Clifford Geertz (1973) notes, social rituals dramatize a culture's fears about phenomena over which they have no apparent control. For instance, Geertz demonstrates that the Balinese cockfight is a ritual enactment of controlling or safely assimilating the very animality that Balinese culture so pervasively suppresses in every other walk of life. Similarly, the ritual of a writer handing over her text to "objective" critics is an enactment of what writers might fear most—that their texts are not their own. Geertz's point about cockfights is that the ritual, rather than challenging Balinese culture, actually serves to reinforce the status quo, which is based on a hierarchy of status—the rich, who bet only on the best, most evenly matched cockfights, remain rich while the poor squander themselves on mismatched or trivial or otherwise unimportant fights. Nothing changes; it is seldom, if ever, that anyone really acquires or loses significant wealth. And that, after all, is beside the point. It is the *play* of the fight that matters.

Similarly it is the *play* of workshop talk that matters more than any desire to change the status hierarchies of the classroom and the world of publishing, with its rungs of writers, agents, editors, and publishers as well as status assignments to small presses, university houses, and commercial publishers. The belief that an individual writer is autonomous and does, finally, control the meaning of her text is an issue not to be challenged but to be ritually affirmed as the object of such meetings. Writers, it is assumed, *need* to believe in this heroic representation of themselves in order to face what seems an otherwise impossible ladder to mount and climb: becoming a writer.

The paradox that the class, guided by the experienced "master," Gerald, sought to immerse itself in was the ritual giving-up of control of their work to the scrutiny of others so that they would ultimately gain a deeper and more permanent control over their text and, presumably, their lives as writers. The writer's talk breaks the ritual code; she cannot be *both* a writer and a reader of her work at the same time. The purpose of giving up control, ritually, is to learn the ways strangers might react to her text and to adjust herself accordingly, so that publishers and editors, the next level of "strangers," will not seem quite so strange.

Just as, according to Geertz, the Balinese cockfight ritualizes the animalistic and assimilates the taboo into a familiar and thus controllable entity, so does a writer listen to the talk of strange readers to bring into herself that Otherness that seeks to control her. Again, it is a ritual that serves to reinforce one's autonomy by, paradoxically, giving oneself over to Otherness. One eats the hearts of enemies in order to garner their strength and power for oneself. Of course, no real control has been lost, because no one really had control to begin with; that is the point of having the ritual at all. One ritualizes that over which one has no control in order to build the illusion that one does have control over the unknown, the unforeseen, the uncertain.

Readers in this ritual believe they are assisting the writer in gaining mastery over her meanings—meanings that are sometimes obscure, veiled in the mysteries of composing, which, like other taboo subjects, is highly private and individualized as well as idealized—by ritually appropriating the writer's text and imposing their own meanings upon it. Readers, like writers, operate under the belief that they are in control of the meanings they assign to the text, that these meanings are obvious and clear, and that in circumstances where they cannot evoke that meaning, it is because of a flaw in the text, not because of uncertainty of the act of reading.

While readers enact this belief in their own autonomy as interpreters of text, they also believe they cannot presume to know or to contribute to the composition of the text, because it does not, finally, "belong" to them. They cannot claim such responsibility, given that production is separate from consumption of textual objects. Their task, as they see it, is to make the ambiguity visible to the writer, who, in turn, tries to internalize the ways of seeing that readers provide, in a way of stepping outside oneself, so to speak, to know what is unknowable to others.

However, though the ritual of the classroom might affirm belief in the autonomy of the writer, critic, and the text, what is actually enacted are the ways in which such meaning really *is* out of the hands of an individual and controlled by a larger agency—that of culture. The ritual both clarifies and obscures this relationship, much as the Balinese cockfight both reinforces and obscures social hegemony with the promise of change and challenges to status. The fear that underscores a writing workshop—that meaning is not solely individual or private—is enacted through its talk. The point of the ritual is to become what one fears most; the Balinese merged with their cocks (as Geertz notes, the *double entendre* is intentional) and writers merge with the voice of culture, which speaks for the belief in autonomy while internalizing meanings inscribed by culture. It is no surprise, then, that the plot of Carrie's life, just like the plot of the writer, is inscribed by the class as the need to gain control. Women and writers (and readers) are Others to be assimilated in the hierarchy of cultural status and control.

Of Writers, Heroes, and Goddesses

If one accepts that there is such a thing as a "voice of culture," what might that voice be? In the graduate workshop, certain recurring words mapped the locus of the class's attention: *obsession, why, control, anger, victim, significance, man, pregnancy, mother, fear, survival, love, smile, intense, bird, information.* Arranged in a field, they might appear this way:

Obsession	*Why*	*Significance*
Control	*Victim*	*Intense*
Smile	*Love*	*Anger*
Man	*Mother*	*Fear*
Bird	*Pregnancy*	*Survival*
	Information	

In the arbitrariness of such an arrangement, patterns nonetheless emerge; the "voice of culture" that this class responded to is plotted by its own language; and within that language, as theorists such as Carolyn Heilbrun and Rachel Blau DuPlessis have argued, are the plots (or myths) that inform the lives we lead, the invisible webs that bind us in culture.

Obviously, numerous narratives are available from the small field of language I've charted, just as numerous narratives are possible from among the members of the class; my rendering of the experience is only one of an infinite number of possibilities. Yet at the same time, these narratives, set in relation to each other, can yield, as Geertz has modeled in his story of the Balinese cockfight, larger patterns of significance.

Read individually, isolated from each other, each individual narrative may seem "small," "subjective," incomplete; one may conclude that such perspectives are, after all, relative, with none more or less significant than others. But if these narratives are connected to other narratives of the culture, broader significances are possible, at once affirming the individual stories while demonstrating a more general meaningfulness rather than remaining in the quagmire of relativism or the foundationalism of the objective stance.

Consequently, the relationship between the classroom ritual that affirms the autonomous self even as it enacts the opposite and the mythos that structures such belief is critical to an understanding of the larger significance of one classroom's interaction. This relationship between ritual and myth is, however, highly complex; rather than attempt to define it in any systematic way, I will instead describe it through the relationship of the ritual of the writing class to a mythos of the autonomous self. If the ritual of the writing class assimilates fears of losing control of meaning, then one mythos that informs such a ritual is that of the heroic quest—specifically, of the writer as hero.

The heroic quest has been considered a universal pattern by myth scholars for many years. The quest plot is said to be found across all cultures and includes both genders. According to the popular myth scholar Joseph Campbell (1968), and drawing from Jungian psychology, the male hero represents masculine aspects of the psyche, while female figures represent feminine psychic forces. Such figures are not, according to Campbell, gender specific; thus, women and men might enact the same quest for meaning.

This view of the hero and the heroic quest as universally representative of self-development and transformation underscores much of American literature in equally essentializing terms, as Nina Baym (1985) has argued. In the graduate workshop, the heroic quest served as a model for a writer's development, with the search for meaning as the object of the quest. Thus, the classroom ritual is intended to prepare the writer-heroes to do the impossible: to control meaning in a world in which there is no control. To prepare themselves, they must learn to give up control in order to gain a larger control: power over the Other presented by the readers in the class.

To become self-realized, it would seem, requires that writer-heroes reinscribe a subject-object hierarchy while they ritually affirm their culturally assigned, marginal status. One never does, in any final sense, triumph over culture. One does, however, become more adept at inscribing the sanctioned codes. Development, in this model, means learning one's place in the social hierarchy.

Even as the heroic quest focuses attention on a single character—his triumphs and trickery in the face of querulous and often unpredictable gods and goddesses—the ritual enactment of the quest underscores how, finally, one does not overcome culture but becomes more fully and complexly inscribed by it. Paradoxically, the deeper one's understanding of that inscription, the freer one presumably becomes. One gives up the smaller self to a larger, transpersonal Self.

However, what essentialist views of myth such as Campbell's overlook is the deeper paradox—the hero both assimilates and transcends culture. Transformation, mythologically speaking, requires both. Essentialism, however, privileges the ascendant aspects of the quest. Thus when Campbell discusses the heroic cycle of departure and return, separation from mother/community/earth, it is as an inevitable, inescapable pattern, always ending in ascension over prior, human limitations. The hero-writer must experience the pain and trials of separation—from the self, from the mother country, from all the ways he used to know himself and his text. As Belenky and her colleagues (1986) have pointed out, the masculine myth requires that confirmation of knowledge typically comes at the end of education (or questing) rather than at the beginning (193). Prior to that time, the hero is not seen to have proved himself as one who possesses control over his destiny.

As the classroom dialogue dramatizes, Beth did not, finally, regain control of her meaning, because that meaning was not solely her possession in the first place. She believed, however, that she should strive for such control. Typically, writers in such classes do not ask, Why is my text being interpreted in this way? (although Beth thinks Kathy is trying to ask just that kind of question). Instead they ask, How must I change my text (and my self) to make my meaning clear?

Surely both questions are useful to ask; however, the latter is privileged in writing workshops, whereas the former informs literature classes (that is to say, the text is viewed as complete; only the interpretations of the text are contested). When the division of labor is polarized between consumption and production of texts, when relations between apprentice and master writers (student vs. teacher) and between texts (manuscripts vs. "great" literature) are rigidly hierarchized, the attention of the writer-hero never strays from an inward gaze in which belief in individual autonomy is validated, even though, outside, the workshop ritually reinscribes the fear that an individual is finally not able to control meaning and is thus never, finally, transcendent over, but always enmeshed in, culture. The dialectic between individual and society, self and culture, text and context, breaks down in face of what Ann Berthoff calls "killer dichotomies," or in other words, antagonistic oppositions.

These two aspects of the hero, as autonomous and as culture itself, coexist in an antagonistic opposition that ultimately prevents writer-heroes from challenging the cultural values already in place. Consequently, within the classroom, heroic "subjects" ironically serve as vehicles to ensure their own "object" status as instruments of the gods (or of the publishing world, of culture). The question then becomes, Whom does this oppositional framework serve? Who can, in the eyes of culture, become knowers and possess (and control) knowledge?

In discussing the valorization of the heroic quest, the problem resides not simply in the quest plot but in the ways such stories are interpreted. By approaching myths from within an oppositional framework that breaks down the dialectic necessary for the transformation of consciousness, our ability to grasp the deeper, more transformative powers of these myths becomes sorely limited. Knowledge becomes idealized as either a product of the conscious, rational mind triumphant over subconscious subversions or as painful but necessary lessons in the school of hard knocks. All is knowable, as objectivists since Descartes have argued.

The other side of the dialectic—what is unknowable, mysterious, chaotic, that into which we are abducted through tragedy, crisis, accident, the unforeseen—is subsumed within the essentialist, transcendent hero. The dialectic of our knowledge of knowledge—as *both* something both sought after *and* something we are abducted into—is broken into polar oppositions. We thus assume in our interpretations that one cannot be a knower if one is out of control (i.e., not dominant).

Consequently, the graduate workshop could not imagine Carrie except as someone lacking control—whether her lack was perceived as an inherent flaw or regarded as a inequitable social condition (e.g., sexism keeps women from controlling their own lives). No other interpretation of Carrie as knower in her own right was offered, because what it means to know is so closely tied to a masculine developmental model that posits rational control and willful seeking as benchmarks of achievement.

However, there is another, quite different story of coming into and thus transforming consciousness—the Eleusinian mysteries, most notably those of Persephone and Demeter. Typically, neither Demeter nor Persephone is regarded as a heroic persona in interpretations of these myths, and only Demeter's goddess qualities (as enraged mother) are explored (Downing 1989); Persephone tends to be viewed as primarily a good daughter who negotiates her life between her powerful mother and Hades, her abductor/husband. As Christine Downing explains in *The Goddess* (1989), the emphasis of most interpretations of this myth is on Persephone's departure from and return to her mother, Demeter. Foremost in our attention, then, is the mother-daughter relationship as one of separation, loss, and grief, punctuated by joyous albeit temporary returns to the daylight world where Demeter reigns. Persephone's powers as goddess are downplayed in favor of her status as daughter to her more powerful mother, who rages so "extravagantly" that the earth is placed in turmoil, mortals quake in fear, and finally the "higher" gods, to keep the peace, strike a bargain so that Persephone will share her time between earth and Hades.

The Persephone/Demeter cycle embodies a powerful metaphor for a state of consciousness or knowing; more specifically, it can also be applied as a metaphor for the activity of composing. The cycle embodies the suppressed or hidden side of the dialectic of the composing process; instead of the masculine hero going forth on a conscious quest for rational knowledge, the feminine hero, Persephone, is abducted into the underworld of the unconscious. In contrast to the hero who chooses his adventure, Persephone is abducted—into the underworld where she ultimately gains her goddess power. The composing dialectic would encompass images of writers as heroic, rational, conscious, in control of their meanings, in relation to images of writers abducted into the chaos and ambiguity of creation, overtaken by an idea, outside "rational" consciousness, in love with or terrified of the object of their attention.

As Downing explains, the problem with understanding feminine or goddess powers in relation to masculine-oriented myths is one of interpretation, not simply missing information repressed by patriarchal culture. The Persephone-Demeter cycle is commonly interpreted through the framework of a heroic quest; Persephone is implicitly viewed as the victim of a quarrel between two more powerful, parental figures. If the heroic cycle is, as Campbell insists, a universal cycle of departure and return, then it is no wonder that Persephone's story would be understood as a departure from and return to the mother. Her story thus is understood to begin with descent into difficulty and separation and to end in the ascension to the daylight world, mother, and reunion.

Downing, however, reinterprets the myth to portray Persephone as a goddess in her own right, noting that her goddess powers come not from her return to the daylight world of her mother but from the descent/abduction into the dark world of Hades. The relationship of Persephone and Hades, Downing says, is rarely given the attention that the separation from the mother has received, mainly because of the patriarchal lens, which values the hero story of ascension and transcendence (which Persephone's return to earth suggests) above all others.

Persephone's real power, according to Downing, comes from being the goddess of death—she not only dwells in the unknown, she is the unknown, is the embodiment of mystery, in contrast to the image of the hero who affirms culture as all that is knowable and thus controllable in the social order. Her power comes from the unpredictable ways in which one's consciousness is transformed in the face of death. It is a generative, though disruptive, power, quite the opposite of the control celebrated in the heroic quest; a power to live more deeply through—rather than, as in the heroic view, to triumph over—uncertainty, pain, and grief.

If to read androcentrically, as Elizabeth Flynn (1986) claims our culture does, means privileging certain ways of knowing and certain states of consciousness, then consider the ways in which Carrie's story was also interpreted through the androcentric lens of the hero. Carrie, as one who lacked control, was an unsatisfactory character to most readers. For Carrie to fit the heroic mold, she had to gain control, overthrow the dark man,

Michael, and go her own way. But if we read Carrie as a Persephone figure, one who is abducted into knowledge of herself, and subsequently into a death of prior, more limited consciousness about herself, by a Michael-Hades figure, a different story begins to emerge, one in which Carrie has power to transform herself through what she already possesses as a knower. Although Carrie can still be perceived as lacking a certain control, nonetheless she has already begun her quest. Like Persephone, she simultaneously is abducted into and willfully chooses her life. She is powerful in her own right, not just in relationship to the male figures in her life.

In the context of the writing classroom, as long as the descent into the chaos of composing (knowledge and transformation of consciousness) is represented as a painful but necessary violence, something to be ritually controlled and thus marginalized rather than fully explored and realized, then the full power of the transformative disruption of composing is relegated to being an obstacle on the way to a validation of the cultural status quo rather than an exploration of the shifting and fluid meanings into which the writer opens herself (and is simultaneously abducted into). Nothing in the cultural arrangement is questioned, and therefore nothing, including the status of writer and woman as objects of a greater, usually masculine, power, has to change. The power to assign meaning remains in the hands of an elite few, the gods of authority, rather than among the many mere mortals.

The problem of changing the power relationships in the classroom as they are culturally assigned is complex indeed, particularly between teachers and students. Though students are perhaps the most heavily inscribed as objects of teacher attention, teachers are in the paradoxical position of negotiating a "killer dichotomy" within their institutional identity—as both subjects over their students and objects in the larger framework of the institution.

In the next chapter, I will narrate my experience of a self-directed writing group, as a comparison to the teacher-sanctioned talk of the academic class. I will compare the ways in which the teacher, as an agent of the institution, is, like the hero, both a controlling figure (to students) and one who is controlled (by the institution and the culture's idea of teacher as Other). In contrast, I will show how a teacherless group, while still enacting cultural myths of the writer, also points toward an alternative representation of teachers in a dialogical relationship with students, connected to, as opposed to simply dominating, or being dominated by, their students.

 # The Self-Directed Group

The Greek underworld is not terrible and

horrifying, but simply beyond life.

—CHRISTINE DOWNING

In the previous chapter, the dialogue between the writer's and the instructor's discourses in the academic class ritually reenacted dominant cultural beliefs about writers, women, and teacher-student relations that preserve cultural hegemony. The mythic basis for these cultural beliefs was that of the ascending hero (interpreted within an oppositional framework against descending gods and goddesses of the Greek underworld). In this chapter, I offer a story of a self-directed writing group as a contrast to the teacher-directed academic class. Members of the self-directed group were students at the same research university as the academic class. They knew each other from classes, held their meetings in the university writing center, and regarded their discussions as contributing to their professional development as writers. In this sense, their interactions, like the academic class, were regulated by the university. Yet at the same time, members expressed an autonomy beyond the usual student role by scheduling their own meeting times and settings and determining by consensus the length of each meeting, the topics, and the direction of the talk. All were experienced participants in university workshops; all wanted a "different" sort of workshop experience than traditional classes could offer. Some were also members of a community-sponsored writing group that met in people's homes once a month. Among the main motivations for this group to gather, then, were the convenience of the university as a common meeting place and the members' shared histories as writers with academic experience who also felt the limitations of that experience.

This second narrative, like the first, is based on an actual discussion

125

of the same story, "Bridge of Flowers, Bridge of Iron," which I also taped and listened to on a number of occasions. The form of this piece is based upon the dialectical notes, similar to the previous narrative; however, the "dialogue" becomes, in fact, a "trilogue" as well as a "monologue" as the discourses break in and out of three voices, represented by the three-column format. This form captures the collective and individual identities expressed in this talk and the blurring that occurred in the process. This form also dramatizes a contrast to the dialectical nature of the talk and the emphasis on the formation of individual identities expressed in the academic class. For this reason, I use the collective pronoun *we* in addition to third-person pronouns. I have chosen to give the writer of this story a different name ("Maura") than in the academic class ("Beth") to emphasize the constructedness of this experience and the differences in the way the writer was constructed and constructs herself in each context. Again, my purpose is not to claim this narrative as an authentic artifact of what "really" happened but to use it as a vehicle for inquiring into the multidimensional interpretations surrounding any cultural event.

As in the previous chapter, the group narrative will be followed by a further interpretation of textual representations of woman, the ritual enactment of the writer as cultural hero, and the informing cultural mythos. I will also speculate on the difference the presence or absence of a teacher makes in such events; both groups enacted similar "heroic" rituals, although they took distinct forms. Yet the self-directed group also provides useful insight into an alternative view of power relations that can usefully inform an academic class. "Teacherless" groups, of course, have their own limitations in empowering members to move into the dominant discourses of society and culture and thus are not superior to academic classes by virtue of their "de-centeredness" (which is, ultimately, a problematic concept, as this second story shows). Yet from the "teacherless" group emerges possibilities for teachers to reenvision their relations with students not only as the objects of their attention, but as subjects who will transform teachers in the underworld of students' imaginative vitality even as students are transformed by teachers.

The Workshop

We meet in a room within a room, the small computer room of the university writing center, to escape the traffic of students and tutors. Even with the door closed, however, the hum of talk and the phone's ring and an occasional knock on the door remind us that the world of clocks and classrooms and deadlines is not far. The four of us, three women and one man, huddle together in wide-armed chairs,

> Wagons circled for
> the night

in the company of several blank computer screens on either side of the room. There is barely enough space for our chairs—not enough room to stand up and leave without some shuffling and repositioning—but enough room for talk.

We have met twice before; on each of those occasions, a fifth person, different each time, has joined us.

We talk at length about each other's work. more than a few would feel like too many. More than a few makes it difficult to talk: hard not to check the clock, hard to carve this time into our schedules.

We are students and teachers— Too many respon-sibilities tugging on us,

important to have time to talk. Sometimes we bring food. Or we put on a pot of coffee.

too hard to make our way to each others' homes.

We share as students and teachers within the academy, yet   An in-between place, a common destination

This is not home.

we decide when to meet, when to begin.

We take time to greet each other, catch up on news, gossip, families. And we end when we have ended.

We do not end when the clock says to. Teenage daughters and committee meetings and reading for exams draw us apart.

We stay as long as we can. Two hours is mostly what we manage, fragile, fleeting, each time a small miracle. We are students and teachers; we have traveled a long way to this upper Hudson Valley.

Coming from Italy and Iran, New York and Colorado, we are a fleeting group. Eventually it will all end not a place to stay and make a life, not a residence.

We expect to keep traveling. It takes everything in us. We are on the move, a place to move out from. A place for visitors, the paradox we live by.

School is an in-between place

To become a resident, we have to leave

Today is a typical fall day in the upper Hudson River Valley, overcast and chilly, a bit of wind stirring up dead leaves. The drapes in the computer room

the room within a room

are open, the light diffuse. One by one we gather; we hug, we talk, we offer food. We get up and run quick errands for more food and coffee, check the mail upstairs in the department office, smoke a cigarette. It takes a while to settle into our chairs, to focus on the work. We know it takes time.

It is better this way. We leave the rush-ing behind.

We have so little time to spend

for a different space, a different way of be-ing, a different kind of talk

we cannot leave eas-ily. Yet we are not so close that we cannot be silent.

Our talk connects this inner room to our lives outside. We sit close enough

Our chairs call out for us and we oblige them, whether words or silence, we listen to our listening.

if silence is needed, which it often is. We speak as long as we need to; everyone will have a turn. We want to know what each person has to say.

Maura has facilitated our group from the beginning. Today it is her turn to have her work discussed. She gave us copies of her story last time we met, and we take them out now and lay them on our laps. She has called our group an experiment,

We want a conversa-tion, different from classroom talk,

reflective of our effort to teach ourselves.

Different ways to talk

**We know the kinds
of talk we crave**

have a different
rhythm and tempo
and texture.

yet it is easy to fall
into old patterns,

**we know what they
are.**

but not easy to name
the new ways, only to
say what they are not.

After we are settled into our seats, Maura begins. "I felt like I was writing very close to this character, that I was inside her. So I want to know better what you see inside or underneath this story as compared to what's on top, what's on the surface. Remember not to tell me what you liked or didn't like. Just tell me what you read."

Neither like nor dislike, but what else is there to say? We don't want Carrie to be in this place, this stuckness, because we don't want to be there with her. To be nothing, a woman with no life, frightens us. We don't know how to talk about it. It is hard not to say we like the story; hard to say, we don't want to be Carrie. We are tired of Carries; we know her life too well.

Darkness within darkness. The smell of smoke but no smoke. The possibility of sound, but no sound. Movement within stillness. She who has no name is the darkness within.

**We count on Denise
to plunge headlong
into strange waters.
"It's open-ended. All
the questions aren't
answered, which is
always hopeful. I
don't know how to**

talk about it and not say I liked it. The landscape is so suggestive. There's a subtle interaction with the character."

Jody says, "Carrie is on an edge—and Susan, too."

What Jody doesn't say is she is stuck. We are stuck. She cannot move. Neither can we. It is a sad story. We say we like it, but not because it's sad. Because it's beautiful. There are, after all, beautiful things to like about it. Still, the words don't rise, they fall away like dead skin.

Denise keeps talking. "The writing is beautiful. The open-endedness is hopeful. How can I talk about the potato rock and not say I liked it? The connotations in the landscape were powerful."

Filling up the silence like water filling up emptiness

Careful words. But no power to move us.

listening to listening, the shape of shapelessness. Swirling in on herself, enfolding the merest speck of sound, a stray mote to feed her. Flakes of skin an irritation in the oyster's shell. Vibration in the dissonance.

In the silence, spiders spin invisible webs;

Between us, vibrating threads capture the dance of dust and mitochondria, binding us as

we fold into ourselves, listening.

computer faces stare, dark, cavernous framed by square, white casings. Voices outside have shrunk to ants in the distance. No one knocks on the dark door. Fluorescent lights burn the backs of our eyes.

Jody says, "The story is exploring what's under the surface, following the edges, tactile: rock, bone. Two strong characters in Carrie and Susan, both walking on edges."

A sad story, a tight place.

"A sad story," says Garratt. "Flowing women down at the water. Granite men

**high up on the
rocks. These are
parts of herself—be-
ing stuck, wanting
to move, up or
down. But she
doesn't know how,
doesn't know how to
enter the under-
world, can't inte-
grate. Michael is the
weight of things she
can't bring into her-
self. He nourishes
and devastates."**

Garratt reads, "When she looked at him lately, as she did
now, all the lightness inside her that she tried so hard to capture
compressed under the weight of his dark eyes looking past her
into some primordial grief that both nourished and devastated
him."

Michael weighs
heavily on us

Consider his dark-
ness

**Denise observes that
Carrie explores his
darkness,**

not her own.

**her movements
down continually
distracted by him.
She sees her way
out only through
him.**

"Michael is very manipulative," says Denise. "Carrie doesn't know
what she wants, so she looks to Michael. And he is very demanding. He
takes her away from herself. Same with her lover, Ben. She can't make
decisions, just falls into something—falls into having a kid, falls into rela-

tionships. No support from Susan, even: Carrie's floundering. Her house is her mind and her body, and she abandons it. Flees from it. Literally between a rock and a hard place."

difficult to speak in
"neither like nor dis-
like." What does she
mean? What does she
need? The old riddle
posed to King Arthur,
"What does a woman
want?" What does a
writer want?

We are mysteries to
ourselves.

We feel her stuckness.
We *are* her stuckness.

Awakening to pain.
Neither this way nor
that. What is there to
say? If there were
lips to speak, if there
were air to gather
and blow gently.
Only pain. Nowhere
to turn, nowhere to
land. Only a dry
static.

Denise says, "There is strength in water, but it's contained by the potholes in the river. Water has only a certain flexibility when it's surrounded by rock. It's a classic hierarchy—women below, next to the water, men above, high on the rock. Both marriages, Carrie and Michael's, Susan and Tom's, are precarious:

Susan took off for a small cove just behind them where a trickle of water slid down into a glassy pool, one of the deepest of the potholes, Carrie knew. Tom and Michael stretched out their legs as they repositioned themselves overhead. Tom pointed to the small whirlpools the rocks created against the flow of the river. Carrie closed her eyes, letting the sun probe her lids, tilting her head far back against her neck.

"Susan is not in a strong place, either. There is so much uncertainty. Resonances of flowing/containment, erosion/solidity. All the elements are there, but they're stuck in their places, men above, women below. The women are imperiled."

Danger among us. We
shift our ankles and
look down at the
pages in our laps

**Outside we hear
voices.**

nothing to hold on to,
nothing to distract us
from ourselves

**Maura leans for-
ward, then back, in
her wide-armed
chair. She breathes
deeply; we all take a
breath and wait.**

"This is so much Carrie's view of things, it's hard to separate what Carrie's feeling from what she projects onto Susan and Tom. It isn't what Susan is thinking as much as it is what Carrie's view is. It's Carrie's inter-pretation of Susan's thoughts. Carrie sees fear in Susan because she is afraid. She sees herself in Susan," Maura says, then reads:

Susan was trying so hard to help her Carrie felt bad that she was holding back. She thought of Susan bending over an especially beautiful flower on the Bridge of Flowers, an electric orange and yellow one, its center thick with pollen, Susan folding its face gently in her hands, bending low to smell it, the tip of her nose dusted bright yellow. And then Tom tapping her nose, grinning, then wiping the smudge off with his finger-tip. Susan's quick glance at Michael, then her, as Tom touched the pol-len. Michael looking away, as usual. But Carrie saw it, though until now she didn't understand it. Susan's look was fear.

in the background
static, dry, crackling,
like a radio in be-
tween channels

The in-between place

a difficult place to in-
habit. What Maura
wants us to see and
what we do, in fact,
see. Dissonance. Nei-
ther here nor there.
Neither like nor dis-
like. We know what
we don't want. But
what *do* we want? We
are stuck in our
stuckness. Static rises.
This time, we do not
fill it in with words
that drop like dead
skin. It vibrates, irri-
tates, makes us long
for water or coffee or
a trip to the bath-
room.

**pressure without is
pressure within.**

We stay in our stuck-
ness and listen to our-
selves

Listen:

Jody is speaking. At first, we didn't notice.

More static cresting
then falling back into
itself

Her voice cracks slightly; she straightens her spine. She removes her
glasses with one hand and turns her wrist outward. We lean forward in
our wide-armed chairs to hear her voice over the hum outside.

distant ants
combing the hive

"Carrie's name in itself has a connotation of caring. She is stuck, but she cares, she is learning things about herself. The house is her body, and it is not. It is herself, and it is not. The house is not just 'me' but 'ours.' The house is also the marriage. 'Me,' Carrie, is outdoors. She is not abandoning herself but abandoning a place that has slowly shut down for her. And it feels like the story is about that process. One way to say it is, Carrie's running out of the house. Another way to say it is, she's leaving a house that can no longer contain her. Leaving is also an act of strength."

"Yes, the house that was, was the marriage house. Deciding to leave opened up a couple of possibilities for her—Ben, whom she doesn't have to stay with, and herself on the rocks. Carrie connects her pregnancy to Ben, but another option is to have the baby alone. Attaching the child to Ben—that's where she's still not free," says Denise.

But with the summer came Ben, and the sharp edge winter had honed in her softened. She opened up the house again, cleaned out the wood stoves. As soon as it was warm enough to leave the doors open, she left and rarely came back, spending her days at the potholes or at Ben's place drawing, and nights at his side. As long as she stayed in the house, Emma would stay. So she left the doors open, hoping Emma would take the hint and leave. She planted a garden, half-heartedly, because they had always planted a garden. But she forgot to water it, and then there was drought. The failed garden became another reason to stay away. Ben told her, "Move in with me."

the story no longer one story. Flight, dissolution, distraction, denial also acts of decision, alternatives neither good nor bad.

In this in-between place, hands are the vessels of vision. No one chooses pain. Who would think it has a flavor? Who would think it has a smell? Who would think you could run your hand along its back and find your other hand, the one

you never use? And
hold it, beloved, the
unborn, the never-
was, the always-will-
be?

**Our chairs creak
like restless boats.
Spiders web our si-
lence while ants
march in the dis-
tance, building
skyscrapers and
superstructures and
spiraling towers.**

One direction is not
enough. One story is
only one story.

A closing is also an
opening.

Garratt says, "The woods are a place of opening for her, leading into
the rugged terrain of her psyche. She is on a weird edge with Ben, who is
and is not part of this terrain. The *I Ching* says return must be treated
with tenderness and care. Care—Carrie—the name is manifest. After a
long sickness, a flowering or blossoming can come, if treated with tenderness. Carrie is the bird at the end of the story, and their marriage is the
crippled cat. She can't bring herself back into the marriage. It's actually a
very caring gesture to leave the bird behind:

> "Oh, look, I think it's hurt!" Carrie cried.
> Michael and Tom turned around as Susan and Carrie bent over the
> bird, which sat motionless.
> "It must be scared to death of us," Susan said, leaning over to touch
> its smooth head.
> Michael had already started walking away when Carrie stood up.
> Susan was wondering aloud what to do with the bird, but Carrie didn't
> want to do anything. It wanted to be left alone. Birds like that, she knew,
> seldom recovered, no matter how you nursed them. Besides, she had a
> cat. Her and Michael's cat, the three-legged one they brought from the
> West.

At first I wondered why she left the bird behind, as if she were abandoning herself. But the second time, I saw caring in that gesture. When she follows Michael over the bridge of iron at the end, I saw two interpretations there, too: she's either letting Michael make all the decisions for her again, or, since she's learning how to treat herself with tenderness and care, letting the bird *be*, crossing the iron bridge is a merging with the grief and darkness inside her. It's a way of embracing, to use, to connect to an old, ancient, rusty part of herself. She has to get across the water, merge solidity/fluidity. The first time, I thought it was sad, that she'd left behind the bridge of flowers. The second time, I saw the possibility that gesture opens up."

How can one travel in opposite directions at the same time? The two stories contradict each other, and yet they are both there, depending on how we choose to look at them. Like looking at a photograph and its negative; the emphasis shifts, light to dark, dark to light. Heisenberg's principle: "The object of observation and the medium of observation in physics are composed of the same world-stuff . . . the act of seeing, therefore, has a material effect on what is observed, altering it in the very process of focusing on it."

We see daylight; we give ourselves

Seeing ourselves seeing.
We see darkness; we are taken

Gaining velocity   leaving stuckness

"But why is it a positive act for Carrie to give up trying to make Michael smile?" Maura asks.

Jody responds, "My first reaction was, Oh! She's giving up the flowers she loved. But then I saw the strength in that gesture. Instead of looking at the externals of the bridge, she saw the bridge as a bridge—as something to get her across the water. It came out of strength. The statement about it has a certain detachment that comes from that strength:

> The iron bridge was old and rusty, a remnant of the industrial past of a village that now lived for tourists. But it would get them across just the same.

It's actually important for Carrie to give up on making Michael smile because she never allowed him his autonomy, seeing him only in regard to herself. Carrie feels jealous at *any* connection he has with another person. She needs to undergo a process of connecting with herself, which is what is happening in the story. The possibilities for change emerge from her growing sense of her own autonomy as a person who creates and makes choices for herself."

We create choices
many stories.   Not one story.

"What does she want to do? That's what she needs to ask herself. By accepting the functional in her life, what the iron bridge represents, she can make the choices she needs to make," Denise says.

Garratt says, "You know, this is a story about a story. Susan tells a story that is also about accepting the functional. She tells about a writer she and Tom heard at a reading. The guy reads poems instead of a story because he is literally short of breath:

> What was it Susan had told her last fall? She and Tom had been to a poetry reading of a husband and wife. The husband had had lung surgery and his voice was raspy and his breath short. They read poems about their marriage, poems of great tenderness, Susan said, because the man was obviously dying and their days were few. No one knew how bad off he was until he read poems instead of a story because his breath was so short.

It's not a traditional narrative, but more poetic. No one knew how bad he was until his breath was so short. It's what Carrie sees versus what is traditionally seen. She is unbalanced in her view—not functional. There's an emotional closure of a paragraph on page 2 to show that's how she sees her creative side—as an afterthought: 'On steamy July days she liked to lie out on the rocks in her swimsuit and, when she was so hot she couldn't stand it any more, leap into the potholes with a huge splash. Sometimes she brought a sketch pad.'"

"Her anger is also an afterthought," says Maura. "Retroactive. The whole structure of the story is retroactive. The present seems monumental—she's always trying to remember, but she can't move out from under the present. Always casting back into the past, but never forward. Her anger is submerged."

We see ourselves in her.

How can she do that to herself? Not the husband, or the house, or the marriage, but *her*.

We think she is a victim. "Yes, that's a problem," says Denise. "Her whole life is focused on her relationship with Michael. The man can do no wrong, so she puts her anger on the other woman, Emma. She isn't angry at Michael for his betrayal, just angry with Emma, her best friend." We try Carrie-as-victim but cannot rest there. Garratt says, "But as long as Carrie is with Michael, she can't express anger.

She is *not* a victim. We try this view, and become unbalanced: Carrie chooses but chooses wrong.

He gives her nothing
to hang on to. He *is*
a salamander—slip-
pery, noncommittal,
stares off into space,
stoic. He won't take
a risk, won't com-
mit, so no one can
get pissed off at
him. He can always
claim immunity,
'Hey, I'm just a sala-
mander.' He's not
giving her anything,
no reciprocity of vi-
bration. Carrie has
never been able to
embrace her anger."
Michael has kept
her down, distracted
her from anger.

               She wanted to be dis-
               tracted.

Are they both to
blame?

               Is neither to blame?

We are now a coun-
seling group on "Re-
alizing Your Anger."

               We gossip about mu-
               tual friends whose re-
               lationship is in
               trouble. There are
               some juicy parts—the
               husband had an affair.
               And oh! It was her
               best friend.

               "Her best friend?"
               "You don't say?"

"He's such a jerk."
"But she just takes it
from him."
"He's so controlling."
"She's just as manipu-
lative in her own way.
Trying to make him
smile. Really! She's
jealous as hell."
"She's insecure."
"He's a bastard."
"She's pathetic."
"He's weak."
"She's strong."
"*She's* weak."
"*He's* strong."

**"Is it just a given
why Carrie is with
Michael in the first
place?" Maura asks,
interrupting the
back and forth,
round and round, a
fast ride that makes
everyone a little
dizzy.**

Anger has a way of
spinning us faster
than we can keep up
with ourselves.

**The question
catches us off guard,
stopping us cold.**

Deferring the anger,
again. Are we angry at
Maura, too?

**The attraction *does*
seem like a given.
Nothing we would
have thought to ask.**

**Maura adds, "It's a
question another
group wanted to
know." It *did* seem
obvious until the
question was put to
us. Now it's strange
to actually consider
what the attraction
might be. We know
other Carries. Her
situation is frus-
tratingly familiar.**

"The dynamic is familiar. They're attracted to each other's lacks. It's pretty common."

"The woman hasn't discovered a self, attracted to a man . . ."

"Who can be angry and creative."

"*So* angry!" Denise exclaims. "He won't give her *anything*! Such a sonofabitch. Withholding, manipulative. Icky power plays."

It feels good to rage at
Michael instead, the
weight over Carrie,
the dark man, the sus-
pended void, the poet
who steals her away
into his underworld.

Falling backward—
too hard to face the
darkness. Always fac-
ing what is left be-
hind. The daylight
face with its last
grieving light, the
warm mother voice,
fading. The spine al-
ready numb. The
daughter's face
turned fully toward

> her, too stunned to
> know what is hap-
> pening. Even the
> mother's extravagant
> rage cannot heat that
> place below.

Denise needs a cigarette. Maura thirsts for an Orange Slice. Garratt wants decaf coffee. Jody rummages for the bagel in her bag, then remembers she already ate it. It is the middle of the afternoon,

> Ants stop marching
> behind the black
> door.

the phone has not rung in a long time, and it seems the message has finally gotten out not to interrupt anymore. The day peaks, and so do we. We settle into our wide-armed chairs, into the sudden quiet that has opened among us, and breathe a long, slow breath.

Jody says, "Carrie is looking for ways to nourish herself. At first it seems she's doing it all through Michael. There's that long part where she asks him about what restaurant they should eat at. But then Carrie seeks out the land as a source of nourishment, even though it's also a deprivation. It doesn't come fully into consciousness, but it's there."

"Carrie wants to *fix* something at home (to eat) but it can't be *fixed*— the relationship, that is," says Garratt. "The decision on where to eat is given a lot of importance."

"It comes early in the story, too," says Jody. "Carrie tries to nourish herself through others. She can't find the source of nourishment in herself, so she displaces it onto others. In the interplay with Michael, she's not just trying to love him—she's trying to love herself."

"I see what Jody's saying, but it needs something stronger, something closer to the surface," says Denise.

Maura says, "It's such a quiet story. Carrie's anger is so submerged. The story needs shading. Otherwise people read Carrie as completely passive, as a nothing who gives so much of herself away, discredit her. Michael has his own way of being angry, which is to shut down. Carrie is afraid of her own anger because she's afraid of his, and his potential for violence. She's looking for a way to negotiate her own anger. She's stopped putting it on Emma, made her peace with her."

Shading.
Chiaroscuro. Dark-
ness, the spaces be-
tween—

Define the form

**How to read the
spaces? If they are
lacking, then power
is absent.**

Carrie lacks self-
knowledge. Worse,
she lacks the knowl-
edge to obtain self-
knowledge. She can-
not move.

**If Carrie *perceives*
that she lacks, then
she knows some-
thing. She has the
ability to nourish
herself but is only
beginning to under-
stand how to use it.
Asking Michael to
leave the house was
a beginning. Leaving
the house herself was
a loss and gain, too.**

Her anger has
prompted decisions,

**Yet she is reluctant
to claim this.**

her anger is obscure.
And so is her desire.

**We listen for her
heartbeat.**

Listen for the rhythm
in between. Listen for
the one who knows.

She is so hard to hear.
We want her to be

louder, brighter, more
visible. We want to
know her differently.

Jody says, "Here's a place where her anger comes in. Carrie wants to
swim, but no one else will go with her. Susan says she doesn't have a
bathing suit, but Carrie says to swim in their underwear. Strip down the
layers. She wants everyone to strip down their layers. But no one wants to
give her what she wants. She's frustrated. She says, 'I'm just a little stick.
I've got nothing to hide.' The irony is she is hiding everything, including
her frustration. She *wants* to enter the water. But she doesn't want to swim
alone. She knows what she wants but wants the others to do what she
wants them to do in order to feel secure."

Denise adds, "She's also angry at Emma."

A weird, witchy en-
ergy circulates
among us.

We circle back on it
again and again.

We feel the edge in
the story. Like Car-
rie, Susan, Michael,
and Tom, the four
of us are charged
and prickly and on

The source is closer
than we suspected:
anger. The thick smell
of ozone before a
thunderstorm, the
crackling release of
lightning, the ground-
shattering rumble of
thunder rolling past.
Anger is among us,
evoked like the dead
dancing at a seance. It
rubs against us like an
electric shock. We
make it dance.
We put ourselves on
the edge, on the line

Dry static in the
background, hum and
crackle and buzz be-
yond the door rise

webs of electricity
dance and skip and
flash

**the edges of our
skins. On the sur-
face, our talk is
winding down. We
point to the text.
"How about . . . ?"
"What if . . . ?"
"Maybe you
could . . . ?" "I need
. . ." "This pas-
sage . . . that pas-
sage . . ." Getting
into details signals
the end.**

being *Helpful* because
we feel helpless. It's
all underneath, like
the story. Smoothing
over. Closing down.
Summarizing. Wrap-
ping up. Soon it will
be time for us to ask
what the writer has to
say, just like in all
those other classes.

throbbing in the air,
a pulse in search of
its rhythm

**Yet we *know* some-
thing else is going
on, too, the electric-
ity ungrounded,
eerie.**

Jody glances at her watch; her daughter will need to be picked up
from school soon. Garratt stretches his spine, thinking about the yoga he
wants to do. Denise contemplates her next cigarette and the piles of
poems scattered across her desk needing to be sorted. Maura yawns, trying to suppress her discomfort and edginess: the talk is incomplete.

But that's the way the
world is. Things go
unfinished. There is
only so much time.
Time's up. We have
done our share. Go
back and play. Shad-
ing. Emotional guid-
ance. Chiaroscuro.
Grounding. But no
one feels grounded

**splintered, jagged,
edgy, raw**

underneath the yawns
and stretches and
glances at the watch.
Wrapping it up? Hell
no. More like mum-
mies toddling back to
their sarcophagi. The
automatic response.
Time and mummies
marching on.

Jody and Denise give closing advice. Jody says, "You can bring in the
tension in small gestures, not large. If Carrie were suddenly to get angry,
it would throw off the whole story. It wouldn't be Carrie anymore."

Denise reacts to the rub of that statement, that Jody felt she wanted
too broad a gesture of anger and tension to shade the story, saying, "I
don't mean anything explosive. I just need more guidance of the emotional in the story."

Ok, good advice.
We've done our job.
We all agree what
needs to be done. Isn't
it wonderful we all
agree? But somehow
we know we don't.
But we say we do. It's
easier to leave this
room and return to
daughters and scat-
tered papers and soli-
tude and students.
Maura is most oblig-
ing; she lets us off the
hook by agreeing.

"You know, I realize that I don't fit in with the other fiction people. I
read more like a poet, the way you all do. The people who read my stories

don't read for the language the way poets do, the way I do. I'm aware of that other readership, aware of how the surface of my stories seems too pretty, and they can't get into the other stuff. You know, how the landscape in this story is really Carrie's emotional landscape."

We looked there instead of here, right in front of us, listening to ants marching in the distance instead of the quiet of our bloodcells flowing through webby networks of silence. We see that what binds us is not blood or veins or wide-armed chairs but the spaces between

It's strange to be praised for something we didn't do. We didn't go that far into the language. We didn't talk about the emotional landscape, what it is, what it means. Maura's polite agreement tells us how to read her work. Finally, it's said. Finally, we know. The emotional landscape of the vibrating room we inhabit, that in-between place that is the room within the room, suddenly shifts. We thought we were angry with the writer of this story. But the writer has been unhappy with us (us including herself, because she is a reader of her story, like the rest of us). Saying, very politely, very nicely, We've ignored her, again. Carrie, that quiet, passive, harmless one, saying in the most careful,

mild voice, I hate
your guts.

the spaces between
give vision.

**drawing us down
and in. The emo-
tional landscape.
This phrase sets
something in motion
for us. We were so
caught in the human
relationships that
we glossed the imag-
ery, treating it as a
backdrop, an object,
not a subject. But
"emotional land-
scape" takes an en-
tirely different
sweep across the
story.**

Not anger but the
silence surrounding
it.

Though you are
loathe to know me, I
am there in the
shadows of the day-
light world that sink
you in their stillness.
I am the one you hate
and your power to
hate. I am the rust in
the flower's heart. I
am the connection to
all life. I am beyond
life. I am the pores
through which life
breathes

Jody picks up the thread into the labyrinth of the paradox we have exhausted ourselves in and tests it for its strength. "You know, the image of the bridge of flowers begins to feel like *only* a place of joy."

Maura nods and clasps her hands in her lap. Jody continues, "But the rocks are like the bones of something alive, an edge where she can claim her powers."

Maura leans into the group. Jody's daughter will wait. Denise's cigarette and poems will follow soon enough. Garratt will get to yoga later. Something has shifted. Maura knows something. We all, suddenly, know something. It is on the tip of our tongues.

Maura says, "The bridge of flowers is really just a tourist attraction. The flowers were planted just for tourists. It's not a functional bridge, like the bridge of iron; it only supports pedestrians. The town itself was built on something harder, more substantial, which was the industrial era. Now the place only lives for tourists, a 'quaint' New England town." Maura leans back, still rubbing her hands, now sliding the ring on her index finger up and down, as if to test its looseness.

"I want more of that," Denise says. "It seems very important."

More. more. The story
is hungry, will devour
us if we don't feed it.

Jody says, "I wanted to put a lot of weight on the bridge of flowers as a place of redemption."

Maura says it's artifi-
cial, not substantial.
Yet something makes
us believe in the
redemption of the
flowers. For we all
want to believe

Georgia O'Keeffe full-
blossomed flowers
swaying in their
heavy-pollened gaze.

"Actually, I see the redemption more in the landscape, with the soft-ness in the water, then the rocks, a surprise. Like a skeleton of the mar-riage. You *need* both, the water and the rocks, the flowing and the stillness, the hard and the soft," Maura says.

"Focusing on the 'other side,' you know, the other bridge, illuminates where Carrie is right now," says Denise. "She deals with the surface, look-ing away. It doesn't exclude the archetypal image of the bridge of flowers that Julie is talking about—there are lots of ways of pushing that image of the erotically female. It can call it into question, doesn't have to sentimen-talize it. But show the contrasts, make them substantial. When the reality is more grounded, the metaphoric value of the images is larger and firmer."

Jody doesn't want to
abandon the flowers.
The flowers are not
evil. They are not
good. They are
something else

we hate because we
believe in the redemp-

tion of the flowers,
but the flowers keep
us from ourselves.
Why do we believe?

> Grounding. The word
> is a drumbeat.
> Grounding. Looking
> for our feet. Ground-
> ing. The balance
> weight, the pull into
> the guts

Jody says, "There is a potential for ambiguity, though at first the archetypes seemed pretty clear: iron equals patriarchy, and flowers equal matriarchy. But that doesn't feel like the terms of the story as Maura describes it. For me, bridges were already a potent symbol. Even when I read the title, 'Bridge of Flowers, Bridge of Iron,' I was already all for the bridge of flowers. I'd sensed how you'd use that. And then there were the flowers and the pastels Carrie drew. And Susan's comment about Georgia O'Keeffe—even though she meant the rocks, I couldn't help but think of her flowers, too. Here, on page 15:

> Carrie thought of Susan bending over an especially beautiful flower on the Bridge of Flowers, an electric orange and yellow one, its center thick with pollen, Susan holding its face gently in her hands, bending low to smell it, the tip of her nose dusted bright yellow. And then Tom tapping her nose, grinning, then wiping the smudge off with his fingertip.

So powerful and erotic. And then here, on page 5:

> When Carrie had brought them across the Bridge of Flowers, a pedestrian bridge on the other side of the river that ran parallel to the rusted iron roadway bridge, Susan stopped to look at the names of the flowers that the Shelbourne Falls people had labeled with small tags. Susan kept pulling Tom away from Michael to show him different blossoms, which he duly admired. Michael, on the other hand, said little about the outrageous colors and shapes of those flowers in the peak of their season.

"*Naming* flowers—in feminism, naming is important. And pulling Tom away from Michael, from what he represents—pulling him away from that dark, heavy stuff. And the outrageous flowers and colors are very erotic, very powerful. Perhaps even claiming more power than you necessarily meant? There's a lot of power in those symbols."

**so much power in
those symbols, the
power of the femi-
nine**

> It is sad to turn away,
> difficult to leave the
> gardens we have culti-
> vated between us, the
> familiar paths and
> rosebushes with pre-
> dictable thorns. We
> can wear gloves to
> protect our hands. We
> pull out the killing
> weeds. We smile
> when we mean I *hate
> you*. Because the hater
> is somewhere else, in
> the dandelions, which
> have long roots and
> reappear each spring.

Garratt follows the tug on the thread. "I sense at the end that Carrie *needs* to use the bridge of iron. It might be that you'd need to texture the bridge of flowers so that the perversity of the flowers is also apparent—an Edenic experience gone crazy. The real beauty is in the potholes and the rocks, a mixture of beauty and ugliness. The flowers aren't perverse enough. We have to turn the archetypes. Carrie sees the negative of the patriarchy but not the positive. And sees the positive of the matriarchy but not the negative. I mean, it's pretty nuts that there are *names* on the flowers. You can't come up with your own names. It's the order that's so perverse."

"And the walking on asphalt," says Maura.

"Everything like Alexander Pope," returns Garratt.

"Carrie sees only one blossom at a time—frames it like O'Keeffe. But she doesn't draw back into the landscape to see the yin and yang. People make the place nice for tourists, not for those who really live there," Maura adds.

But Jody is unwilling to abandon the power she initially felt in those images. "The large flowers and the bridges are very powerful symbols," she says.

"The *contradiction* is the most powerful," adds Denise. And though she has contradicted Jody, it doesn't feel like a rubbing against, but a movement with.

First it was a choice—
this story or that?
Who is to blame? But
now the contradic-
tions mean

moving against is
moving along

not just something
lost; not only some-
thing gained:

**the ebb and flow of
movement.**

the hand of the un-
derworld, just beyond
the pollen face.

**Like Carrie, we be-
lieve in the redemp-
tion of the flowers.**

flowers are not always
good.

Maura says, "Someone told me that the bridge of flowers symbolizes the early part of marriage, the passionate part you want to live in for-ever—especially men, or at least men in midlife crises like Michael. They can't see themselves living outside that initial passion. But Carrie, too, looks wistfully at the young couple in the water, nostalgic for that time in her and Michael's marriage:

She stared across the rocks at a younger couple in bathing suits jumping in the water together, meeting in the deepest part of the potholes then turning on their backs to float. Carrie said to Susan, still dangling her feet in the water, "Let's go swimming." She said it loud enough for the men to hear.

"Yes, floating," says Garratt. "Of course they would be floating."

"If you don't get a sense of the artificiality of the bridge of flowers . . . see, that's why Michael is attracted to Emma. It's not *false*, maybe, but *volatile*. Not a place to live."

"Not a home. More like a restaurant."

"A tourist attraction. Yes, that helps so much. That's really central. Everything shifts."

"Like in the Frost poem, 'Fire and Ice.' The last line sounds like the last line of the story," says Jody, reciting,

> *Some say the world will end in fire,*
> *Some say in ice.*
> *From what I've tasted of desire*
> *I hold with those who favor fire.*
> *But if it had to perish twice,*
> *I think I know enough of hate*
> *To say that for destruction ice*
> *Is also great*
> *And would suffice.*

"It all turns on the metaphors in this story," Maura says. "Other readers moved me along up to a point, but it's like I have to teach people how to read my stories."

The afternoon slips away, but no one is in a hurry to leave. We talk and stretch and move around, slowly, as if we have been at sea a long time and are on strange legs for land. The silence disperses in a stream of quiet chatter as we gather up our things and prepare to open the black door to the world outside, like ants into waning daylight. We might meet again; we might not. It is difficult to enter that quiet place, to turn away from our familiar gardens and mothers and daughters and fathers and brothers and husbands and wives and lovers. And in fact, we don't just enter; we are also taken, as Carrie is taken, as Persephone, enacting the mystery of departure, which is also arrival. It is the other side of daylight, the mystery of mysteries. The weeds grow deep within us; their roots point to nourishment for the writers, the travelers, the Carries within us.

Women and Relationships

As in the academic class, a major focus of the self-directed group's attention was Carrie and her marriage to Michael. Carrie's is the point-of-view through which the story is narrated, so it is not surprising that both groups would pay a great deal of attention to her character. However, perhaps more interesting is how Carrie is discussed by both groups largely in relation to others, particularly the men in her life, Michael and Ben, but also, in the second group, in relation to Susan and to her best friend (and Michael's lover), Emma. Thus the tendency in both groups was to read the woman in the text in relation to someone else (or, as the self-directed group later discussed—and Linda commented in the academic class—in relation to some*thing* else—the landscape). Both workshops interpreted Carrie's story through the heroic framework of a woman trying to overcome various obstacles in her life (the obstacles taking on different forms, depending upon the reader). Yet readers assumed that she, unlike male heroic figures, lacked the ability to become autonomous and independent. In the academic class, this masculine bias, which favors male heroic figures over female ones, became evident during a discussion of Barry's story.

In Barry's story, Carrie's male counterpart was a nineteen-year-old named Kevin who, like Carrie, had a problem with control; he habitually slammed into cars "accidentally," persistently blurted out the wrong thing at the wrong time, and generally executed bad timing with a young woman whom he had loved in high school and presumably still loved, though she had gone away to college, leaving him behind. However, Barry's hero in this coming-of-age story was perceived as comic and sympathetic rather than unreliable and/or confusing like Carrie. The class thought it "natural" for Kevin to fall in love with an angelic young woman who dressed in white and radiated a mysterious magnetism that caused him to sink to the depths of oafishness in her presence. She floated above the horizon of Kevin's attention, as incomplete, elusive and "flat" as Michael, but to the class entirely acceptable.

The class considered Kevin "realistic," his growing up story familiar and therefore poignant and funny. To them, it was sad but funny the way he acted out his awkwardness, smashing into cars, stumbling over introductions to his girlfriend's new boyfriend, haunting fast-food dives at odd hours of the morning and night. When it was suggested that Kevin was, in fact, an angry young man, that the "accidents" weren't accidents at all but symbols of his inner turmoil, including his rage at the angelic girlfriend, the class changed the subject. The expression of anger was just as taboo for a male character as a female character. Yet Kevin was considered "realistic" while Carrie was seen as "flawed" or "lacking" something.

Unlike the interpretation of Beth's story, which focused on Carrie's relationships, the class's readings of Barry's story emphasized Kevin's maturation. His relationships with his father, friends, and, most significantly, his girlfriend, were understood as reflective of his states of mind, supporting plots to the main drama of his emerging adult consciousness. Though the plot was considered bittersweet and funny, readers also assumed that a significant change took place in Kevin: he had "gotten over" his angel and thus would stop "accidentally" bashing in cars. Instead, Kevin remained faithful to his favorite fast-food haunts, where he would sip coffee and reminisce (as writers are presumably wont to do) over the good old days of carefree youth. By the end of the story, Kevin is perceived to be well on his way toward growing up, gaining a sense of self and independence by abandoning his hopes for his angel.

This emphasis by the academic class on the male character's individual development (rather than his romance, friendships, or familial relationships) contrasts with the representation of Carrie's development, which is described in the context of her marriage to Michael by both the academic class and the self-directed group. Although both workshops expressed the desire to see Carrie gain autonomy and independence, they also read her as entangled in a web of relationships whose dynamics remained obscure to them. Because her marriage occupied so much of Carrie's attention, both workshops spent considerable time analyzing, describing, raging, and puzzling over it. (Kevin's preoccupation with his angel did not, however, lead to similar speculations.)

Thus, discussion in both workshops emphasized the significance of Carrie's marriage to Michael. The self-directed group even explored some of Carrie's other relationships, including her friendships with Susan and Emma. Both groups interpreted Carrie's development through her relationships with others. However, the axes of the debates in the two groups were different. In the academic class, the oppositions were marked by those who believed Carrie was a realistic character and those who did not. In contrast, the self-directed groups were all "believers"; they recognized Carrie as familiar from the start. Their frustration lay not in the text's seeming obscurity, as in the academic class, but in its painful familiarity. To identify with a story of victimization was to have to relive a part of their own histories. And since nothing, in the end, seemed to change, the effort to connect with Carrie was experienced as oppressive.

Thus, the self-directed group argued over not *whether* but *how* to believe Carrie. Jody and Denise represented opposing positions; Jody saw Carrie as a knowing, responsible agent who, like Michael, sought to manipulate others into doing things she was too afraid to do by and for herself. Carrie's invitation for the others to swim was a case in point, according to Jody, as was Carrie's desire to *make* (control) Michael's smile. Denise, on the other hand, saw Carrie as a victim, oppressed by Michael's withholding nature, unable to connect with herself, while constantly looking to others for the nourishment she so desperately needed. Garrett mediated between both views, validating each in turn, while Maura was preoccupied with her own emerging questions about who she wanted Carrie to be.

These opposing views of Carrie were not, however, perceived by the self-directed group as contradictions that canceled each other out or were resolved only through a hierarchy of choice. As I have discussed in the previous chapter, the oppositions are joined by a shared assumption: a woman is out of control. More specifically, the self-directed group linked control (i.e., independence and autonomy) to the theme of nourishment. Carrie was perceived to lack an ineffable something that would allow her to generate the emotional, spiritual, physical, and psychological sustenance she had tried, without success, to manipulate from others. Carrie, therefore, is represented as impoverished, needy, and dependent. Even as Carrie tried to gain control over herself through others, she failed, just as she failed to win Michael's smile. Worse yet, even those who might have been predisposed to help, such as Susan, didn't recognize the veiled gestures through which Carrie communicated her desires.

Thus, both workshops interpreted Carrie through what she lacked, casting her as Other than themselves. Some sympathized, but no one empathized, because Carrie was perceived to be somehow responsible for her lacks and had to fill them—a heroic yet impossible task for one so lacking in heroism as Carrie.

The Writer as Subject

Like the academic class, the self-directed group projected a lack of control onto both Carrie and the writer of the story. However, because of Gerald's presence in the academic class as a teacher/authority, the anger experienced by both writer (for having lost control, ritually giving over her meanings to the group) and readers (who are equally unable to control the story's meaning) is marginalized, most notably by Gerald himself when he dismisses Kathy's interpretation of Carrie as angry. One role of the teacher in the academic class was to defer a direct confrontation between readers and writers. For instance, Gerald settled the argument over whether or not Kathy's interpretation of Carrie as "angry" was viable, insisting that such a view was "only" Kathy's "interpretation." In order for the ritual of affirming the autonomous writer to occur, a "master" needs to orchestrate the heavy current of emotions channeled among participants.

Part of the ritual's success relies upon a master's ability to background apprentices' anger in favor of the "higher" gains of control that the ritual promises. One might compare it to the physical suffering experienced by a ballet dancer, whose body is twisted and pushed well beyond its normal functions in order to present the graceful lines and movements of the dance. With the appropriate instruction, dancers learn to train their attention on the deep experience of the dance and away from any anger they might feel from the pain and distortion of their bodies. Similarly, the "deep play" of the Balinese cockfight (Geertz 1973) made the immediate, physical risks (a cock, armed with razor-sharp spurs, would sometimes rush out into the crowd and severely wound mesmerized onlookers), the potential loss of capital, and the larger pain of social inequities bearable in the deep experience of a good match. In the academic class, students expected and wanted Gerald, as their teacher, to train their attention on the ritual of heroic autonomy; anger would serve only to divert the class's attention in unproductive and possibly even violent ways, just as anger might spoil a ballet production or a well-matched cockfight; the "deep play" or engagement that students experienced was what mattered the most. Students willingly "gave up" their authority as subjects to Gerald symbolically to participate deeply in the "play" of discussion. The belief that they had such authority to give up in the first place was a necessary fiction for facing the impossible task of assigning meaning in an uncertain world.

Therefore, it was necessary for Gerald, as the sanctioned authority, to maintain the object ("objective") status of both writer and reader by deflecting any overt signs of anger. To allow an emotion such as anger to become visible and thus knowable and speakable would immediately shift the object status of students to a subject status: one cannot be angry without being angry at someone. Anger would transform the apparently neutral class into chaos, with no clear status ranking, since Gerald, as subject, would also be open to question. Thus, Gerald's insistence on maintaining anger as a taboo subject kept the ritual of heroic initiation on track while affirming culturally inscribed hierarchies, including his own subject status as "master."

Although the self-directed group did not include a teacher/authority, members had internalized the cultural inscriptions of the writer's role well enough that even without a "master" present, control remained a central issue. However, because no one person was "in control" of this group, the subject of anger was accepted, though still quite restricted, deflected to the characters in the story, particularly Carrie and Michael. For instance, anger toward Carrie was not actually named, but instead was again redirected on a number of occasions toward Michael, who was perceived to be "withholding" and "manipulative," someone who "takes Carrie away from herself." The group's representations of Carrie, though less obviously charged, nonetheless were suggestive of anger: "She can't make decisions, just falls into something"; she's "afraid," "dependent." Carrie incites a more covert anger in readers, who recognize her familiarity and hate the powerlessness with which she is portrayed. Such covert anger is also part of what the group projects, again in an indirect way, onto the writer, who seems equally powerless to control the meanings of her text, to "save" this woman character from herself and from Michael. Though anger is named and directed overtly toward Michael, anger toward Carrie and the writer remained covert, a taboo issue, and thus unspeakable.

Even without the controlling presence of a teacher/authority, the self-directed group kept Carrie and, in turn, the writer and themselves in an object status for a long time. They deflected their rage at the powerlessness they each felt to change Carrie's story into something more vital and nurturing, rather than the familiar story of oppression they had come to know so well. Maura's attempt to direct the group to forego evaluation ("neither like nor dislike") is as much a paradox as Carrie; what does Maura (or Carrie) want? It's King Arthur's riddle: What does a woman want? But how can one know what a woman or a writer wants if she is Other than oneself? How can one make that imaginative leap when meaning is enacted as privately held, the writer's text autonomous, the self singular and transcendent—when the script of the heroic quest is itself the ritual being enacted? When heroic ritual emphasizes others in relation to self (as Barry's story demonstrated), not self in relation to others (as Carrie so doggedly tries to enact, to the dismay of her readers), what hope is there for a Carrie who seems endlessly mired in the quagmire of her own indecision?

Perhaps because there was no one person in control, no Gerald to act

as peacekeeper for overheated and "unproductive" emotions and gate-
keeper to heroic initiation, the subject of anger did take hold in the self-
directed group. At the same time, they kept the subject on apparently
safer ground by making Michael a focal point of their anger. By keeping
Michael within their control, marking him off as Other, ritually inscribing
him as "oppressive," "weighty," and "dark," they made him function as a
kind of voodoo doll for the group, while the real object of their rage,
Carrie, the writer, the writer in themselves, was ritually bound to the
object of that rage: the dark side of the heroic persona. The group's carefully channeled anger served only to bind them even closer to the belief in
autonomy—if only Carrie were more independent, if only the writer were
more creative, if only they could come up with a different story, then . . .
what? The only power they knew was the power of the hero, and yet it
was that power that seemed to keep them powerless. They desired and
despised it at the same time.

Yet the absence of teacher/authority did create different conditions for
the talk of the self-directed group even as they continued to adhere to the
same cultural inscriptions as the academic class. Some of the ritual codes
of workshop talk were displaced; Maura, for instance, spoke more and
more often, referring the group back to Carrie's anger, the need for "shading," a "chiaroscuro" that would highlight the subtler dimensions of her
fleeting, almost imperceptible emotions and states of mind. A shift occurred, giving Maura an opening to speak; and as the discussion went on,
she spoke more frequently, though always on the same theme: Carrie's
rage, Carrie's need to be understood. She was careful, however, to keep
the subject of anger indirect; to claim such emotions herself would risk
whatever objectivity and thus "mastery" they all might have over the
meaning not only of the story, but of their own lives, not to mention
jeopardize the friendships among them. They did not want to give up on
the very beliefs that kept them bound to powerlessness, because they
didn't believe they were powerless or out of control to begin with. How
can one function if meaning is out of one's control? Otherwise, why
would anyone want to be a writer?

Yet in Maura's persistence to speak, and the group's desire to appease
her—perhaps to avert potential conflict and possibly the end of friendships—a slip in control did occur, quietly. In giving what is ritually the
writer's last speech (the speech before the story is laid to rest), Maura
thanked the group for discussing issues they did not address. Maura's
praise for the group's attention to "language" and the story's "emotional
landscape" showed the group, finally, what mattered to Maura—Carrie in

relation to the land. Although the writer had carefully described the setting, neither group understood it as anything but Other, a backdrop to events rather than a subject in its own right.

Perhaps it was emotional blackmail on Maura's part, a "womanly" strategy, to assign blame through speaking praise, to speak "slant," as Emily Dickinson has written, to protect herself from possible confrontation, providing easy access to denial if the need arose. The fact that Maura spoke might not, in and of itself, be remarkable, since speaking was simply another form of the symbolic return of control to the writer. What *was* remarkable was that the criticism within her remark was heeded and the needs buried within those remarks finally addressed. The writer then became a subject whose message implicated readers as subjects in their own self-hate. To face the writer's rage was to confront the face of the dark one within themselves, the other face of the hero.

Of Writers, Hades, and the Other Face of the Hero

Our understanding of the hero and, in turn, the image of the writer as cultural hero has been impoverished by our culture's splintering of the hero into oppositional and thus unresolvable dualities. The talk of these two writing workshops represents these dualities. Each group foregrounded a different, and apparently opposing, aspect of the hero. The academic class emphasized the "light" face of the hero, who ascends from "merely" local origins and transcends common relations to become "universal" as Culture. His triumph is celebrated through legends, such as *The Odyssey*, that affirm his memory and thus the structures of culture. The self-directed group, however, focused its attention on the "dark" face of the hero, as represented by Hades. Hades is a descending rather than ascending figure, who abducts the unsuspecting, innocent Persephone into the mysteries of death. He is violent, volatile, and unpredictable, a constant threat to the stability of daily life and the structures of culture. Although the "light" Odysseus appears to contradict the "dark" Hades, both draw upon the same power: the power of fear. Both are fearless in their ability to overpower obstacles and in that fearlessness invoke fear in others.

Fear was experienced by each group, although it took different forms; the academic class ritually affirmed fear as part of the heroic challenge. Heroes, after all, have to learn to conquer fear. The self-directed group, however, experienced fear as oppressive, something they felt helpless to change. In either case, fear was perceived as a major obstacle to the writer's quest for meaning; for some it was a necessary challenge; for others, a debilitating reality.

Both groups identified Michael as the dark hero in the text of "Bridge of Flowers, Bridge of Iron," finding him equally undesirable. Yet Michael is a poet whose brooding, solitary habits fit quite well the heroic portrait of an artist like Bern Porter (see chapter 3)—self-sufficient, totally dedicated to his art, unmoved by public opinion, unafraid to flaunt "conventional" social mores. He is the kind of individualistic, trailblazing personality that "apprentice" writers want (or are supposed to want) to become. Neither workshop, however, embraced him as such. The academic class questioned whether Michael was "really" so bad (they couldn't answer for themselves, finding the story's "evidence" inconclusive) or if Carrie's perception of him was distorted. The self-directed group quite openly despised him *and* believed in him (for them, the evidence was more than sufficient). The academic class searched for Michael's light or "positive" aspects; the self-directed group focused on his darkness or "negativity." Both workshops, however, rejected him as an artist.

The difference in the two groups' emphases is the result of the teacher/authority's presence. For the academic class, the purpose of enrolling in a class was to learn from someone with a "mastery" of the subject. To learn from the master, students necessarily give themselves up symbolically to the master's instruction. The writer ritually surrenders her personal meanings to the group's authority; the student gives his individual authority to that of the teacher, who knows more about the "larger" world of academic (and in this case, also publishing) life. The myth behind the transference of mastery is that of the transcendent (ascending) hero. The teacher represents one manifestation of it as one who has battled and conquered the dragons of public acceptance. The teacher is the "insider" who presumably will assist students into becoming like herself—a master of meaning, a hero in control of her destiny. In order to learn, one must believe in and trust the teacher's good will to use that mastery humanely.

But as I illustrated in the previous chapter, what the myth of heroic ascendance actually reinforces, when understood in opposition to the descendant or "negative" hero, is the fear of being out of control. This fear of the loss of control, in turn, reinscribes a hegemonic teacher-student relationship. Students must give themselves over wholly to the "master," who knows better than they the way to transcendence. Yet what they are really enacting is their fear of being taken over in this way. The belief is that the teacher, once the course is through, will return the students' "text" of self, just as readers ritually return the text to the writer. What in fact happens in both cases is just the opposite: the writer and the student learn to internalize the "Other" in the form of the "cultural" text embodied in reader and teacher.

In the self-directed group, the descendant hero became an icon that the group resisted, the dark side of the teacher/authority from whom they had hoped to become liberated, only to find themselves bound all the more tightly in their fear. In some ways, the self-directed group was freer than the academic class to express their resistance, less constrained by the teacher's authority; having a majority of women in the group made it safer to express fear and anger. And for the women, the costs of trying to become the transcendent hero were perhaps more painfully apparent in their experience as Others in a male-dominated culture. In contrast, raising the issue of difference in the academic class jeopardized the ritual initiation into the mysteries of writer-as-hero. Difference, in this context, was an anomaly to be eradicated and overcome. But neither group can be said to have "overcome" fear; quite the contrary. They both inscribed it that much more deeply.

Just as the two positions on Michael (the positive image of a man worthy of love and admiration or the negative images of "withholding," "manipulation," "oppression") are two sides to one larger image of a fearsome hero, the two opposing views of Carrie represent a woman out of control. If Michael is a Hades figure, then Carrie is his wife, Persephone, underworld consort to Hades. Understanding Persephone's mythos, however, requires some reinterpretation to know her not simply in relation to others but as powerful in her own right.

According to Christine Downing (1989), the Persephone mythos typically is understood in the context of the ascendant hero. Persephone's abduction by Hades is represented from the perspective of her mother, Demeter. Demeter's loss and subsequent rage and grief inscribe Persephone primarily as a daughter (Persephone in relation to her mother) rather than as a goddess, as mystery itself. Persephone's complex relationship to Hades and her emergent identity as goddess are typically marginalized in this interpretation. The "ascendant" aspect of the mythos, that is, Persephone's abduction and return to her mother Earth, is emphasized over the "descendant" story of coming into her powers as Goddess. The "ascendant" story focuses on Demeter's loss rather than Persephone's maturity, suggesting that women's lives are necessarily a cycle of separation and reunion with the mother.

Similarly Carrie's story is understood through the "ascendant" mythos, focusing on Carrie's loss of self and powerlessness. She is either "insane" and therefore outside "normal" life or an unsuspecting victim. In both cases, she remains subordinate to the apparently more potent, creative/ destructive powers of Michael/Hades. She is interpreted as one seeking to free herself from, rather than understand herself in relation to, the Dark One.

If we instead read Persephone and Carrie in relation to both the ascendant and the descendant mythos, as both abducted by and giving themselves over to the underworld, we arrive at a more complex portrait of the mythic hero. The hero is thus one who both ascends and descends, who chooses the initiation to quest and is chosen (abducted) into that experience. Even as the "light" side of the heroic image ritually inscribes the cultural code, Persephone (and Hades) are there to disrupt it. The heroic ritual seeks to stabilize culture through the promise of individual autonomy and fixed, knowable meaning; the underworld resists such stabilization, inscribing instead the changing nature of and mysteries beyond culture and the uncertainty of meaning. In Bakhtin's (1981) terms, the "hero" (subject) of discourse follows similarly contradictory impulses as centripetal (bringing in, unifying) and centrifugal (pushing out, decentering), the site of struggle in meaning making.

If we interpret the writer through this mythic framework, we understand that the myth informing initiation rituals (such as writing workshops) suffers a similar impoverishment with its emphasis on the ascendant and its suppression of the mysteries of composing—its recursiveness, ambiguity, chaos, and uncertainty. Both workshops represent this dichotomy of the heroic writer between the superior, ascendant hero and the subordinate mysteries; each emphasizes the necessity for control in the act of composing. The academic class ritually enacted giving up and reinstating greater individual control over meaning, whereas the self-directed group dramatized their rage and fear at being controlled by meanings that were outside their power to change. In either case, composing power was equated with an ability to control meaning, even as the fear that no meaning could, finally, be controlled was ritually inscribed. Both groups viewed control as necessary yet dreaded and even feared; by ritually giving up control and internalizing the Other, they risked becoming the Other and losing self.

The instructor, who has "mastery" over the meanings of his text, embodies the ascendant hero. He, like his students, began as an apprentice (one who is controlled) but rose to a master (one who controls). As the ascendant hero, the instructor is a fixed point students align themselves with. Yet the descendant hero tells another story: that mastery is contingent and meaning always changing. One will always have to return to the underworld of composing, the struggle for meaning. The ascendant mythos divides students' attention between the text of their lives as they know it and an ideal text they aspire to become. Masterful composing is the result of matching self to ideal, apprentice to master. Yet students will always fail, always remain subordinate to the greater powers of the instructor. They will always be inscribing the instructor's text, albeit in a consistently less perfect form.

Therefore, to become the ascendant hero is to become the teacher. One learns how to separate one's attention from one's home or local knowledge and cast it toward the larger knowledge of the gods (or, in this case, of Culture). Yet by inscribing the ascendant hero, divided as the hero is between idealized control and objectified Other, teachers simply perpetuate their disempowerment. Teachers as ascendant heroes, similar to writers, are inscribed by culture as all-knowing and all-powerful, yet utterly despised and blamed even in their apparent victimization. The ascendant ritual of initiation ensures that teachers as well as students keep their attention divided and the narratives of their multiple lives separate and disconnected.

Thus, the mythos of composing that prevailed in both groups was a story of separateness, keeping the "texts," or narratives, of production (i.e., the composing process) separate from the narratives of consumption (i.e., interpretation). Writers remain silent, and readers, having ritually seized control over the textual artifact, underscored the gaps, the lacks, the failures of the writer's attempt at control. Both writer and reader could continue to view each other as objects, their meanings as private and no one else's, and nothing, ultimately, had to change in the texts that were discussed as long as the texts of the writer's experience of composing remained separate from the text of reader's experience of reading. The significance of composing, in this context, is its ability to maintain the status quo, ritually enacting an appropriation of the writer's text while at the same time ensuring that nothing, in the end, really would change.

However, in the self-directed group, one moment did, finally, offer the possibility of connection between writer and readers and consequently presented an opportunity for change. That moment, as I've mentioned before, came when Maura "praised" the group for their insights into the language and "emotional landscape" of her story. This is not to claim the "superiority" of the self-directed group over the academic class; what each group learned was significant though different in its mode of knowing; the academic class entered the discourses of the "master" teacher, a necessary move as writers seek public autonomy and power, while the self-directed group explored the language they already had and developed one collaboratively, effectively blurring the discourses of self and Other. Each mode is limited, yet each can, if seen in relation to the other, inform each other.

However, at this point I wish to draw attention to what can be learned from the self-directed group, specifically their ability to move between the various discourses of the conversation to generate a collaborative reading of the story. As teachers, we might take for granted the importance of learning a "master" language; but the important role of "local" or "native" languages in learning is, I believe, less understood in the context of practice.

Maura's comment provided readers with a key to understanding her reading of the story. Though Maura masked her need to be understood (and her anger in not being understood) in the guise of praise to the group, her need was still heard and addressed. *Why* she was heard remains a subject of speculation; what is significant, however, is *that* she was. For readers, Maura's phrase *emotional landscape* pointed to an entirely different set of relationships with regard to the story's setting. The story's preoccupation with rocks and water, bridges and flowers, had been interpreted by both groups as a backdrop to the more compelling human drama. When Maura described the setting as "emotional," the landscape became a subject in its own right, emphasizing Carrie's relationship to nature and, symbolically, to her own "nature," that is, her understanding of herself (as well as pointing to the writer's understanding of her own text).

The landscape, as a silent Other, expressed the dichotomies of Carrie's "nature" (how she constructed her reality) but at the same time offered a clue as to how to move beyond those dichotomies into more fluid and nourishing relationships. The key images were the two bridges, symbolic of the movement in and out of the rock-bound fluidity of Carrie's psyche and her perception of her marriage. The first bridge, the bridge of flowers, had initially been interpreted as a symbol of the feminine, with its erotic flowers, sensuous colors, and serene arrangements. Carrie identified with this bridge, proudly introducing Michael, Susan, and Tom to its sensual delights. Carrie identified the second bridge, the bridge of iron, with Michael, who chose to cross that bridge rather than the bridge of flowers to return to town. Its hard, rusty construction, dull surface, and utilitarian function embodied many stereotypes of the masculine, in contrast to the "softer," more aesthetically pleasing bridge of flowers. In giving up on "her" bridge, Carrie, readers assumed, had given up on her own feminine self in favor of the masculine cruelty that the bridge of iron represented.

Maura, as it turned out, discovered something altogether different in the meanings she ascribed to each bridge. As Maura said, the stereotypes of masculine and feminine mask qualities of each bridge that are ultimately more meaningful to Carrie. The bridge of flowers, after all, was not place to live but a "tourist" sight, a domesticated version of the feminine. From this angle, the little name tags beneath each plant, the carefully paved walkways, the trimmed and weed-free plots seemed absurd, even dangerous. The bridge represented the trap of an idealized self and an idealized view of marriage in which Carrie was caught. What she really needed for herself and her marriage weren't flowers and promises but a way over the river—not a place to stand, but a way to move. The bridge of iron was in fact the better bridge for her, painful as it was for her to turn away from the more beautiful vision. And the dark man, Michael, also held a clue toward her own realization of the powers within, the goddess power of Persephone. What she had wanted from Michael all along were his creative powers; in finding that she could not obtain them through him, she began to recognize that she, too, might have similar powers within herself and would not have to rely upon his to develop her own. She was learning to discriminate power over (as she experienced with Michael's domination) from power through Others, power in connectedness, including a connection to the oppressor within herself.

Power, in this new context, is a matter not simply of control but of challenging familiar meanings embodied in cultural archetypes that seem entirely natural and "real." The power of composing comes from an ability not simply to control or stabilize meaning (which is necessarily contingent) but to also render it visible and subject to contestation, subverting expected and familiar representations into the strange and uncanny and, in turn, making that which is strange and uncanny seem familiar and expected. A genuine power of writers, then, is in their ability to make the familiar gardens of conscious life and culture strange, so that we can better see the contradictions we enact between the many lives we lead, the many stories we narrate to and about ourselves, and see them as meaningful rather than anomalies.

As these narratives illustrate, composing is a difficult task to undertake, and one that is completed only temporarily. Composing represents an alternative way of seeing in relational rather than dualistic/oppositional modes. Reading the act of composing, the experience of practice, mythically means understanding the ascendant and descendant heroic mythoi in relation to each other. Such an alternative suggests a model and a method of composing and interpreting narratives of practice that put writers and readers, teachers and students, in relation to a common enterprise of composing meaning. Thus may we move between and among the various texts of our lives for the nourishment necessary to not only survive but flourish.

🌱 Representations of Power

Perhaps one of the most powerful themes the academic class and the self-directed writing group dramatize is that cultural inscriptions, possibly even more than institutional authority, reproduce cultural beliefs and values; in some respects, the teacher as authority figure did not have to be present for cultural myths to be enacted. These inscriptions are so deeply embedded in the images of daily life that they are practically invisible, and thus unconscious. In this respect, cultural myths *seem* real and inevitable because the power of myth lies in its appeals to verisimilitude, to common sense—instead of beliefs and values that undergird myths, we tend to see a "reality" unmediated by consciousness, because even as it affirms, myth also conceals its origins. In this sense, myth has no beginning or ending. It simply *is*. The only access we have to it is through the representations—such as stories—by which it constitutes itself.

How cultural inscription operates in the collective imagination is thus a complex question. On the one hand, it comprises the narrative structures of our belief systems. On the other hand, it entails ways of understanding, or interpreting, those structures. Inscriptions are thus the objects as well as the instruments of interpretation. As Clifford Geertz (1973) notes, we know the narratives of culture only through other narratives. There is no first or final story to hearken back to, no originary myth, only interpretations and the interpretations of what those interpretations mean: "webs of significance" on which there is no "objective," outside perspective, and of which there is no subjective "essence." And, as Carolyn Heilbrun (1988) has pointed out, the way we live our lives is largely determined by the way we represent our lives to ourselves, through the stories we tell about the lives we lead. The lives that are available to us, then, are shaped by these representations. That is what makes these stories (and in turn, what these stories mean in relation to each other) so vital, because they are the inscriptions, the meanings, that we are born into and, aware of it or not, are shaped by. Understanding their significances illuminates the complexity of any effort to change the power rela-

171

tions between teachers and students in a hierarchical status arrangement such as those inscribed in the classroom and between genders.

Understanding the ways power is represented in these inscriptions can lead us to alternative images of power and power relations—between self and other, teacher and students, writers and readers, females and males—that inscribe difference. As Wendy Doniger O'Flaherty (1988) has commented, mythic power is not wholly dependent upon language, although our *knowledge* about our language practices or, as Ann Berthoff (1981) says, thinking about our thinking, is—at least in a culture in which literate, written knowledge is, arguably, privileged over all other modes of knowing. The acquisition of power in and through culture requires, as social constructivists have noted, access to the culture of power—its languages, rituals, codes of behavior, and so on. But what that power is and how to get it remain issues of much debate.

These issues become even more complicated with respect to cultural difference. If writers and students are inscribed as "heroes" who rise above their lowly status to triumph over their native cultures, those who are "born" heroes may prosper while those whose differences are perceived as obstructions to their ascension into power will forever strive to overcome those differences. In the framework of heroic ascension, students' attention becomes divided by false oppositions, enlisting them as guardians of their own oppression, while those who are born "heroes" can proceed to claim their "natural" inheritance.

The narratives underlying stories of ascendant heroic power are those of control—self-control as well as control over others through stabilizing meaning. Control is the dominant story of education and intellectual development, as well as of "heroic" models of composing. Control is valued highly, even (as the writing groups dramatized) as it ritually inscribes fear of its inevitable loss. Some strive all their lives to gain such control, but are excluded from ever, finally, obtaining it, because of the obstacles their "difference" presents. Presumably, only those born in control can have that kind of control—over the language, over ways of meaning, over the stories we tell about ourselves. And to maintain such control, one must be in control of a lesser, subordinate group, onto whom the fear of losing control is ritually inscribed. To be in control means displacing one's fear of loss onto Others who lack the "native" abilities to gain control for themselves.

Alternative Stories of Power

But there are alternative stories of power; the struggle to articulate them as well as to determine whose stories should count is at the heart of the debate over writing pedagogy and literacy. If the ascendant view affirms heroic initiation into self-control and power over others, a dialogical view casts power as relational, power through others rather than power over— an image of collective identity and action advocated by feminists such as Starhawk in *Dreaming the Dark* (1988). From this perspective, Persephone's story takes on new meaning as a metaphor for the writer in the academy and the culture at large. In the heroic narratives of ascendance, her goddess powers, in contrast to her familial roles, have been simultaneously marginalized and idealized and her "native" powers symbolically appropriated. Her development will always be regarded as incomplete and thus lacking in contrast to the "rising" hero. Yet in the dialogical view we would understand the struggle for meaning more complexly—as both a call to action as well as an abduction into the unknown.

Why is this complexity missing in the stories we write, teach, and live by? What are the conditions that have privileged some stories of composing more than others? Although Others' differences signify alternative narratives of power—especially the power of the writer and the power of composing—such alternatives are generally not valued by the dominant culture. Because the experiential knowledge of "practitioners" is regarded as less "universal" and thus less generalizable than the knowledge of critics, theorists, and researchers, the story goes, its "subjectivity" is valued less as a mode of knowing than the presumed "objectivity" of the others.

The story of power as control was enacted in each writing group as the power to control one's emotions (that is, the subjective self), most notably that of anger. Anger was perceived as a highly powerful, as well as potentially disruptive force, generating elaborate social rituals to control it. The various strategies each group employed to control anger, and how, as a potential source of power, it was denied or directed, provide a key to understanding each group's construction of power: its meaning, accessibility, and value. We can thus better understand representations of anger as both a threat to group consensus and a powerful, though risky, resource for focusing attention and energizing imaginative thinking.

Anger as a Metaphor for Power

I will now discuss the two groups to illustrate differences in the ways anger, as a metaphor for power, is constructed. I will also discuss the significance of the academic versus the self-directed contexts in which these discussions took place. Finally, I will return to the arguments posed by social constructivists over how to empower students by providing access to the culture of power; I will argue for a more inclusive and reciprocal model of power, and of composing and the teaching of writing, in which student writers are not snared in the double bind of being *either* "insiders" *or* "outsiders" but actors and knowers capable of not only entering but re-visioning the dominant hegemonic structures of the institution.

In the academic class, power meant control—over one's self, one's text, and one's emotions—paradoxically inscribing the impossibility, yet also the necessity, of controlling meaning. The class enacted this view of power in a number of instances. First, students constructed their role in naming those places in the writer's text where she had lost control of her writing. Such moments were characterized by readers' doubt. For instance, several students were skeptical of the "negative" portrayal of Michael; other students found Carrie's passivity and devotion to Michael, despite his betrayal, unrealistic; and there was the question of whether Carrie was pregnant, which in turn raised the question of whether she, as the consciousness through which the story was told, was "reliable." Students and teacher alike highlighted places in the text where their interpretation had been confused, uncertain, or, in some instances, obstructed. These were understood as interruptions and thus implicitly (and sometimes explicitly) framed as problems for the writer to solve. Such problems were perceived as slippages on the part of the writer, problems that denoted places where the writer was not in control of her text or her meaning, that required fixing, whether editorial or conceptual.

Although it is not unusual for a writing class to offer more concrete suggestions for such problem solving, in this instance students and teacher were more preoccupied with interpreting the story's content than with offering concrete advice. For instance, although Karen repeatedly asked for more information about Carrie and Michael's prior history, she did not state what that information might be. Gerald and Carl suggested that clarification about Carrie's presumed pregnancy and more information about her relationship with Michael would be useful, but again, they did not say what those might be. In their symbolic roles as appropriators of the writer's text, readers recommended changes to the original text, although at the discussion's end they returned textual control back to the writer. The myth of authorial autonomy is thus reinscribed, as if to say, It's your text, after all, not mine. If you grant me control over my reading, then I will grant you control as author. The ritual requires readers to act as though the text is, ultimately, the writer's to control; as readers, they can't tell a writer how to solve problems. They can only frame problems they encounter and make broad (or sometimes, very narrow) editorial, as opposed to conceptual, recommendations. That is why the writer sits silently throughout the discussion—for her to speak is to challenge the autonomy of her readers' readings and to jeopardize the objectivity they claim as outsiders to the production of the text. The lines of production and consumption of texts are quite clear in this way, and for a reader or a writer to cross that line is a highly problematic (though not necessarily impossible, as Maura demonstrates) act.

Thus power in the academic class is a matter of who controls the text at a given moment. For the system to work, writers must symbolically give up control of their stories to the readers. In the end, it is assumed that writers will gain more power over their texts through the insight students and teacher offer as to where writers' control has lapsed. This model of power as control assumes that writers already possess autonomous control over their language and the forms that language takes, and that it is primarily a matter of learning how to identify these lapses for themselves that will lead to self-control as writers, and thus autonomy from groups such as the academic class. In short, workshops serve to prepare writers to leave the workshop community for a life of solitary work. Writers learn to anticipate an editor's response before they submit a manuscript, the assumption being that once they know the problem, they, being in control of the text, will know how to solve it eventually. Writers are, thus, educated to identify and frame problems in such a way as to be able to address them. They are not, however, educated as to how to solve those problems, since that merges into the territory of the production of texts, a territory that readers, respectful of the author's ownership, tread upon lightly, if at all.

Power as control was also enacted in the class's interpretation of Carrie, as well as the writer, Beth. Both are perceived to be out of control. Beth, as mentioned before, is perceived to have lapses in control over her text. Carrie is suspected of being an unreliable character, lacking control over her emotions as well as over her life. Of central concern to the class is Carrie's desire for love. She is mysteriously "obsessed" with winning and maintaining Michael's smile—in other words, his approval and love. Her behavior seems "unnatural"; no one understands why she cares so much about Michael. Thus, some students, such as Karen and Barry, suggest that perhaps Michael isn't really all that bad if Carrie loves him so much. Perhaps it is Carrie who has the problem—and that problem is a lack of control over her desire for love and approval.

Beth, like Carrie, is perceived to have given over to certain excesses in her writing. Like Carrie, her excesses or "obsessions" reflect a lack of control or restraint in her perception of Michael and Carrie. Exaggerations are evident; the unreliability in Carrie's character is thus also suspected of reflecting a similar unreliability in the writer. Beth's vision seems to be faulty. In their effort to be helpful, the class members take great pains to frame the story's apparent contradictions and suggest corrections. Though mysterious, Beth's story is nonetheless "solvable." As the narrative of objectivist inquiry claims, in the end, all is knowable—if only writers work a little harder at controlling their vision as well as their sentences.

If self-control is the benchmark of power in this context, then the subject of anger is a highly charged one, because an angry person is perceived as not exercising self-control and is therefore a threat to the fragile structures of social order within the class. However, such an emphasis on emotional restraint only deepens the contradiction being enacted: self-control is ritually affirmed while the fear of losing control (in this case, getting angry) is reinscribed. If emotions like anger were not regarded as so powerful, then control over them would not be so imperative. Anger is a complex issue: If the class were to grant that Carrie is angry, they would also have to grant that the writer, as well as themselves, might also be angry about symbolically giving up control of their texts to others when they cannot even claim such control to begin with. Anger, in this context, is a destructive rather than constructive force, violent and chaotic, disrupting the carefully ordered classroom story of control. Anger represents something unknowable and thus invisible in the text; and because it is such, it is not of interest to the class. The class's mission, instead, is to *solve* mysteries, not reveal them, to discuss what is knowable and visible. Anything else is an anomaly, a distraction from orderliness. To challenge the existing order is to risk utter chaos and meaninglessness.

Power as Connectedness: Transpersonal Consciousness

This view of power as control, specifically control over one's desires, is a familiar theme in the ascendant heroic myth. It is a view that represents goddess figures such as Persephone as victims who are nonetheless held responsible for lacking the self-control to resist their unconscious desires for taboo experience. It assumes that a Persephone, or a Carrie, or a Beth, for that matter, can and should cultivate this self-control—and at the same time it acknowledges the tragedy that they will never finally achieve it. That tragedy is what Homeric versions of the Persephone story (Downing 1989) teaches: Persephone does return to the daylight world and her mother, but only during certain times of the year, and never permanently. She is doomed, at least in Demeter's eyes, to permanent exile.

Yet Persephone does gain mythic power as the queen of the underworld and Hades' consort in a realm beyond life, beyond what is knowable and representable in human experience. Persephone embodies the mysterious—is mystery, the unknown. If power in the anthropocentric realm of conscious life is focused on self-control—of one's actions, thoughts, and emotions—then power in the underworld of Hades is focused on connectedness. It is the site where the corporeal loses its self-contained form and is transfigured into a dynamic interplay of paradox. Unlike the impersonal/ultrapersonal power of the Olympian gods, this power is transpersonal. If the goddesses are, as Downing (1989) suggests, what they symbolize, then Persephone is mystery, the mystery of mystery. She reveals the unknowable and the unfathomable because she is the unknowable and the unfathomable. Her power is not to *solve* problems or resolve paradoxes, but to *represent* what is unknowable. From this perspective, contradictions are not mysteries to be solved, but significant in themselves; not anomalies to be erased, but meaningful events.

To read Persephone, Carrie, and the writer(s) in the classroom as enacting anger casts a very different light upon them. Anger makes them knowing subjects, because to be angry, one must be angry at someone or something. One is an actor rather than merely a passive object of attention and abduction. In the case of Carrie, it is unacceptable to some readers that Carrie is angry, because it suggests that she has a responsibility as a participant in her relationship with Michael; she is not only a victim or insane; instead, she actually seeks to exert a similar control over Michael by *making* him smile. Carrie, therefore, desires not only love but power: the power to control others. Likewise, to grant that Persephone might have unconsciously desired the taboo experience of exploring her sexuality is to acknowledge that power, not simply displaced love, was the object of her desire. And for the writer, anger would suggest that she desired power as a reader, as a consumer of text as well as a producer. Anger would transform her into a reading subject, not simply the object of classroom talk. And because she would have to be angry at some*one*, everyone in the class would be knowing subjects and thus be responsible for what they said in a way that would jeopardize the "free" exchange among readers.

So the ultimate self-control is of controlling one's emotions—keeping them in check, holding back, refraining from excesses, trying, in effect, to achieve a neutrality that erases the subject from the statement. One aims to be impersonal in one's commentary, for impersonality is perceived to be the most helpful in maintaining group cohesion and the tenuous lines of goodwill and unity. Anger has no place in such a fragile balancing act. It's seen as an anomaly, at best an immature play for attention, at worst a struggle for control over others. For if anger prevails, chaos reigns, and the class might as well pack it in since the pursuit of meaning through talk would no longer be possible.

In a mythos that casts the hero as being completely in command of himself, physically, mentally, and emotionally, as giving up the self, as Joseph Campbell describes it, in order to achieve a greater power and dominion, then such a lapse signals danger not only for the hero but for everyone behind him. The hero is the human negotiator with the gods, and to lose him would be to lose control over everyone's lives in the face of capricious, often whimsically destructive "supernatural" (i.e., cultural) powers. Anger represents an attachment to the mortal world that heroes cannot afford to trifle with. Such is the case with the teacher as hero; if teachers lose their status as negotiators with the gods, then students lose any hope of gaining control over the "real world" of academia and publishing.

To become a heroic success, writers must also learn to control anger in face of "gods" who serve as editors and publishers and agents, or, if they choose a more academic path, committees, departments, administrators, and reviewers. Thus, the classroom serves as a preparation for facing the "real" world of work. It provides an audience of readers who are known to writers not as subjects but instead as whimsical gods who will accept or reject writer's work capriciously. It is the writer's task to try to outsmart them, to become a trickster, like Odysseus, however temporarily. The more writers are able to achieve that, the more legendary their status among other mortals becomes, and they may attain that semi-godlike status of renown in the public realm. So, the ascendant hero story is not simply enacted in the reading of writers' work; it also represents writers' ways of being in the world, as heroes overcoming an adversarial world as best they can, to become the ultimate tricksters in a world of the powerful, unpredictable gods of publishing.

The self-directed writing group also enacted this representation of power as control, although in somewhat different ways. Power was something that the members perceived themselves to be lacking; they were frustrated, for example, at their (and the writer's) powerlessness to change what seemed an inevitable outcome in Carrie's story—the continued victimization of an oppressed woman. Carrie had no control over her life, and they, as readers, had no power to change that reality. They were just as powerless as Carrie, and they were angry about that, though that anger was displaced largely onto Michael as an icon of male domination. To name this anger directly, to face, in essence, an anger that they turned onto themselves as a result of their own feelings of inadequacy, was to admit that they completely lacked control. Power as control was something they felt themselves to be lacking yet perceived as necessary even though they despised its oppressiveness in their own lives. Unlike the academic class, in which control was a sign of heroic achievement, the self-directed group identified that control (in the form of Michael's suppressed anger) as an instrument of oppression while continuing to deny its presence within their own interactions.

However, the drama enacted within the self-directed group was not only the tragedy of failed attempts at self-control but a challenging, though also painful, turning toward self-awareness of the group's dynamics. For most of their discussion, the members of the self-directed group inscribed Carrie (and, symbolically, the writer and themselves) as lacking control. However, this changed when Maura suggested a key to understanding the story through its language and "emotional landscape." As in the academic class, the self-directed group interpreted Carrie as someone lacking—in this case, a tragic, though regretfully familiar, woman "stuck" in a marriage that doesn't nourish her but that she cannot bring herself to end. It is a "space," as Denise described it, that no one, including the readers of the story, wanted to inhabit. They resisted entering that space because it seemed so limiting, so much like "spaces" they had known themselves and did not wish to symbolically inhabit. Thus, they deflected Maura's direction to speak in "neither like nor dislike" and instead discussed the "beauty" of the prose as a maneuver to avoid engaging with the text on other levels. On the other hand, since this group did affirm Carrie and her anger as believable, they seemed to generate some interpretive momentum; naming the "space" Carrie inhabited as frustration was also a tacit acknowledgment of the group's frustration in their inability to meet Maura's direction and engage with the text from an interpretive rather than evaluative approach.

In contrast to the academic class, which debated Carrie's plausibility as a character, the self-directed group debated in what way she might exist. Like the academic class, this group's representations of Carrie alternated between Carrie as a victim and Carrie as a manipulator. First the group raged against Michael, Carrie's victimizer and oppressor. Later, the discussion returned to Carrie, whom Jody described as responsible for manipulating Michael's smile. Both representations, however, contain anger—not only toward Michael but toward Carrie as well; both deflect some of the blame and anger they project onto Michael back to Carrie. They were angry at Carrie for making them enter an uncertain space, although they sympathized with Carrie's domination by Michael. These opposing representations—Carrie as victim, Carrie as manipulator—came from the same sense of Carrie as "stuck," out of control of her life. However, only the anger at Michael is openly acknowledged and even enacted in outbursts by the group; anger toward Carrie, and toward the writer and the group, is deferred, maintaining Carrie as Other than themselves, ensuring her object status as apart from rather than connected to themselves, while also maintaining the separateness of group members as autonomous and self-contained.

Preoccupied with controlling their anger, the self-directed group nonetheless enacted this control differently than the academic group did. Although no teacher/authority established and maintained boundaries between readers and writer, the self-directed group, having internalized cultural inscriptions about the production and consumption of texts, exerted these pressures on each other, first by making Michael (and, covertly, Carrie) the objects of their rage. By ritually inscribing their anger onto the characters in the story, they thus symbolically controlled it. They ritually enacted their fear of the inability to control their destinies through their representations of Michael and Carrie, which provided a sense of power over the characters as objects of their rage and feelings of inadequacy. Without a teacher's presence, the group could thus name their anger as such, but only to displace it onto an acceptable Other, Michael.

While the self-directed group covertly raged at Carrie's powerlessness through Michael, they also identified with Carrie's powerlessness by naming the subtle forms Carrie's anger took. One example offered by Jody was the exchange between Carrie and Susan about whether or not to swim, where Carrie's frustrations at her needs not being met surface, however faintly. And yet even this identification with Carrie wasn't enough to alter the feelings of powerlessness the group experienced through the more familiar plot of oppression. When Maura tells the group what she thinks the story needs, the conversation seemed to be winding down into particular suggestions for highlighting Carrie's anger. But in fact the talk had begun to trail off rather than wind up or down, because the issues of anger and control had not yet been fully revealed. The subject of anger

had been broached—anger as a force in Carrie's life was named and affirmed—but only to be projected onto Michael and Carrie, objectified, in
essence, as something Other, something outside of the group, a focal point
of attention not connected to themselves.

Because the subject of anger had not been grounded through a connection to themselves, it lingered and charged the group's silences, which
finally exerted so much pressure that the group began to reconnect with
their responsibilities within the linear, temporal world of duties and deadlines. The group resisted, claiming their anger at Carrie (and symbolically,
the writer whom Carrie represents) as their own self-directed, and self-
oppressing anger as agent of hate. They would have had to claim, in essence, that they *were* Carrie, agents in their own oppression.

If, to claim power, Carrie must experience the full range of her emotions, including anger, the writer must also be able to explore her own
emotions, including those that jeopardize the familiar plots into which she
is inscribed (and that she inscribes herself into) in everyday life. Power, in
this sense, is inscribed by a deeper view of relationships, one that differs
from the models of control and domination in which one group subjects
another to its objectified hatred and fear. Power can also, from this perspective, generate connectedness: anger puts Carrie in touch with her own
powers as someone who knows what she feels. As the self-directed group
pointed out, Carrie's gesture of leaving the wounded bird behind represented that paradoxical view of anger, as both controlling, in leaving a
helpless bird to die, and compassionate, in knowing she could not do
anything to help it survive. The group interpreted the bird as a symbol of
both Carrie and her marriage. By coming into the experience of her anger
more fully, Carrie is propelled into making decisions for herself rather
than falling into the wake of other's choices.

Although I think both groups in their own ways ritually enacted the
values and beliefs of the writer as cultural hero, the self-directed group, in
a moment of ambiguity, also posed the possibility for re-visioning power
relationships between readers and writers, as well as teachers and students. That moment, as I have mentioned before, came when Maura
praised the group for addressing issues they had not, to any great extent,
discussed. After Maura spoke, the rest of the group experienced the contradiction between what she said and what they knew, as a group, they
had accomplished, and recognized the significance of that contradiction as
Maura's dissatisfaction with the discussion. They then acted upon that
contradiction by discussing the very issues that Maura had named as critical to an understanding of the story. They realized Maura had been more

concerned with the relationships among the images of nature that reflected, in her eyes, Carrie's "emotional landscape," her silent, inner self, than with the interpersonal relationships around which they'd focused their discussion.

Why that shift in the discussion's focus actually occurred is a matter of speculation, for the self-directed group had enacted the same heroic representation of writer and marginalized representation of woman as the academic class. Perhaps because social relationships among the members had existed prior to the group's formation, members felt more responsibility to attend to one another's dissatisfaction with the group. But what is most remarkable is that the contradiction and, in turn, Maura's dissatisfaction, veiled as it was, were heard at all. Like so many of Carrie's gestures of frustration and anger, Maura's dissatisfaction was so slight as to be barely recognized. It wouldn't have been, in most circumstances. Yet it was, and because it was, the group attended to another, deeper layer of significance of the story surrounding the archetypes of masculine and feminine images symbolized by the two bridges.

The writer, initially inscribed as out of control of her text, became a knowing subject with surprising ideas, ideas that she had been exploring tacitly through the background images of the story but the significances of which she had been unable to articulate. She had felt the possibilities of a different view of power relationships, including the marital relations between Carrie and Michael, but had not been able to name them as such because the apparent oppositions divided everyone's attention, including her own. The deeper significances lay in an interpretation of the contradictions of these images as meaningful rather than as a "problem" to be solved.

That the self-directed group did break through to deeper significances of the writer's story does not, however, mean that this group was more successful than the academic class, nor that "writing without teachers" leads to better workshop talk than teacher-led classes. The powers to anticipate "alien" readings of one's work, to test the text for weaknesses, to identify problems are all, of course, of great use to writers and necessary for developing not only the ability but the authority to write and speak. The self-directed group was less effective than the academic class in developing such habits of mind. However, the self-directed group does dramatize a different kind of talk—interpretive and descriptive rather than strictly evaluative—that allows reciprocity between the writer and the readers, the text and its critics, the writer and her text as knowing subjects. Such talk engages the writer in her own developing sense of meaningfulness and assists her in the articulation of it to herself and to others, not so much for the purposes of persuading readers to read the text "her" way (the fear of "spoiling the pot" of the objectivist myth) but to participate in constructing interpretations of her text, negotiating her roles as both reader and writer. The different kind of talk yields a different enactment of power, power as connection, that exists in a dialogical relationship with the enactment of power as control.

Reinscribing Power in Relation

In Christine Downing's rereading of the Persephone mythos, the goddess powers she restores to Persephone are similar to the representations of power that the self-directed group enacted in the end, not only with regard to the writer of the story, but symbolically with regard to the writer in themselves whom they had been inscribed to hate. To read as Persephone is to read mythically and symbolically; the contradictions become meaningful rather than anomalies to erase or mysteries to "solve." As Linda in the academic class put it rather wistfully, it is to read the *absences* in the story. Persephone, as Downing notes, represents a way of seeing life from beyond life, the imagined perspective that death, the loss of "one-in-selfness," as Downing calls it, affords. And this is also writers' imagined perspective, to inscribe themselves into the mysteries beyond familiar interpretations of daily life, beyond the grief of the mother/daughter separation and into the possibilities of power as mystery itself, of a transpersonal world where the apparent contradictions of conventional life and thought are transformed into meaningful events.

Thus, the power of the writer is not represented as simply the heroic myth of ascension and domination; it is also a longer and deeper cycle represented by the One who resides within. It represents not only the knowable and visible (the objectivist story) but what is not knowable and visible, describing the ordinary mysteries of life and death as significant in their connectedness rather than as idealized and thus diminished as separate and opposed.

For writers whose own ways of knowing their experiences are inscribed as Other in the culture, it is critical to be able to claim this alternative consciousness that opens up beyond linear, ascendant time, to reinscribe a different, more reciprocal representation of power. All writers, in a sense, enact Persephone each time they enter their own chaos of meaning making, bringing language to thought and thought to language. Yet for those whose differences have been effaced in the myths and rituals of culture, it may be even more crucial to "revision" the old ways of seeing and being through the metaphors Persephone represents. If the hero must give up self in order to find a more expansive identity, the Other first goes inward, to construct a self that is otherwise denied in the social roles available to her and find a connectedness between the apparent contradictions her difference represents. Both stories, of course, matter; but they matter more when understood *in relation* to each other rather than as separate and opposed in significance.

The story of writers in academia is one of apprentices learning the power relations of a world that is hierarchical yet unpredictable, dominated as it is by the greater powers of publishers, teachers, administrators, reviewers, and editors. Power is something writers are shown they currently lack; to attain it, they must learn self-control and discipline, not only socially but in the conventions of their texts. The point of such an apprenticeship is to learn how to give up their former identity to become one with power-as-control. Without this power, writers lack the ability to progress upward on the social or cosmological ladder. Thus, writers let themselves be initiated into the rituals of control in order to gain control—one must give up control of one's life in order to gain this larger control. If writers have no power initially in the classroom, it is because as part of the initiation they must learn to give up control of their meanings in order to understand how they and their texts are "read" by others, with the understanding that they will then be able to convey the meanings they want to convey. Teachers, as "masters," assume such control, and writers must trust them for guidance through the mysteries of the academy and the publishing world at large, learning the "tricks" that will make them master "tricksters."

Power in the self-directed group also signified a loss of control in order to gain power. However, that power not only was perceived as a different, if only temporary, gaining of control, but also suggested the possibility of a new connectedness with Others, a reconfiguration of old ways of thinking and being in the world, a new set of relations forged from the old. Rather than the one-way transaction of master transforming apprentice, an initiation into the mysteries of the "real" world of academics and publishing, the power of the writer depended upon the transformation of each member of the group. That power was enacted in the transaction of constructing and negotiating the meaningfulness of the texts of the group. Power was a shared force that bound as well as liberated, an ability to relate to paradox as complex experience rather than only opposition, to have relational perception, which is dynamic, rather than oppositional perception, which is linear. Or rather, to understand the dynamics of an interplay between two apparent contradictions in perception.

Reinscribing the Social

When social constructivist theorists represent the empowerment of student writers, power means control over, more than meaning of, the contradictions of lived experience. It is a narrow representation of power that serves to reinscribe the ladder of status already in place. The social constructivist classroom is constructed within a model of the world that says that power is a matter of who has control—over money, resources, status, as well as meanings and texts. And what these theorists regard as necessary is to initiate students into the culture of power, as Lisa Delpit (1988) has so powerfully argued in her article "The Silenced Dialogue." However, I don't think they are questioning, as Delpit does, the assumptions behind the representations of power in academia and society in general; rather, they seem to accept those terms as the "reality" in which they must work.

This is not to say that Bartholomae and Bizzell, in particular, deny the barriers "basic" writers face in succeeding—academically, economically, and politically—because they can be so easily thwarted by a lack of comprehension of the ways of academic discourse. And though I think they are right to argue that teachers, as representatives of the academy, do have something to offer students in ways of thinking about the world more complexly, there is also a heavy price attached to learning those ways, at least in the assimilation model that these theorists imply. The pertinent question is, What does it mean that they reinscribe social hierarchies? Whose interests does it serve? In reflecting upon my own experiences in the academic writing class and the self-directed writing group, I don't think it is a matter of replacing the academic "hero" model with the nontraditional "goddess" model, of flipping the hierarchy. Both models exist. But the ways the academy and our culture value these models complicate any effort to bring into the classroom alternative representations of the world, power, writers, women, and students. One may articulate such representations, but at what price? What is it that makes it so easy to enact the same stories over and over? What does it mean that despite its best intentions a class cannot interpret the woman in the story or the woman writer/student as anything but tragic, both victim and agent of her own victimization? On the other hand, what does it mean that a group of writers, gathered together on their own initiative, can represent alternative readings of the Other in the texts and connect them to their personal stories?

Composing Difference

Composing signifies not only the activity of writing texts in the classroom but also composing the text of one's self and one's life. Thus, when Bartholomae and others want students to become empowered in the academy, they are also asking them to take on the ways in which the academy composes them—to re-figure themselves as powerful, knowing presences. However, to become this, students must, in the process, erase the differences they bring to bear upon their ways of experiencing learning. Among these differences is that of gender. To gain power, status, authority, and control institutionally, one cannot be a woman. One must give up, or at least suspend, control, and become vulnerable to the shaping forces of academic discourse. The ideal suggested here is that more students of marginal status will be brought into the mainstream in order to change it, and in turn, the academy. But I don't think anything real can change if students learn to choose between ways of being in the world that, on the one hand, limit their choices in the social hierarchies of work and world and, on the other, breed devaluation and even self-hate for the "native" ways of knowing they bring to their classroom experience.

This book represents my inquiry into the paradoxes of institutional inscriptions placed upon me as a women in the academy. Conventional forms of research require that one take out what the writer and woman know experientially. Thus, to gain academic authority, my work must conform to specific ideas of what counts as research. I have chosen, however, to turn research methodology into a question about itself—why and how we value what we do, in order to better understand the assumptions that shape our representations of student, writer, teacher, and woman. I value, at the center of my research, the narratives that otherwise go unspoken in representations of classroom and research experience.

I have revised my stories to include the possibility of being both a writer and a woman inside as well as outside the academy. The revised plot reads: Gains of power do not necessarily require losses of control. I am modeling, as Wendy Doniger O'Flaherty so elegantly does, ways to represent as well as interpret the stories we live by through the stories of

Others, who are also ourselves. Fictions constitute themselves in this self-reflexive way, just as we learn language by using language; language breeds language. Writing generates writing. Stories create stories.

Revisioning Research: A Different Sort of Question

If we approach representations of the woman/writer/student in the text as human constructions, then they are available for critique and revision. They do not have to be the helpless Persephone, an unconscious player in her abduction into experience and exile. They are not Carrie, the woman whose need for love is so consuming that she will give up control of her life just to be with the man she loves. Nor are they Beth, the writer who sits silently, her story unspoken and unrealized. Nor are they Maura, who praises when she means to critique.

To begin revision means thinking about what makes such stories possible. As Christine Downing has demonstrated, it is looking at the ways in which the ascendant hero story has erased knowledge of the connectedness of goddess stories. In terms of writing classrooms, it means considering the ways teachers of writing are implicated in the academy, the ways it reads us and our students, to better understand the constraints in which we operate and turn them into enabling forces. The irony of representing the teacher as the ultimate source of power (i.e., control in composition theories) is that teachers (particularly teachers of writing), in the scheme of the educational hierarchy, in fact have very little control over their classrooms. In addition, what they do is greatly undervalued compared to the vast amounts of money, resources, and personnel devoted to research that is often directed at erasing teacher input into the curriculum. When compositionists discuss empowering students, it can finally be understood only as ironic; teachers are as much Other in academia as are the students and writers they are supposed to empower. Teachers are teaching students to be controlled, just as they are, not in control.

But within a framework of power as connectedness, in which we come to know the Othernesses of students through an interpretive stance of reading their textual "anomalies" or contradictions as meaningful acts, we might begin, as Clifford Geertz (1982) has proposed in cultural anthropology, "to figure out what the devil they think they are up to" (58). And it is not from some posture of *noblesse oblige*, the giant bending down to hand the midget a piece of sky (the image of Gulliver strapped down by thousands of Lilliputian guy wires should be enough to discourage such altruism). Rather, there is a reciprocity involved, whereby students can help us understand our own complex stories in the academy as teachers, the messiness and confusion and sometimes outright terror of a context where one is easily misunderstood and even penalized because one's values and ways with words seem foreign and at times threatening to the powers that be.

The question that students so readily ask teachers (especially in the required composition courses)—"What's in it for us?"—is a good question for teachers to ask theorists who advocate the practice of social justice in the classroom. The abstractedness of such a utopian ideal masks, I think, the real problem, which is that teachers are as limited, albeit by somewhat different constraints, as students are. To project teachers as some higher power of control is to mystify the real lives of teachers in academia. Teachers are inscribed in these theorists' texts as selfless, morally and spiritually higher creatures, similar to Victorian notions of the angel in the house. Teachers are supposed to bring social justice to bear within their classrooms without considering their own cultural inscriptions. Expressivists and social constructivists alike imprison teachers in the same mythology of woman as all-giving, all-nurturing, the goddess of bounty as separate from the goddess of death and destruction, which represents that programmed self-hate that they may project onto students as "lacking"—confidence, skills, power, and knowledge.

What's in it for teachers to listen to the differences of their students as meaningful? They might begin to hear themselves differently, as similar to *and* different from students, the dynamic interplay of apparent opposites, which will make them value their own ways, as well as students', of knowing and being in the world of the classroom. Teachers' stories, like women's stories, students' stories, goddesses' stories, have been effaced, rendered subjectless by plots of cultural hegemony and hierarchies of what counts as research and scholarship. But they can be remembered, restored, and revalued in cooperation with students. As feminists have noted, it is a political act to reinscribe the image of woman; so it will be to reinscribe both teachers and students of writing. The questions we ask will change, and that is the beginning of revisioning what we already know in our lives to be true.

🍃 Epilogue
Writing, "That Old Classic"

In a book that emphasizes the importance of narrative as a mode of knowing, it seems fitting to end with a story. Ann Berthoff asks in "Rhetoric as Hermeneutic" (1991), "If we put it this way, what difference would it make to our practice?" (283). The particular story I want to tell here is one that will help me address a question that has arisen as I have written and rewritten this book: What difference has it made to my practice to tell these stories? I would like, then, by way of this last story, to dramatize what difference telling stories has made in my approach to teaching and my attitudes about myself as a writer, scholar, and woman.

During my first semester as an assistant professor (after nine years of graduate and part-time teaching), I asked my freshman writing class to compose a character sketch of the author of their textbook, Ann Berthoff. The students had been struggling for a few weeks with the language and concepts of that text, many expressing awe and intimidation with someone whom they regarded as in command of words, but words that seemed to exclude them and their own language and experiences as writers. Their experiences as writers were neither as satisfying nor as successful as Berthoff's seemed to be; in turn, my expressions of pleasure and trust in the "chaos" of composing only heightened their sense that their experiences of failure, frustration, and struggle were meaningless both to Berthoff, as a "master" writer, and to me, their teacher-writer. By representing myself as not only a teacher but as a writer (who also struggled but found the struggle worthwhile), I seemed to be silencing students who had experienced writing and writing instruction as messy, difficult, and confusing, not to mention boring, repetitive, and rote.

By asking them to characterize the textbook's author, I expected their sketches would dramatize their tacit assumptions about writers and writing, thus making them more available for reflection and critique. Writers' powers clearly seemed Other to them, something they admired yet feared.

189

I expected that through the process of observing and reflecting upon their images of writers and writing they might be better able to reenvision those images in ways that did not exclude their experiences. In turn, they could reflect upon and critique the implicit values about writing present in their sketches.

Many students wrote sketches that were eventually revised as stories about what kinds of writers they were or would like to be. A first draft by Gary (not his real name) seemed well on its way to becoming a longer story; he had written such a perfect parody of the writer-teacher that I laughed even as I cringed a bit, for in his portrait of the powerful teacher-writer I felt a critique of not only Ann Berthoff, but myself, a teacher who loved writing to the point of obsession. Here is the first draft of Gary's sketch:

Ann E. Berthoff

"Good morning class!"

"Good morning Ms. Berthoff."

"I hope all of you had a splendid summer. I was able to do a number of intellectually stimulating things, and you all will have the chance to read about it in my journal. I had copies made for everyone. You may pick them up after class, if they are to heavy for you have a janitor help you."

"Did you write in your journal everyday, Ms. Berthoff?"

"Yes, I wrote every hour on the hour for five minutes. You just never know when a rare thought might pop into your head."

"Did you want to hear about our summer, Ms. Berthoff?"

"I'll hear from everybody just as soon as someone takes attendance while I write in my journal."

"I'll take attendance Ms. Berthoff."

"Why, thank you Jeff." Ms. Berthoff writes in her journal. "My class seems unusually energetic today. Why, I ask. Is it because it's Monday? Is it because it's sunny with a high of 92? Is it because it's the first day back? Is it because Taco Bell now serves breakfast? Is it because I wore my blue sweater? Why are they so energetic? I like that word . . . energetic. It means, full of energy, wild, ready to go. But where are they ready to go? Are they ready to go home? Are they ready to go out? Are they ready to go to lunch? Are they ready to go to the moon? Where are they ready to go to?"

When I first read Gary's draft, I admired his parodic skill—the self-absorption of the teacher as performer; the endless, pointless questioning without response; the thinly cloaked aggression beneath the outward cheerfulness; the obsessive concern with writing each and every minute, drawing the writer away from the immediate life around her. The students were little more than servants to the teacher-writer's "genius," keeping the classroom running while the great writer sat and pondered the moon. And of course the great writer doesn't even include her students as potential writers—she attributes their "energetic" appearance to their desires to leave school and act in the world rather than desires to write, despite the students' expression of interest in her journal. They are readers of great writing, but not writers themselves.

Fresh out of high school, Gary also didn't miss a beat in skewering the rituals of schooling: the sing-songy greeting, the expected questions, the monotonous routines. Underneath the conventional forms was a war of resistance and insincerity—students catering to the teacher-writer's ego as a way to escape the meaningless act of writing; the teacher-writer writing about her students' desire to escape. Both students and teacher-writer knew where each other stood, yet they completed the ritual just the same, *pro forma*, in tacit agreement that nothing had to happen, nothing and no one had to change as a result of their classroom experiences.

I wrote this response to Gary:

> Gary,
>
> Your Ann B. seems completely obsessed with writing—her own, that is, not her students'. What makes this story funny is the exaggeration of someone so caught up in making sense of the world that the opposite begins to happen—she makes no sense at all. She loses touch with reality because she's so caught up with philosophizing about it. And what's even funnier is that the students, who apparently had Ms. B. the previous year, are pretty cheerfully accommodating Ann's obsessiveness. I mean, they greet her enthusiastically, they ask her about her journal writing, they offer to take attendance while she talks. It's as if they're holding out for Ann to listen to them; when they ask her, "Did you want to hear about our summer, Ms. Berthoff?" it's bizarre because it's obvious she couldn't care less about their summer because she cares only about her own experiences. What's odd, then, is that the class, knowing this about her, still seems to expect that she is, at some point, going to get interested in them. Why do they not only put up with her, but actually seem to encourage her? It's one thing to sit in class and just resist by not participating; it's another to assist her in her nonsense!
>
> So while the caricature of Ann is funny, the students, in the end, bother me. They are not funny but actually a bit disturbing. If they know she is like this, why do they still seem to expect something more from

her? Surely her journal entries, even if they are fascinating, would get boring eventually. And aren't they frustrated that she doesn't really seem to want to listen?

Though I saw the students in Gary's story as complicit with the teacher-writer in maintaining their separate worlds and identities, I represented them to Gary as passive, herded through the expected hoops, hoping that Gary would, in fact, confront the question of whether or not the students really were conforming to the teacher's absurd expectations. I wanted the students to be different, to openly challenge such conventional exercises in jumping through ritual, requisite hoops. I wanted Gary to confront the students' passivity—how could students put up with such an autocratic teacher? Overall, my response focused on the students as the "problem" more than the teacher; I accepted the failings of the teacher as a given, but found the "passive" students unacceptable and "disturbing."

Before turning in their drafts, students had exchanged papers with a peer and wrote letters to each other characterizing their partner's portrayal of the teacher character. Then they answered each other's letters and turned them into me with their drafts, knowing all along that I was part of their audience, an "eavesdropper" on their "conversation" about each other's writing. I read these letters after I wrote my own response, so as not to be too influenced by their viewpoints (the intentional fallacy still holding sway over my approach to the writing workshop).

To my surprise, Debbie wrote Gary that his Ann Berthoff seemed to her to be cheerful, curious, and caring—hardly the self-absorbed "genius" engaged in a tacit battle of resistance with cagey, superficially obedient students that I had constructed through my reading. Here is Debbie's letter to Gary:

Dear Gary,
    I came up with five words to describe Ann Berthoff's character after reading your story. They are: cheerful, pleasant, energetic, observing, and curious.
    When I read your story, the first time words came to mind quickly. I could really picture this woman bouncing into the room with a big, happy smile. She seemed full of energy ready to really reach these kids. She seems like she's just waiting for some class room response. Waiting for that one student reaching out for help. She also seems somewhat strict but not too crass, that's what makes me think of her as pleasant.
    At the end of your story she seems to slow down a bit. She's watch-

ing the students. As she's observing she's asking herself about what she thinks she sees. She must be very curious to ask some of those questions.

Debbie

Perhaps Debbie was being careful in her comments, unwilling to offend Gary and/or me; or perhaps she just missed the irony?

Although Debbie's response initially puzzled me, I decided that she was probably just being careful—after all, she knew I was reading over her and Gary's shoulders as they corresponded with each other. Gary's letter back to Debbie, however, was even more puzzling:

Dear Debbie,

   I got the feeling from your letter that you were able to picture my character easily. I tried to portray a very cheerful and generous teacher who expected good things from her students. This is how, in your response, you described her. You also put down as one of your words that she was curious. I didn't mean to put that as one of her qualities but after I went back over the story I did see how you were able to get that. In the last part with her writing in her journal, [she] does come across as a person who is inquisitive. I also wanted to get across the point of my character being comfortable with her job, I feel this is important to the character sketch because it gives the basis for her cheerfulness and enthusiasm. I wasn't sure if you picked up on that.

I could no longer attribute Debbie's "naive" reading simply to guardedness, caution, or lack of sophistication, since Gary so clearly confirmed that reading. Suddenly, I was an "alien" in the students' "community" as writers and readers. After reading their letters, I added a final paragraph to my response to Gary,

I just read your and Debbie's letters, and I am really stunned at how different our interpretations are. I really thought your story was a parody (making fun of) Ann. I did not see her as gentle or nice or interesting at all. Quite the opposite. I was even more stunned that you and Debbie saw your character similarly. I had to check to make sure we were all talking about the same story. I still don't think of her as fun or pleasant, though I do see that she feels comfortable with her writing. Why do you suppose I got such a different reading than you two?

Gary's letter back to me helped clarify some things but confuse others:

Dear Mrs. Cain,

You brought up alot of good points in my character. I did try to make my character seem overly obsessed in her own writing. When she asks the class about their writing she does that out of habit. She is not actually curious about their writing but maybe even wanting to bring up the topic of writing without scaring the students off. I used the students to try and display what could happen with a teacher that was too involved in learning rather than teaching. The students showed a bit of amusement at Ms. Berthoff's enfatuation with her writing.

I don't know why you were not able to see my character the same way I did. I was making a joke of the character but I also tried to give her the appearance of a gentle, warm, teacher.

Sincerely,
Gary B.

Gary's letter gently resisted my re-presentation of the students as passive victims; instead, the students patronized the "whims" of their somewhat self-absorbed but harmless teacher, quietly amused by her writing "obsession." Perhaps they were also amused that the teacher thought she might "scare them off" by introducing writing—amused that the teacher thought she had that kind of influence over them? The teacher's "enfatuation" with her own writing was a sign that her own learning as a writer mattered more than her students'; being a writer mattered more than being a teacher. The joke, apparently, was her obsession; but her gentleness and warmth took the edge off her character and thus redeemed her in the students' eyes.

I commented in the margins of Gary's letter to me that I didn't see why he thought writing might scare the students off, nor did I see the students' amusement, and that I saw the "joke" as more "pointed" than a gentle poke. I asked him whose learning the teacher was more involved in—her own or her students'—thinking that Gary might see the teacher's learning as in competition with the students'.

Gary choose to revise this paper for his final portfolio. In his revision proposal, he explains why:

The character sketch of Ann Berthoff was an interesting paper. It allowed us to use little information and alot of imagination to create a person through our eyes. I tried to convey the character as a teacher that loved her work and attacked it with a certain energy that would encompass her to the point of her not paying attention to her students. I choose this paper because of the different messages I got from the readers. I feel that if I can change the approach of my paper it would be more clear. I used a setting of a classroom with a conversation between the students and Ann Berthoff. If I could change that maybe to a different viewpoint perhaps an outside observer maybe I could add a few more details and convey my message a little clearer.

Gary certainly appeared to get the message that his first draft was not understood (at least by his instructor) in the ways he wanted it to be. He chose instead to focus on the students' talk among themselves rather than a "conversation" between students and teachers—a move that seemed designed to give more attention to what the students thought of the teacher in their own voices, rather than leaving it up to the reader to interpret their attitudes through the ways they interacted with the teacher. Aware of the conflicting readings generated by his first draft, Gary revised his story so that the students' "private" conversation became the story's focus, rather than the teacher-as-performer:

Character Sketch Revision

The sun was just beginning to shine through the east windows, striking the newly cleaned desktops. The light sent a comfortable glow around the room which was already filled with impatient students.

A student in the second row said to his friend, "I wonder where she is. It's not like her to be late."

His friend responded, "Maybe she had car trouble. You know how she still drives that old classic car."

Molly, a girl that sat in the same seat in the front row for every class, turned and said, "I think she is just getting old and probably forgot what day it is. You all know how forgetful she can be. Like last year 2when she promised me a recount in the class president elections, she just totally forgot."

"I don't think a recount was going to help you anyways" replied the boy closest to her. "Besides Mrs. Berthoff counted them herself and she is real good at keeping tract of things."

"Yes" exclaimed the other boy, "she writes in her journal every day after class just to record what happened in class that day. She even puts down what some of us said that she thinks is funny or worth noting."

"Ya like everytime Molly is wrong about something" joked his friend. Molly ignored them. "I don't think she is getting old at all. She is one of my favorite teachers, if it wasn't for her and her writing drills I would still be writing as bad as I was before."

"Yes, I would also. I think Mrs. B. is the best, even though she is kind of strict with us. She can be the nicest lady around but if you don't do your assignment you had better like sitting in the hall finishing it."

Just then Mrs. Berthoff came into the room to explain to the students why she was late. It turned out that she was half-way to school when she remembered today was test day so she went home to pick up the test. Proving once again her dedication to the class.

What's striking about Gary's revision, besides the fact that he chose to do it at all (his urge to extend his meaning sustained rather than inhibited), is the shift to the students' world without the teacher, their voices now individualized rather than a group chorus, their "private" thoughts and feelings revealed to "eavesdropping" readers. The teacher is the object of their attention, observed, debated, and ultimately judged. Her writing now has a point—it's a record of them, the students, though the record keeping seems focused on "keeping tract of things"—assignments, deadlines, conversations, and (perhaps) errors. She may be a little obsessed with "keeping tract," a little too strict in holding students accountable for all their work, but that's OK because they are learning from her "writing drills." No one gets away without writing!

"Mrs. B" (an affectionate, though regressive, revision of the more manic "Ms. Berthoff") may be so obsessed with record keeping that she is forgetful, so tied to the written text that she can't rely upon her memory to get her through the day. That, not old age, is what the boys argue as the explanation for her absentmindness. Thus, it's not surprising that she "forgot" their tests. Her writing is a symbol of both her obsession and her "dedication," which the students find amusing (because it makes her forgetful) yet admirable because she is so completely devoted to her work.

I think Gary probably came closer to getting across what he had in mind in his revision—that is, the writing teacher as the "strict but nice" elderly woman, dedicated to the point of obsession (and, as a result, sometimes forgetful). The eccentric performer of the first draft, colorful as she may have been, was clearly too "alien" to Gary's readers and possibly to Gary as well. "Mrs. B" fits more familiar images of the good writing teacher, images Gary is concerned with reproducing rather than challenging. In his revision, Gary does seem to come closer to what he might have had in mind while composing the first draft.

Can Gary's writing, then, be regarded as "improved"? Is his revision a "better" piece of writing than the original? Is he now, as the two boys claim, a better writer as a result of all this writing and writing about writing?

I will answer those questions by first returning to the question I posed at the beginning of the chapter: What difference has it made for me to tell these stories, to write this book? The difference is that my understanding of Gary and his "progress" as a writer has deepened; my readings of my students, my teaching, my writing are richer, more complex. Including the writer's voice in the construction of my response to his writing has not "spoiled" or unduly influenced me, as the objectivist myth encoded in the intentional fallacy suggests. The writer's view is another story, another text among the various texts I read as a teacher. What Gary had in mind did, finally, matter in my assessment of his overall learning and development.

What difference has Gary's revision made to his attitudes toward writing, to his intellectual maturity, to his facility with the written word? In some ways, the revision comes as a disappointment, a "tamer" representation of the teacher, the sharp parody and ironic humor of the original extracted. One might argue that the original was more "honest," closer to Gary's "true" feelings. The teacher's absurdities are more colorful, her idiosyncrasies funnier, her "performance" the deeply ironic underside of the teacher-centered classroom.

But Gary didn't want or intend such a broad parody. If anything, he admired the teacher's "performance" as a sign of "dedication" and seriousness. He was not, in fact, critiquing the teacher-centered classroom at all. If anything, he was skeptical of the student-centered classroom. When Gary wrote in his letter to me, "I used the students to try and display what could happen with a teacher that was too involved in learning rather than teaching," I was intrigued and a bit disarmed. His revision clarified his intentions for me: to Gary, the teacher was a bit too obsessive with "keeping tract" of the students—too involved in observing them, in learning about them, and not involved enough in "teaching." Teachers weren't supposed to learn from their students—they were supposed to *teach* them. In turn, students were supposed to learn—they didn't teach, either each other or their teacher. Learning and teaching remained separate, mutually exclusive activities for Gary. The roles had to remain clear. His revision was a return to a more familiar image of teaching that was more comfortable for him, presumably more easily understood by his intended audience. Even the change in names, from *Ms.* to *Mrs.*, from surname to initial, signifies a step backward into the tried and true.

Yet there are also some steps forward for Gary. He came up with a new strategy for conveying what he had in mind—removing the teacher character from center stage and replacing her with student dialogue that, for Gary, represented a more balanced rather than parodic representation of the writing teacher. OK, so she's a little obsessive about her students, making them write when it's often the last thing they want to do. But after all, the students feel they've learned something. Molly's ageist remark is challenged and put to rest. It's still OK to laugh a little at "Mrs. B's" absentmindedness, but it's not at the expense of her age—it's because the students know she really cares about them. Gary's representation of the teacher is an attempt at a richer, more humane characterization—an aim strengthened and developed through the process of dialogue.

Without question, the old myths about teachers in general and women writing teachers in particular are recovered and intact in Gary's text. "Mrs. B." is the gristmill of social civility, taming the wild students, drilling into them self-discipline and order. She's a "classic" (why else would she drive "that old classic car"?) of mythic proportions, humanized by her endearing shortcomings the way the Greeks created gods with equally human failings.

And yet—and yet, *there* are the student voices, missing in the first draft. There they are, talking to each other, even having a little fun at the teacher's expense. Gary's critique of the student-centered classroom makes a little more sense. Sometimes the practices of a student-centered class-room *do* keep students as objects of teachers' attention. Sometimes teachers *need* to be teachers—need to be authoritative subjects, not in-tense spectators, even sincere coaches.

The students in Gary's story are waiting impatiently for the teacher, who is late. Where has she been? When will she come back into the story? Her students miss her, even (especially) Molly, the girl who sits in the front row, in the same seat, watching "Mrs. B" intensely, eager to be called upon, wondering if she can still be president.

No, Gary didn't give "that old classic," writing, an overhaul, though it is certainly due. At best, he managed a tune-up. But enough to get the teacher on the way back to the class, the writer on the road to controlling his own meanings. Molly *could* be president. Even the teacher can make mistakes; perhaps the record *was* wrong.

It's all still possible. This is, after all, a true story.

Or is it? Where does Gary's story end and mine begin? Where does mine end and his begin? Where does the truth lie?

To evaluate Gary's learning, to assess the professional judgments of practitioners, to weigh the truth of women's experiences as women—these are interpretive activities that require such a blurring to occur for new forms, new namings, to occur. Gary's story ends with a heightened sense of what he has in mind—who writers are, what teachers should do and be, what power students have to write themselves into their own stories. He is far from finished with this story—I wish he had written at least one more draft—but he's made some important moves toward realizing a more complex, critically minded reality. Thus, in the end, a new beginning. For me, to see the teacher-writer through Gary's story is to understand the limits as well as the powers of the student-centered classroom, particularly for women. The problems I posed to Gary's representation of students as servants to the teacher yielded a less interesting story because, in the face of this more powerful, authoritative reading, Gary retreated to more familiar images. Yet Gary did find a way to respond to this power, albeit in small, tentative ways, by writing the teacher out of the story scene and the students in. My interpretation mattered in helping Gary shape his own, as a point of resistance, as well as a model of forming: the students had to change. But so did the teacher.

My story begins with Molly, the teacher's pet, the good-girl student who sits in the same front-row seat every day. Molly blames her election defeat on the woman teacher's age and, subsequently, her forgetfulness. The "old classic" seems to stand in the way of the "new model" of woman. The boys resist Molly's challenge of the "old," taunt her ambitions. But Molly knows something they don't: something written can be rewritten; "errors" can lead to new truths. Teachers' "errors," too, can lead to such truths. Women, teachers, writers, students, Others can re-present their errors as differences in the institutional story by telling their truths, to themselves, to their students, to each other, to those who make them the object of their attention.

Finally, the subject speaks, and that is what has made the difference—to my teaching *and* my learning.

Note

Thanks to the many teachers who have given me their insights into Gary's work. Without the richness of their many readings, I would have only skimmed the shallows, I would have missed the depths.

Works Consulted

Aisenberg, Nadya, and Mona Harrington. 1988. *Women of Academe*. Amherst: University of Massachusetts Press.

Alcoff, Linda. 1988. "Cultural Feminism versus Post-Structuralism: The Identity Crisis in Feminist Theory." *Signs* 13: 405–36.

Alcosser, Sandra. 1989. "Causing Each Tentative Voice to Speak." *AWP Chronicle* 2 (October/November): 1, 3–4.

Atwood, Margaret. 1983. *Surfacing*. New York: Warner.

Bakhtin, M. M. 1981. *The Dialogic Imagination*, ed. Michael Holquist, trans. Caryl Emerson and Michael Holquist. Austin: University of Texas Press.

Bartholomae, David. 1980. "The Study of Error." *College Composition and Communication* 31 (October): 311–27.

———. 1985. "Inventing the University." In *When a Writer Can't Write*, edited by Mike Rose, 134–65. New York: Guilford.

———. 1986. "Released into Language: Errors, Expectations, and the Legacy of Mina Shaughnessy." In *The Territory of Language: Linguistics, Stylistics, and the Teaching of Composition*, edited by Donald A. McQuade, 65–88. Carbondale: Southern Illinois University Press.

Bartholomae, David, and Anthony Petrosky. 1986. *Facts, Artifacts, and Counterfacts: Theory and Method for a Reading and Writing Course*. Upper Montclair, N.J.: Boynton/Cook.

Bauer, Dale M. 1990. "The Other 'F' Word: The Feminist in the Classroom." *College English* 52 (April): 385–96.

Baym, Nina. 1985. "Melodramas of Best Manhood." In *The New Feminist Criticism*, edited by Elaine Showalter, 63–80. New York: Pantheon.

Belenky, Mary F., Blythe M. Clinchy, Nancy R. Goldberger, and Jill M. Tarule. 1986. *Women's Ways of Knowing*. New York: Basic Books.

Berthoff, Ann. 1981. *The Making of Meaning*. Upper Montclair, N.J.: Boynton/Cook.

———. 1987. "The Teacher as REsearcher." In *Reclaiming the Classroom: Teacher Research as an Agency for Change*, edited by Dixie Goswami and Peter R. Stillman, 28–38. Portsmouth, N.H.: Boynton/Cook.

———. 1991. "Rhetoric as Hermeneutic." *College Composition and Communication* 42 (October): 279–87.

Bishop, Wendy. 1989. "Valuing the Community of Undergraduate Creative Writing." *AWP Chronicle* 2 (October/November): 5–6.

———. 1990. *Released into Language*. Urbana, Ill.: National Council of Teachers of English.

Bizzell, Patricia. 1984. "William Perry and Liberal Education." *College English* 46 (September): 447–54.

———. 1986. "Foundationalism and Anti-Foundationalism in Composition Studies." *Pre/Text* 7 (Spring/Summer): 37–57.

———. 1990a. "Beyond Anti-Foundationalism to Rhetorical Authority: Problems Defining 'Cultural Literacy.' " *College English* 52 (October): 661–75.

———. 1990b. "Collaborative Learning, Language, and the Authority of Teachers." Response to Kenneth Bruffee. Paper presented at the Conference on College Composition and Communication, March, Chicago.

———. 1991. "Power, Authority, and Critical Pedagogy." *Journal of Basic Writing* 10 (2): 54–70.

Boomer, Garth. 1987. "Addressing the Problem of Elsewhereness: A Case for Action Research in Schools." In *Reclaiming the Classroom: Teacher Research as an Agency for Change*, edited by Dixie Goswami and Peter R. Stillman, 4–12. Portsmouth, N.H.: Boynton/Cook.

Brannon, Lil. 1985. "Toward a Theory of Composition." In *Perspectives on Research and Scholarship in Composition*, edited by Ben W. McClelland and Timothy R. Donovan, 6–25. New York: Modern Language Association.

———. 1993. "M[other]: Lives on the Outside." *Written Communication* 10 (July): 457–65.

Britton, James. 1982. *Prospect and Retrospect*, ed. Gordon M. Pradl. Upper Montclair, N.J.: Boynton/Cook.

———. 1987. "A Quiet Form of Research." In *Reclaiming the Classroom: Teacher Research as an Agency for Change*, edited by Dixie Goswami and Peter R. Stillman, 13–19. Portsmouth, N.H.: Boynton/Cook.

Brodkey, Linda. 1987. "Modernism and the Scene(s) of Writing." *College English* 49: 396–418.

Bruffee, Kenneth A. 1984. "Collaborative Learning and the 'Conversation of Mankind.' " *College English* 46 (November): 635–52.

———. 1986. "Social Construction, Language, and the Authority of Knowledge: A Bibliographic Essay." *College English* 48 (December): 773–90.

———. 1990. "Collaborative Learning, Language, and the Authority of Teachers." Paper presented at the Conference on College Composition and Communication, March, Chicago.

Cameron, Deborah. 1985. *Feminism and Linguistic Theory*. New York: Macmillan.

Campbell, Joseph. 1968. *The Hero with a Thousand Faces*, 2d ed. Princeton, N.J.: Princeton University Press.

Chopin, Kate. 1972. *The Awakening*. New York: Avon.

Christ, Carol P. 1986. *Diving Deep and Surfacing*, 2d ed. Boston: Beacon Press.

Deen, Rosemary. 1986. "The Lively Order: The Author's Authority and the Teacher as Monarch." In *Audits of Meaning*, edited by Louise Z. Smith, 213–28. Portsmouth, N.H.: Boynton/Cook.

Delpit, Lisa. 1988. "The Silenced Dialogue: Power and Pedagogy in Educating Other People's Children." *Harvard Educational Review* 58 (August): 280–98.

Doniger O'Flaherty, Wendy. 1988. *Other People's Myths*. New York: Macmillan.

Doty, William G. 1986. *Mythography: The Study of Myths and Rituals*. University of Alabama Press.

Downing, Christine. 1989. *The Goddess: Mythological Images of the Feminine*. New York: Crossroad.

Dugan, Penelope. 1991. *A Pedagogy of Inclusion*. Ph.D. diss., State University of New York, Albany.

DuPlessis, Rachel Blau. 1985. *Writing beyond the Endings: Narrative Strategies of Twentieth Century Women Writers*. Bloomington: Indiana University Press.

Ebert, Teresa L. 1991. "The 'Difference' of Postmodern Feminism." *College English* 53 (December): 886–903.

————. 1992–93. "Ludic Feminism, the Body, Performance, and Labor: Bringing *Materialism* Back into Feminist Cultural Studies." *Cultural Critique* 23 (Winter): 5–50.

Elbow, Peter. 1973. *Writing without Teachers*. New York: Oxford University Press.

————. 1986. *Embracing Contraries*. New York: Oxford University Press.

Ellsworth, Elizabeth. 1989. "Why Doesn't This Feel Empowering? Working Through the Repressive Myths of Critical Pedagogy." *Harvard Educational Review* 59 (August): 297–324.

Flynn, Elizabeth A. 1988. "Composing as a Woman." *College Composition and Communication* 39 (December): 423–35.

————. 1990. "Composing 'Composing as a Woman': A Perspective on Research." *College Composition and Communication* 41 (February): 83–89.

————. 1991. "Composition Studies from a Feminist Perspective." In *The Politics of Writing Instruction: Postsecondary*, edited by Richard Bullock and John Trimbur, 137–54. Portsmouth, N.H.: Boynton/Cook.

Flynn, Elizabeth A., and Patrocinio P. Schwartz, eds. 1986. *Gender and Reading*. Baltimore: Johns Hopkins University Press.

Freire, Paulo. 1992. *Pedagogy of the Oppressed*. New York: Continuum.

Frey, Olivia. 1990. "Beyond Literary Darwinism: Women's Voices and Critical Discourse." *College English* 52 (September): 507–26.

Geertz, Clifford. 1973. *Interpretation of Cultures*. New York: Basic Books.

————. 1983. *Local Knowledge*. New York: Basic Books, 1983.

Gilligan, Carol. 1982. *In A Different Voice*. Cambridge: Harvard University Press.

Goswami, Dixie, and Peter R. Stillman, eds. 1987. *Reclaiming the Classroom: Teacher Research as an Agency for Change*. Portsmouth, N.H.: Boynton/Cook.

Gould, Eric. 1981. *Mythological Intentions in Modern Literature*. Princeton, N.J.: Princeton University Press.

Grondahl, Paul. 1989. "Bern Porter Turns Your Discards into His Poetry Collage." *Times-Union* (Albany, N.Y.), 17 November, C-10.

Haake, Katharine. 1989. "Claiming Our Own Authority." *AWP Chronicle* 2 (October/November): 1–2.

Hairston, Maxine. 1985. "Breaking Our Bonds and Reaffirming Our Connections." *ADE Bulletin* 81 (Fall): 1–5.

Harris, Joseph. 1989. "The Idea of Community in the Study of Writing." *College Composition and Communication* 40 (February): 11–22.

Heath, Shirley Brice. 1983. *Ways with Words*. New York: Cambridge University Press.

———. 1987. "A Lot of Talk about Nothing." In *Reclaiming the Classroom: Teacher Research as an Agency for Change*, edited by Dixie Goswami and Peter R. Stillman, 39–48. Portsmouth, N.H.: Boynton/Cook.

Heilbrun, Carolyn. 1988. *Writing a Woman's Life*. New York: Ballantine.

Herndl, Carl G. 1991. "Writing Ethnography: Representation, Rhetoric, and Institutional Practices." *College English* 53 (March): 320–32.

Hillman, James. 1975. *Re-Visioning Psychology*. New York: Harper & Row.

Hirsch, E. D. 1987. *Cultural Literacy*. Boston: Houghton Mifflin.

Holbrook, Sue Ellen. 1991. "Women's Work: The Feminizing of Composition." *Rhetoric Review* 9 (Spring): 201–29.

Homer. 1937. *The Odyssey*, trans. W. H. D. Rouse. New York: Mentor.

hooks, bell. 1989. *Talking Back: Thinking Feminist, Thinking Black*. Boston: South End Press.

Hurston, Zora Neale. 1978. *Their Eyes Were Watching God*. Urbana: University of Illinois Press.

Ingalls, Rachel. 1983. *Mrs. Caliban*. New York: Laurel.

Janangelo, Joseph. 1991. "Pedagogy of the Rich and Famous: How Can We Empower Students Who Are More Powerful than We Are?" Paper presented at the Conference on College Composition and Communication, Boston.

Jarratt, Susan C. 1991. "Feminism and Composition: The Case for Conflict." In *Contending with Words*, edited by Patricia Harkin and John Schilb. 105–23. New York: Modern Language Association.

Jewett, Sarah Orne. 1982. *The Country of the Pointed Firs*. New York: Norton.

Kingston, Maxine Hong. 1976. *The Woman Warrior*. New York: Vintage.

Knoblauch, C. H., and Lil Brannon. 1984. *Rhetorical Traditions and the Teaching of Writing*. Montclair, N.J.: Boynton/Cook.

――――. 1988. "Knowing Our Knowledge: A Phenomenological Basis for Teacher Research." In *Audits of Meaning*, edited by Louise Z. Smith. 17–28. Portsmouth, N.H.: Boynton/Cook.

Kohlberg, Lawrence. 1984. *The Psychology of Moral Development: The Nature and Validity of Moral Stages*. San Francisco: Harper and Row.

Kuhn, Thomas S. 1970. *The Structure of Scientific Revolutions*, 2d ed. Chicago: University of Chicago Press.

Labov, William. 1970. "The Logic of Nonstandard English." In *Report of the Twentieth Century Annual Round Table Meeting on Linguistics and Language Studies*, edited by James E. Alatis, 1–43. Washington, D.C.: Georgetown University Press.

Lather, Patricia. 1991. *Getting Smart: Feminist Research and Pedagogy with/in the Postmodern*. New York: Routledge.

Lévi-Strauss, Claude. 1963. *Structural Anthropology*, trans. Claire Jacobson and B. G. Schoepf, vol. 1. New York: Basic Books.

Lu, Min-zhan. 1991. "Redefining the Legacy of Mina Shaughnessy: A Critique of the Politics of Linguistic Innocence." *Journal of Basic Writing* 10 (1): 26–40.

Martin, Nancy. 1987. "On the Move: Teacher-Researchers." In *Reclaiming the Classroom: Teacher Research as an Agency for Change*, edited by Dixie Goswami and Peter R. Stillman, 20–27. Portsmouth, N.H.: Boynton/Cook.

McQuade, Donald. 1992. "Living in—and on—the Margins." *College Composition and Communication* 43 (February): 11–22.

Miller, Susan. 1991. "The Feminization of Composition." In *The Politics of Writing Instruction: Postsecondary*, edited by Richard Bullock and John Trimbur, 39–53. Portsmouth, N.H.: Boynton/Cook.

North, Stephen M. 1987. *The Making of Knowledge in Composition*. Upper Montclair, N.J.: Boynton/Cook.

Pearson, Carol, and Katherine Pope. 1981. *The Female Hero*. New York: Bowker.

Perry, William Graves. 1970. *Forms of Intellectual and Ethical Development in the College Years*. New York: Holt, Rinehart and Winston.

Phelps, Louise Wetherbee. 1991. "Practical Wisdom and the Geography of Knowledge in Composition." *College English* 53 (December): 863–85.

Ponsot, Marie, and Rosemary Deen. 1982. *Beat Not the Poor Desk*. Upper Montclair, N.J.: Boynton/Cook.

Ray, Ruth E. 1993. *The Practice of Theory: Teacher Research in Composition*. Urbana, Ill.: National Council of Teachers of English.

Rose, Mike. 1989. *Lives on the Boundary*. New York: Penguin.

Rosenblatt, Louise M. 1978. *The Reader the Text the Poem*. Carbondale: Southern Illinois University Press.

Schniedewind, Nancy. 1987. "Feminist Values: Guidelines for Teaching Methodology in Women's Studies." In *Freire for the Classroom*, edited by Ira Shor. Portsmouth, N.H.: Boynton/Cook-Heinemann.

Scholes, Robert. 1985. *Textual Power*. New Haven: Yale University Press.

Schuster, Charles I. 1985. "Mikhail Bakhtin As Rhetorical Theorist." *College English* 47 (October): 594–607.

Shaughnessy, Mina P. 1977. *Errors and Expectations*. New York: Oxford University Press.

Shor, Ira. 1987. *Critical Teaching and Everyday Life*. Chicago: University of Chicago Press.

Silko, Leslie Marmon. 1978. *Ceremony*. New York: New American Library.

Sommers, Nancy. 1992. "Between the Drafts." *College Composition and Communication* 43 (February): 23–31.

Starhawk. 1988. *Dreaming the Dark*, new ed. Boston: Beacon Press.

Sternburg, Janet, ed. 1991. *The Writer on Her Work, Vol. II: New Essays in New Territory*. New York: Norton.

Trimbur, John. 1989. "Consensus and Difference in Collaborative Learning." *College English* 51 (October): 602–16.

Walker, Barbara. 1987. *The Skeptical Feminist*. New York: Harper & Row.

Winter, Kate. 1993. "Another Kind of Captivity Narrative." *Written Communication* 10 (July): 438–44.

Woolf, Virginia. 1929. *A Room of One's Own*. New York: Harcourt, Brace and World.

Yaeger, Patricia. 1988. *Honey-Mad Women*. New York: Columbia University Press.

Index

Abuse, 112–13
Alcoff, Linda, 7, 9, 10
Alienation, 5
Androcentrism, 122
Anger, 181; acceptance of, 161; control of, 178, 180; displacement of, 179, 180; expressing, 165; marginalization of, 159–60; objects of, 162; power of, 173–76; and self-control, 176; as taboo, 158, 160–61
Antifoundationalism, 32
Authority: decentering, 30; of dominant discourse, 2; exercise of, 19; giving up, 160; institutional, 18, 171; of knowledge, 33; lack of, 4; metalinguistic practices of, 17; rhetorical, 33; of students, 160; textual, 32
Autobiography, 3
Autonomy: ability to achieve, 157, 158; authorial, 174; belief in, 117, 162; giving up, 52; heroic, 120, 160; individual, 115, 166; public, 168; reaffirming, 116, 160; of self, 118; of writers, 115

Bakhtin, Mikhail, 2, 14–15, 47, 166
Bartholomae, David, 20, 25, 33–36, 185
Bauer, Dale, 15, 30
Baym, Nina, 44, 47, 50, 119
Belenky, Mary, 18, 20, 25, 31, 32, 51, 119–20
Berthoff, Ann, 8, 17, 36, 70, 120, 172, 189
Bildung, 43, 44
Biography, 21

Bizzell, Patricia, 20, 25, 29–33, 39n2, 185
Boundaries: learning within, 54; production-consumption, 114–15; reader-writer, 115; self-Other, 53
Brannon, Lil, 3, 16, 17, 20
Bridge of Flowers, Bridge of Iron, 72–83
Britton, James, 3
Brodkey, Linda, 20, 47
Bruffee, Kenneth, 20, 24, 25, 26–29, 30

Cameron, Deborah, 9, 10, 18, 19, 24, 27
Campbell, Joseph, 49, 51, 119, 122, 178
Classroom: dialogue, 69–123; examination of social inequities, 30; feminization of, 30; interaction, 118; opening up of, 28; power relationships in, 123; practices, 24–26; ritual, 119, 160; social order in, 176; status hierarchies, 116, 172
"Composing as a Woman" (Flynn), 17, 18
Composition, 186–87; cultural representations of, 1; expressivist theory and practice in, 23; feminization of, 23; gender in, 4, 17, 19; heroic models of, 44, 172; inequities in, 23; inquiry into, 1–2; knowledge-making in, 6; metaphors for, 121; myths of, 18, 47; power of, 173; relational modes in, 169; representations of, 5; resistance in, 48; significance of, 167; social constructivist theories in, 13; status of, 5, 8; stories of, 19; theory and practice, 4; transformative disruption of, 123
Conflict, and identity, 1

Consensus, 28
Control: of anger, 173, 178, 180; cultural, 117; of destiny, 120; in dialogue, 161; of discourses of power, 10; in education, 172; gaining, 51, 122; idealized, 167; lack of, 115, 122, 159, 164, 172, 174, 175, 176; maintenance of, 172; of meaning, 12, 119, 120, 122, 161, 166, 169, 174, 184; as oppression, 179; Otherness in, 116; and power, 113, 175, 178, 184, 185; rational, 121; of self, 51, 172, 173, 176, 177, 184; of social processes, 8; stories of, 51; of text meaning, 116, 117
Critical Teaching and Everyday Life (Shor), 30
Critical theory, 5
Cultural: assignment of status, 119; beliefs, 125, 171; "codes of power," 25; control, 117; differences, 172; empowerment, 23; feminism, 7, 9, 14; forms of myth and ritual, 19; hegemony, 125, 188; identity, 47; ideologies, 47; images, 12; inscription, 69, 119, 161, 171; interpretations, 72; literacy, 32, 36; myths, 44, 69, 115, 171; politic, 24; power, 23, 24; prescription of gender, 1; shaping of women's experience, 42; status, 25, 117, 123; values, 12, 120, 171
Culture: assimilation of, 119; contexts of, 1; dominant values of, 9; and gender, 5; internalized meanings of, 117; male-domination of, 42, 165; metadiscursive activities of, 10; myths of, 18, 184; patriarchal, 122; of power, 172, 174, 185; rituals of, 1, 184; stabilization of, 166; structures of, 163; transcending, 119; "voice of," 117–18

Deen, Rosemary, 26, 27
Delpit, Lisa, 185
Demeter, 121, 165, 177
Determinism, 8–10
The Dialogic Imagination (Bakhtin), 14
Dialogics, 14–15
Dialogue: academic classroom, 69–123; on *Bridge of Flowers, Bridge of Iron*, 83–123; effect of teacher presence on, 164; and

gender, 112; and identity, 1; narrative, 72; processes of, 198; self-directed group, 125–70; between two discourses, 70
Discourse. *See also* Language; abnormal, 28; academic, 33, 34; access to, 10, 13; alienating, 12; appropriation of, 24; argumentative, 5; bringing into dialogue, 14; centrifugal impulses in, 47, 166; centripetal impulses in, 47, 166; classroom, 69–123; consensual, 27; correction, 7; dialogic theories of, 15; dimensions of, 10; dominant, 2, 5, 7, 27, 33, 35, 37, 125; expressive, 3; feminized, 5; gendered, 9; hierarchy of, 16; interactions among, 15; literary, 3; marginalization of, 28; multiple, 43; national, 39n2; normative, 27, 28; open-ended, 14; oppositional, 48; of power, 13, 25, 29, 38, 39; practitioner, 6; privileged, 16; of research, 5; of resistance, 47; scholarly, 7; subject of, 166; "talking back" in, 2, 11, 13, 14; theories of, 3, 47; uncertainties of, 70; women's access to, 9
Dissensus, 28
Domination: classroom, 123; and language, 5; male, 113; myth of, 183; patriarchal, 30
Doniger O'Flaherty, Wendy, 11, 12, 24, 172, 186
Downing, Christine, 121, 122, 125, 165, 177, 183
Dreaming the Dark (Starhawk), 173
Dugan, Penny, 3
DuPlessis, Rachel Blau, 20, 42, 43, 46, 118

Ebert, Teresa, 13, 18, 24, 38
Eiseley, Loren, 2
Elbow, Peter, 25, 30, 51
Eleusinian mysteries, 121
Ellsworth, Elizabeth, 27, 37, 38, 47
Empowerment, 125; and changing language practices, 24; cultural, 23; feminist critique of, 37–39; linguistic, 33, 37; of marginalized groups, 8; myths of, 36; personal, 23; of students, 37, 38, 174, 185, 186

Energy drain, 27
Essentialism, 119
Experience: exclusion of, 190; feminized, 10; interpreting, 12; knowing, 183; and language, 8; lived, 1, 51, 185; male-dominated, 43, 47; meaning of, 13; narratives of, 23; nature of, 10; personal, 112; stories of, 55–68, 72–83; truth of, 11; value of, 32; women's, 7, 9, 42, 43, 46, 51, 55–68, 72–83, 198
Expressivism, 20, 23, 24–26, 188

Fear, 163–64, 164
Feminism: cultural, 7, 9, 14; and linguistic reform, 5; poststructuralist, 9
Fiction, 2, 21; as genre, 2, 14, 15; marginalization of, 14, 16; as mode of inquiry, 14–15; seen as false, 2
Flynn, Elizabeth, 17, 18, 19, 23, 122
Foucault, Michel, 71
Freire, Paolo, 26
Frey, Olivia, 5

Geertz, Clifford, 2, 36, 115, 116, 118, 171, 187
Gender: in composition, 4, 19; cultural inscription of, 1, 9; and culture, 5, 24; and dialogue, 112; hierarchies, 2, 8, 172; and identity, 19; inequities, 37; and language, 5; and linguistic reform, 5; moral and ethical development in, 19, 49; relationships, 44; in research, 4; roles, 30; status arrangements, 172; stereotypes, 169; and subjectivity, 5; and teacher privilege, 35
Genres: blurred, 2, 3, 70; fiction as, 2, 14, 15; of self-reflective narrative, 2–3
Gilligan, Carol, 18, 19, 25
The Goddess (Downing), 121

Hades, 165, 166, 177
Hairston, Maxine, 5
Harris, Joseph, 34
Heath, Shirley Brice, 36, 37
Heilbrun, Carolyn, 20, 21, 42, 69, 118, 171

Herndl, Carl, 17, 18
Hero: ascendant, 125, 164, 165, 166, 167, 172, 176, 178; autonomy of, 120; as culture itself, 120; descendant, 165, 166, 167; duality of, 163, 164; gendered, 20, 119; teacher as, 20
The Hero with a Thousand Faces (Campbell), 49
Heteroglossia, 14
Holbrook, Sue Ellen, 4
Honey-Mad Women (Yaeger), 15
hooks, bell, 47

Identity: collective, 125, 173; conflict in, 1; constructing, 43, 44, 69; cultural, 47; in dialogue, 1; gendered, 19; individual, 125; local, 47; masculine, 3; narratives of, 1; national, 47; nature of, 10; personal, 1, 50; poststructuralist deconstruction of, 13; of power, 35; professional, 1, 50; search for, 44; subjective, 17; and truth of experience, 11; of women, 50; writer's, 44
In a Different Voice (Gilligan), 18
Inquiry: into composition, 1; as fact, 11; fiction as mode of, 14–15; hermeneutical, 10; instruments of, 16–17; lore as, 6; nature of, 11; pedagogical, 17–18; phenomenological, 16
Intentional fallacy, 192, 197

Janangelo, Joseph, 35
Jarratt, Susan, 5, 30

Killer dichotomies, 120, 123
Knoblauch, C.H., 16, 17, 20
Knowledge: about language practice, 172; appropriation of, 7; authority of, 33; confirmation of, 120; of consciousness, 123; construction of, 17, 70; discovery of, 70; experiential, 10–13, 21, 26, 173; idealized, 120; institutional hierarchies of, 4; knowing, 39, 42, 54; of knowledge, 121; making, 2, 4–5, 6, 8; meaning of, 10; modes of, 5, 14, 173; objects of, 32;

Knowledge (continued)
of practice, 5, 6, 7, 8, 15, 39, 173;
production of, 30; of researchers, 173;
written, 172
Kohlberg, Lawrence, 49

Labov, William, 27
Language: bringing thought to, 183;
changing, 23, 24, 36, 37; and
communication, 10; control of meaning
through, 12; correction, 23; and
domination, 5; and empowerment, 33;
and experience, 8; and gender, 5, 8; as
instrument of inquiry, 16–17; and
meaning, 8–10; meaning replication
through, 18–19; and models of male
experience, 42; and myth, 12, 13, 172;
objectification of, 8; postmodern theories
of, 24; of practice, 4, 5, 37, 172; and
reality, 3; of research, 4, 5; and social
control, 9; as substitute for reality, 9;
theories of, 8; women's relationship to, 9
Larson, Richard, 5
Lather, Patti, 17, 18, 21
Learning: alternative models of, 25;
assimilationist models of, 33; binary
opposition in, 26–29; collaborative, 25,
26–29, 30, 31; experiencing, 186; expert
novice model, 29; gender bias in, 32;
process-oriented, 30; reciprocity models,
37; social contexts of, 25; and teaching,
53
LeGuin, Ursula, 43
Linguistic: determinism, 8–10, 19, 23;
distortions of practice, 8; empowerment,
37; reform, 5, 12, 13
Lives on the Boundary (Rose), 3
Lore, 6, 7

Marginalization, 8, 123; and access to
institutions, 13; of discourse, 7, 28; of
fiction, 14; of students, 25, 37; of
women, 17, 46
Meaning: assigning, 123; construction of,
18–19, 53, 70; control of, 119, 120, 122
161, 166, 169, 174, 184; of experience,

13; internalization of, 117; knowable,
166; of knowledge, 10; linguistic
determinism in, 8–10; making, 2, 10, 13,
50, 53, 166, 183; mastery of, 116–17;
metalinguistic forces in, 9, 10; of myth,
11; negotiation of, 15, 30–31; personal,
23; possibility of, 10; private, 53, 117;
quests for, 46; rendering visible, 169;
replication through language, 18–19;
social construction of, 8–10; social
control of, 9; stabilizing, 172; of stories,
11, 39; as two-valued relationship, 8–9
Metaphor: anger as, 173–76; for
composition, 121; for power, 173–76; in
stories, 11, 49; writing as, 173
"Mikhail Bakhtin as Rhetorical Theorist"
(Schuster), 15
Miller, Susan, 5
Mythography, 11
Myths, 1, 121; of academic life, 43; of
authorial autonomy, 174; communication
of, 13; content of, 11; contradictory, 24;
creating new, 12; cultural, 19, 41, 44, 69,
115, 171, 184; derogatory connotations
of, 2; of empowerment, 36; as events, 11;
function of, 11, 13; gendered, 119–20;
heroic, 44, 47, 51, 118–19, 176;
institutional forms of, 19; masculinized,
44; meaning in, 11, 12; power of, 12, 19;
reinterpreting, 47, 122; and ritual, 118;
universality of, 49; of writers, 45

Narrative(s): classroom, 3; connected, 118;
of culture, 111; dialogue, 72;
ethnographic, 3; of experience, 23; and
experiential knowledge, 10–13; gendered,
14, 111; of identity, 1; and ideology, 46;
individual, 118; and models of male
experience, 42; power of, 14; quest, 46;
reliability in, 112; self-reflective, 2–3;
and ways of knowing, 3, 21
Naumann, Rosalie, 4
North, Stephen, 6, 7, 8, 15, 18, 19, 23

Objectivity, 5, 16, 36, 115, 160, 173
Odysseus, 163

Oppression, 180; control as, 179; in race and class, 47; of women, 179
Other: boundaries with self, 53; fear of loss in, 172; internalizing, 166; objectified, 167; representation of, 19, 159

Patriarchy, 54, 122
Perry, William, 31, 32, 49
Persephone, 121, 122, 123, 163, 165, 166, 173, 176, 177, 183
Phelps, Louise, 8
Plots: heroic, 51; psychosocial conventions in, 43; quest, 42, 48, 53, 119, 120; romantic, 42, 44
Plurality, 43
Positionality, 32
Positivism, 19
Power: access to, 5, 7, 8, 10, 38; acquisition of, 172; alternative images of, 172–73; of anger, 173–76; to assign meaning, 123; of composition, 166, 173; as connectedness, 176–83; and control, 113, 175, 178, 184, 185; cultural, 23, 24, 172, 174, 185; discourses of, 13, 25, 29, 38, 39; energy drain in, 27; exercise of, 19; gaining, 122; heroic, 172; hierarchies, 2; identity of, 35; institutional, 10, 18, 23; lack of, 51, 178, 184; metalinguistic practices of, 17; mythic, 12, 19, 172; of narrative, 14; over others, 119, 172, 173; public, 168; reinscribing, 183–85; relations, 7, 28, 29, 123, 125, 171–72, 173, 184; representations of, 171–88, 172, 183; structures of, 13; of teachers, 27, 167, 188; textual, 32; of writers, 169, 173, 175, 183, 189
Practice: appropriation of knowledge in, 7; classroom, 24–26; feminization of, 4–8, 18; interpreting, 24; knowledge in, 5, 8, 15, 39; and language, 4, 5, 37; legitimating experiences of, 15; linguistic distortions of, 8; misrepresentation in, 7; and research, 4–8, 15–17; resistance in, 8; scholarly discourse in, 7; self-reflective, 2–3, 4; silences in, 8; status of, 8; stories of, 11; of students in schools,

52; subordination of, 5, 10; and theory, 4, 8
Production-consumption boundaries, 114, 115, 117, 175

Reality: accounts of, 41; adversarial, 25; alternative models of, 25; changing, 179; of conflict, 32; empirical, 3; interpreting, 38; and language, 3, 9; pragmatic, 6; reinterpretations of, 14; shaping, 69
Reform, linguistic, 5
Relationships: of binary opposition, 26–29; dialogical, 123; dynamics of, 158; entanglement in, 158; gendered, 44; to male-dominated culture, 42; power, 123; ritual-myth, 118; society and individual, 44; teacher-student, 26–29, 34–39, 125, 172, 189–99; women and, 157–59
Research: and classroom life, 4; conventional, 186; discourse of, 5; dominance of, 6–7; gender in, 4, 17–19; genres outside of, 2; language of, 4, 5; nontraditional, 2; objectivist foundations of, 15–17; phenomenological approach to, 1–4; positivist, 17; and practice, 4–8, 15–17; revisioning, 187–88; subjectivity in, 17; traditional, 3
Resistance, 191; collective, 20; in composition, 48; discourses of, 47; expressing, 165; in practice, 8
"Rhetoric as Hermeneutic" (Berthoff), 189
Rhetors, 31
Ritual, 125; classroom, 119, 160; of culture, 1, 19, 184; in dialogues, 115; giving-up of control, 116; heroic, 166; institutional forms of, 19; and myth, 118; reinforcement of status quo, 116
Rorty, Richard, 28
Rose, Mike, 3, 4, 20

Scholes, Robert, 16
Schuster, Charles, 15
Shaughnessy, Mina, 25, 33
Shelter, 55–68
Shor, Ira, 30
"The Silenced Dialogue" (Delpit), 185

Social: change, 24; constructivism, 13, 23–
39, 185, 188; control, 9; hierarchies, 27,
31, 119, 185; inequities, 25, 30, 37;
intervention, 24, 37, 38; justice, 12, 20,
34, 36, 188; norms, 46; order, 176;
privilege, 35; reinscribing, 185–86;
status, 27
"Staffroom Interchange" (Flynn), 18
Stories: about ourselves, 171; classroom
dialogue on, 69–123; of composing, 19;
of control, 51; of culture, 21; heroic, 49,
51, 53; institutionalization of, 51;
interpretation of women in, 185–86;
meaning of, 11, 39; metaphor in, 11, 49;
and myth, 13; of power, 172–73; of
practice, 11; production of, 115; roles of,
13; self-directed group dialogue on, 125–
70; significance of, 171; teacher-student
relationships, 189–99; of women's
experiences, 42, 43, 55–68, 72–83
Students: access to dominant discourse, 37;
authority of, 160; in binary opposition to
teachers, 25; empowerment of, 37, 38,
174, 185, 186; as heroes, 20, 25;
interpretational abilities, 36; lack of
control in, 51; learning in prescribed
boundaries, 54; preparing for "real" life,
52, 178; subjectivities of, 28, 29; teachers
learning from, 197; trust of teachers, 34,
35
Subjectivity, 5, 10, 16, 17, 21, 23, 28, 29,
36, 173

Teacher(s): access to power, 27, 29; as
agent of change, 29–30; and assertion of
authority, 30, 31, 180, 198; in binary
opposition to students, 25; classroom
roles, 160, 180; effect of presence on
dialogue, 164; exclusion from power, 35;
giving power to students, 26, 27, 36; as
hero, 20, 33–37, 123, 178; interventions
of, 37–38; invisibility of, 25, 30, 31;
learning from students, 197; as master, 3,
4, 27, 116, 160, 161, 164, 166, 168;
nurturing roles, 30; power of, 167, 188;
rhetorical authority of, 33; as rhetors, 31;

and social justice, 34, 188; subjectivities
of, 29; values of, 31
Teaching: collaborative, 26, 27; energy
drain in, 27; expert-novice model, 29; as
feminized activity, 4; lack of authority in,
4; and learning, 53; masculinized identity
of, 3
Thomas, Lewis, 2
Trailing spouse phenomenon, 35
Transformation, 13, 53, 119; of
consciousness, 123; discursive, 71;
processes of, 50
Trimbur, John, 28, 29, 32

Values: of academia, 31; acceptance of, 31;
cultural, 12, 120, 171; dominant, 9;
institutional, 5; teacher, 31; in women's
experiences, 32

Weaver, Barbara, 5
Winter, Kate, 35
Women: and abuse, 112–13; access to
discourse, 9; cultural beliefs about, 125;
cultural identity of, 47; cyclical lives of,
165; experiences of, 7, 9, 32, 42, 43, 46,
51, 55–68, 72–83, 198; identity of, 43,
50; interpretation of in stories, 185–86;
marginalization of, 17; oppression of,
179; as Other, 117; pressures to define
selves, 47; and relationships, 157–59;
relationship to language, 9; and research,
17–19; status of, 123; textual
representations of, 125; trivialization of
writings of, 44, 45; victimization of, 112–
13, 179, 185–86; as writers, 41–68
Women of Academe (Aisenberg and
Harrington), 43–44
Women's Ways of Knowing (Belenky), 18,
31, 51
The Writer and Her Work (LeGuin), 43
Writers: autonomy of, 115, 116; basic, 33;
construction of identity, 44; cultural
beliefs about, 125; enfranchisement of,
33; as heroes, 46, 118, 122, 125, 163;

myths of, 45; object status of, 114; power of, 169, 173, 175, 183, 189; returning text to, 115, 162, 174; status of, 123; as subjects, 159–63; women as, 41–68
Writing: from identity of privilege, 35; in isolation, 52, 164, 175; as male tradition, 41–55; as metaphor, 173; psychosocial conventions in, 43; quest plots in, 42; romantic plots in, 42; scenes of, 20, 44–46; trivialization of, 44
Writing a Woman's Life (Helibrun), 42
Writing Without Teachers (Elbow), 30

Yaeger, Patricia, 15